Religion
In a Material universe

Religion
In a Material universe

Tony Equale

The Institute for Economic Democracy

Institute for Economic Democracy
IED Press
PO Box 309
Appomattox VA 24522

10 9 8 7 6 5 4 3 2 1

Equale, Tony.
  Religion in a material universe / by Tony Equale.
     pages cm.
  Includes bibliographical references and index.
  ISBN 978-1-933567-45-7 (pbk. : alk. paper) -- ISBN 978-1-933567-46-4 (ebook)
  1. Religion and science. 2. Nature. 3. Matter. I. Title.
  BL240.3.E68 2012
  200--dc23
                    2012048468

IEDPress.com
Cover design by B. Sidney Smith

DEDICATED TO THOSE
who embrace the human condition
and are not offended by what "God" has made

Lawyers have a stock Latin phrase, *cui bono?*, which means "Who benefits from this"? a question that is even more central in evolutionary biology than in the law. Any phenomenon [like religion] in the living world that apparently exceeds the functional, cries out for explanation. The suspicion is always that we must be missing something, since a gratuitous outlay is, in a word, uneconomical, and as economists are forever reminding us, there is no such thing as a free lunch.

Daniel Dennett
Breaking the Spell, 2007

contents

preface

After *An Unknown God* was published in 2008, I realized that I had not laid out the philosophical and scientific assumptions on which it was based. *The Mystery of Matter* was conceived to make up for that; it came out two years later. This book follows. It is meant as the next logical step in the elaboration of a coherent view of our existential situation.

Religion in a Material Universe concludes that religion is the poetic expression of a natural donor-recipient relationship that is constitutive of what we are, but whose "donor" side remains unknown ... even to the extent of its separate existence from us. We are necessarily related to the source of our existence — *whatever it may be* — for the very same reason that we are necessarily related to ourselves. If there is another volume, and it is my intention that there shall be, it will be focused on the nature of that relationship, its development and full-flowering.

In the days when such terms were still in use, that still unwritten fourth volume might have been called "Prayer in a Material Universe." I'm not sure I will call it that. The literal and root meaning of "prayer" *is petition.* I am not comfortable with that category, except as a metaphor. Relationship embraces many things; *getting what we want isn't necessarily one of them.*

Aristotle in the *Nichomachaean Ethics* talks about three kinds of friendship distinguished by what is desired. We are all familiar with the first two: there is friendship of *utility*, when you cultivate a friendship in order to derive some benefit from it; then the friendship of *pleasure*, whose only purpose is fun. Finally there was the friendship of disinterested love, based on the recognition of inherent goodness and embraced *for the sake of the other.* This kind of friendship has no purpose at all. It delights in the sheer joy of "being-with" and "be-holding" the beloved. It is contemplative, and something akin to worship.

If, for some reason that book does not get written I would hope that you, dear reader, will follow that clue and find out for yourself how Aristotle's category may apply to our existential situation.

Tony Equale,
Willis VA, April, 2012

prologue

This prologue is intended as more than an introduction. It doesn't only try to ready the reader's mind and appetite for what follows; it is also meant as a preparatory chapter, providing foundational material for the rest of the book.

Because the essays in this volume are a sequel to *The Mystery of Matter,* this prologue needs to construct the bridge from that book, which was a philosophical reflection, to this one, which is about religion.

The world as cosmo-ontology describes it in *The Mystery of Matter,* would seem to have no place for religion. This may be considered the "null-hypothesis;" and as these things go, this book will try to say just the opposite. Why is the null-hypothesis the intuitive response?

Traditional religion in the West, at least since the beginning of the common era, has insisted that human destiny is tied to a world other than this one, populated by beings other than material, whose *existence* is not apparent, and for which, in fact, no evidence exists. The burden of *The Mystery of Matter* was the philosophical justification of the proposition that *existence* is ... always, everywhere and only ... *material energy* and nothing else. There is, in other words, no other world; and there is no such thing as "spirit" referring to a different "kind of being" — Descartes' *"second substance"* — that operates on a set of principles and determinants that are different from the material around us.

Please don't misunderstand. I have no intention of ever denying the existence or character of *phenomena* that we have heretofore attributed to a separate "spirit," like human intelligence, creativity, morality, the desire for immortality, nor their importance for human life. But I now understand all such phenomena to be the expressions of a potential within matter itself. In a sense, nothing has changed, reality remains exactly as we have experienced it except for our metaphysical projections, i.e., what we think all these things really are and what mechanisms are engaged in their activation. *The Mystery of Matter* attempts to substantiate that there is only one thing out there, and it is *matter's energy to exist* on display in the infinite forms that populate our planet and the universe in which it spins.

new atheism

At the center of this question for me is the challenge of reductionist science and the "new atheists" that derive their energy from it. I am referring to Daniel Dennett and Richard Dawkins among others, who are material reductionists.[1] They reduce everything to matter *as it appears in its most primitive forms studied by physics and chemistry*. This implies an important distinction: *there is also a way of looking at matter as it appears in its most elaborated forms, like human beings.*

Those men share a strident antipathy toward religion, which predictably has earned them their sobriquet, *atheist*. But just as to be anti-religion is not necessarily to be atheist ... so too, to be materialist is not necessarily to deny the existence of a *transcendent material dynamism* in the universe, the source of our human selves and our sense of the sacred. I am a materialist, but this is where I part company from the reductionists. They deny any such dynamism. I am speaking of *material energy* as the very mystery of *existence* itself that displays a depth and significance that deserves to be explored on its own terms. For I claim *matter's energy is the energy to exist.* The implications of that statement are transcendent. They explain our experience, our world, and everything in it.

What the anti-religion people denounce is the fantasy that there is *another world* different from this one, built of a different kind of *existence,* that explains and controls what goes on here and of which religion has infallible knowledge. I agree with their denunciation, totally. *There is no other world.* I can easily understand why they fulminate against the religions whose rival claims to the "truth" about that non-existent world have been used to justify some of the worst intra-species violence that humankind has unleashed upon itself. But that is not all. The "atheists" excoriate religion for explaining disasters, from earthquakes to genocidal holocausts, as events consciously "permitted" by a supposedly loving personal "God" — who resides in that other world — who could prevent these horrors if "he" wanted, *but inexplicably chooses not to.* The fact that believers

---

[1] Daniel Dennett, *Breaking the Spell, Religion as a Natural Phenomenon*, Penguin, 2007; Richard Dawkins, *The God Delusion*, Haughten Mifflin, Boston, 2006.

are not fazed by such patent absurdity reveals the extremes to which people will go to preserve their illusions.

Religionists who claim, for their part, to eschew "naïve" providence, insist that "God" *absolutely respects* the natural order. But these same people are loath to explain the so-called miracles that are adduced as proof of their own religion's unique status with "God," and the encouragement they give their members to ask this "God" for a wide range of favors that by-pass the natural order. They can deny it all they want, but miracles are, in fact, the very stock-in-trade of the western religious enterprise. Religion built on this kind of other worldly "God" is called "supernatural theism."

The "God" characterized by theism is a "God" of intervention and miracles, a hovering micro-managing providence, a "person" who saves us from the very same death that his own alleged intentional design of the universe is said to have created. The real "God," I submit, does none of these things, as we may have noticed, and therefore is not the kind of "God" characterized by theism. In the real world, theism is simply not tenable. I am not a theist.

I take my stand with science. It is the one and only arbiter of the "facts." There are no physical "facts" known to religion that cannot be observed and verified by science, but don't get me wrong, *that doesn't eliminate religion.* There is nothing supernatural, *but that doesn't discard the sacred.* There is no other world, *but that doesn't eradicate the unfathomable depths of this one.* There are no miracles of any kind and never were, *but that doesn't deny matter's self-transcending creativity.* There is no "revelation," *but that doesn't mean we do not intimately understand who we are and how we are related to existence.* And the anthropomorphic **humanoid** "God" that all the religions of the book claim literally "intervenes in human history," simply does not exist, ... *but that doesn't mean there is no "God."* We all have a "God." "God" is *the source of our existence.*

The "God" that actually does exist, is the self-donating, self-extruding source-matrix of the *material energy* responsible for the *existence* and character of this universe and ourselves as part of it, exactly as it functions and exactly as we see it with our telescopes and microscopes and endoscopes and exactly as we describe it with our mathematical measurements.

It bears emphasizing that, even in the perennial categories developed by our own tradition, the "divine" characteristics of *matter's existential energy — existence —* are staring us in the face. *Material energy* is neither created nor destroyed, thus approximating to the *esse in se subsistens* which is the classic "definition" of "God;"[2] it is the universal matrix in which all things "live and move and have their being" which was exactly Paul's characterization of "God" that he gave at the Areopagus in Athens;[3] it is responsible for the existence of every form and function in the universe which was the salient point of the Genesis account of creation; it has displayed a self-transcending creativity whereby new things — including living and intelligent things — emerge from a seemingly limitless potential, the sharing of its very "self," which evokes a *kenosis* (self-emptying) acknowledged by some as the unmistakable hallmark of divinity.[4] And, most important of all, the "things" that emerge from and remain immersed in this matrix universally display a **conatus** — a drive for continued existence — that reveals the interior dynamism that they receive from their existential source. All things bear a striking resemblance to what they are made of. They are its image and likeness.

All things have but one interest and one goal, derived from one energy with one self-explanatory purpose — **esse, "to be,"** *to exist.*

religion?

Traditional theistic religion, by insisting, as it does, on a metaphysically separate "spirit," cannot accompany us into the world that *The Mystery of Matter* reveals; and those who think they can simply "tweak" our perennial religious terminology to make it fit, risk sliding us back into an illusory dualism by the back door, *and our last state would be worse than the first.* Let me be clear: *matter's existential energy* is not "spirit," it is matter. A superficial attempt at a semantic syncretism — taking "energy" as "spirit" — would belie the scientific reality and would have us continue to maintain two contrary worlds with their corresponding concepts to which we would have recourse as the needs demanded. It is a dysfunctional practice we have employed in the West for 500 years at least ... and we are schizoid because of it*!* Our new unitary vision is better off, perhaps,

---

[2] *Esse in se subsistens*, "Self-subsistent being." cf Aquinas, *Summa Theologiae*, I, q.3 ff, *passim.*
[3] *The Acts of the Apostles*, ch 17
[4] Pope John Paul II, *Fides et Ratio*, 1998

not being contaminated with any association with traditional theism, and especially the "G" word.

The "G" word, of course, is "God." I use it reluctantly, fully aware that even the quotation marks cannot eliminate the permanent scar of humanoid theism it carries. Our vision offers a new ground for understanding this amazing universe and our insuppressible sense of the sacred ... and it opens the door to religion in a new key: one that plumbs the depths of this world and ourselves as its progeny, rather than trying to blast us at escape velocity out into another.

The *mystery* that I speak of does not refer to an enigma to be solved, but rather, in the sense of the Greek word *mysterion*, "the place where the numinous resides, and reveals itself."[5] With this perspective the material universe becomes the sacred ground from which religion sprouts and in which it remains rooted and draws its life. Such a religion will not look to another world for explanations, nor will it direct us there for "salvation" or our ultimate destiny. If it "saves" us at all it will be by healing the schizoid notions that up to now have split us asunder — body from soul, person from person, individual from community, humankind from the earth.

This book will be guided by the observed and verified presence of a dynamism in the matter of the universe that accounts for its existence and character, its vastness in space and time, and the complex self-possessed, intelligent forms that it has evolved, the most developed of which, to this point and to our knowledge, is the human species. This resident power — *matter's energy* — accounts for the sense of the sacred in us ... and the sense of the sacred is a phenomenon we have to clarify, find a way to *understand*, and decide how to live with.

But that's not an easy task. The final chapter of *The Mystery of Matter* identified *material energy* as fundamentally unfathomable. We cannot *"know"* it because we cannot objectify it. But we *understand* it intimately for we ourselves are *material energy;* we understand it from within. If we enquire after it, it is *material energy* that is enquiring after itself. As with looking at a mirror reflected in another mirror, the self-images recede to infinity. There is nothing to see but ourselves looking at ourselves looking

---

[5] *The Mystery of Matter (MM)*, IED Pr., 2010, preface. *Mysterion* is translated into Latin as *sacramentum.*

at ourselves looking at ourselves. In other words, we see nothing beyond our direct experience of our own *existence.*

> At the end of my reflections, the discovery of the *emptiness* at the heart of *being-here* puts me at a dead-end. ... I am aware that the apparent contradiction we encounter in the way *matter's energy is-here,* leaves us at the edge of a void. We have reached the end of our earth-bound knowing. From a conceptual point of view, the rest is ***darkness.*** ... What I claim is the only thing left ... if one has the temerity to go there ... is *relationship.*[6]

This is the fulcrum, "the still point of the turning world."[7] At a certain point, all "knowing" stops and the only possibility left is ***relationship — an embrace*** — built on our intimate *understanding* of *existence that comes from interior experience, for we are matter's energy* and we cannot relate to it from the outside. We *must* embrace it one way or another; we have no choice, because it is ourselves. Once this is realized another focus comes into play, i.e., *how to do that.* Can the metaphors of our traditional religions bear the burden of *accurately expressing* and *authentically sustaining* our *relationship* to the transcendent existential energy in this material universe — our source, ground and matrix — ourselves? Or must we devise new ones?

Since "knowing" has ended, we have no recourse but to metaphors. Metaphors refer to what we *understand* but cannot objectify. They are ***symbols*** of what cannot be known or expressed in conventional terms. They communicate *understanding,* which I define as an intimate cognitive embrace that is a work not just of the mind, but of the whole human organism in all its integrity. The presence of the body with its ***conatus*** is an intrinsic element of this ***connatural understanding and its expression.*** It confirms the relationship itself to be a function of *material energy.* Our *relationship to ourselves* is the starting point and the endpoint of our relationship to the material matrix "in which we live and move and have our being." *It is the still point of the turning world.*

virtuality and the self

Metaphors are symbols; and the human being is a symbol-making animal. It is what we do. "New atheist" philosopher, Daniel Dennett, has suggested a way of understanding the products of the

---

[6] *Ibid.* p.257
[7] T.S.Eliot, *Four Quartets,* "Burnt Norton."

human symbol-making capacity as *virtual reality*. Disregarding any literal take on the computer robotics that he uses as the model of human intelligence (and matter itself), *virtuality* is a helpful image, a metaphor for the symbolic construct we call culture. For while culture is a "fact" and *exists*, it is a different kind of fact from that studied by the physical / biological sciences. Culture, the mother and synthesis of all symbols, is a collective work of the human imagination. Works of the imagination exist and are very important to us — like all works of art — but their reality depends upon us for their creation, character and continued existence.

On the other hand, the primitive organic evolution of *matter-energy* does not depend on "mind" for its existence or character. It depends rather on a resident dynamism, the **conatus,** an existential energy focused exclusively on continuing in existence, *surviving* ... and to that end it evolves, "finding" new combinations and interrelationships that permit continued existence. Human intentionality enters into this process, but only much later.

Originally there is no mind or purpose to *material energy* other than "to exist" ... and even that is not a choice, because whether they wanted to exist or not, these elaborations would not *be-here* if they had not stumbled upon the right combinations ... and, once they did, they fell into the "trap" of existence from which there is no escape. We did not *choose* to exist; and none of what you and I and everything is made of can *ever stop existing.* It corresponds to the 1st law of thermodynamics: *matter-energy is neither created nor destroyed.*

There are other realities, however, that *are* virtual, the products of mind. "Mind" is itself a virtual reality, a metaphor if you will for our conscious intelligence. While we tend to associate mind with the brain, we really have no idea where exactly this mind, our thinking, resides. The brain is the prime suspect because when key areas are damaged or genetically deformed, "mental" behavior and even self-identity is altered or extinguished. But "mind" suffuses the whole organism; and all kinds of human activity, like intuition and connatural *understanding,* are as much the work of hormones and other bodily components as the brain.

Nor can the brain claim to be the "self." The self pertains to the whole organism and the brain is clearly subordinated to it as to a higher unity. Where, then, does the "sense of self" come from? In our dualist past it was attributed to a "soul," an *immaterial* entity separable from the body.

But all kinds of organisms exhibit a "sense of self," *even those, like para-mecia, that have no brains or neural structures of any kind;* still they pur-sue food and mates and they flee from predators. Not even traditionalists would say that they had "souls." Their "selves" are the products of organic integration. It reveals the fundamental *communitarian nature* of material existence: *matter's energy integrates individuals into higher unities in or-der to survive.* In our case, the human "self," in a further step, is sub-sumed into an even "higher" integration: it is the co-product and co-author of human society.

society

Society is not a "thing" nor a force. It is a *virtual* reality, a human creation that tends to act like a *superorganism*. Its existence and character is *virtual;* it cannot be determined by looking at any other factors than human thought, choice and behavior.

Virtual realities are real but they are virtual. To call them "virtual" doesn't mean they don't exist, but it does mean that both their existence and their character are exclusively dependent upon human perception, projection and choice. Virtual realities have no independent existence or character. They are the product of mind(s) and selves. Aspects of them can be measured and studied by science, but they are not "things" or en-ergies with an independent existence. My social "self," who I think I am, is one of these virtual realities.

The individual biological organism is not the "self," though it can be confusing to try to make the distinction, for society's "self" is organically grafted onto it and *they are not distinct.* The "self" is an *avatar,* an "identi-ty mask," devised in society by our symbol-making capacity; it is a symbol that "gathers" and "stands for" the biological organism, created for the purposes of social interaction. But the "symbol" draws its existence and character from choice ... initially the choice of our immediate *family,* then increasingly of ourselves in conjunction with wider circles of *society.* It is therefore in a virtual context that those things I most identify as "myself" are determined: my name, my gender, my language, my character, my values, my beliefs, my interactive role in society, my means of survival, and my participation in the reproductive cycle and its rituals. That which most intimately and exclusively defines me is a *virtuality* — a symbol — created in collaboration with the society in which I live. Were my individu-al organism, biologically unchanged in any way, to have been inserted from birth in another time, place, family and culture — a different virtual world — I would be a different "self" altogether ... with different goals, values, convictions, antipathies, preferences, etc., and of course, destiny. *I would be "someone" else.*

The socially constructed and sustained "self," since it is not distinct from the biological organism, comes under the protection of the **conatus**. This "self" avoids death at all costs despite being a social fiction; it is treated as if it were the organism itself. We've all experienced this, in ourselves and others. It is all too common for people to make a life or death issue out of the perceived needs of their social self: their career, their preference for a partner, where they live, how they are respected by their peers, their level of remuneration as a function of social recognition, their feelings of betrayal, of being belittled, demeaned, marginalized, etc.

It is this socially constructed self that Buddhism calls "unreal" and counsels us to transcend because it is the principal source of the pain that we inflict on ourselves and others. The social self is real, but its reality is only virtual. We are not constrained to obey its commands and satisfy its demands. Biological survival is rarely threatened by its demise. We are radically capable of deconstructing the self created by society and constructing a new one, a different one — the one we want. But most ascetical programs, recognizing the social etiology of the self, advise us to pursue such a transformation integrated into an alternative community that will support the new identity, or the effort will fail. Buddhists call that community the *sangha.* Historically, it was a monastic community (western monasticism had a similar history), but it need not be. All programs of radical personal conversion offer the same advice. Addicts and alcoholics are encouraged to work out their problems in a "therapeutic community" or in a 12-step group. And the "new man" that emerges, bears the stamp of the new society that has helped it come into *existence* and into which it is integrated. For Augustine of Hippo, joining the Christian church was exactly such a choice. It "saved" him from the viral sexual addictions he had contracted as a member of the Roman elite, and on the basis of his liberating experience he attributed to the Church "supernatural" powers it did not possess. His interpretation dominated Christian thinking in the West for a thousand years.

Virtual reality is ultimately malleable. How I perceive my "self," what responsibilities I feel toward socially encouraged goals and values ... and that includes my attitude toward things as apparently bedrock organic as death ... are all changeable. They are realities we ourselves have created.

Virtual reality, because it has been created in, by and for society, very often looks and feels like it is immutable; for it is constantly reinforced and reconfirmed by others. That makes the "self" feel biological. The **conatus** reacts to perceived threats to its survival accordingly. People kill or die to protect this social self's place in the social world. Recognizing this, many have opted to change the values that define their social self. But no one will ever try to change unless they have some insight into the *virtuality* (the "unreality") of the self as constructed in collaboration with society.

religion in a virtual world

In the epigraph cited at the beginning of this book, Daniel Dennett speaks about a phenomenon "in the living world that apparently exceeds the functional." He is referring, of course, to religion. He asks, *cui bono,* "who benefits" from it? ... what possible purpose could religion serve "in this living world"? He is asking it that way because for him there is no other category of explanation for an expenditure of energy made by any biological organism than biological survival. Religion doesn't appear to have any value for biological survival ... *but by his standards that is impossible.* Therefore, he is convinced there must be some biological benefit provided by religion that we have yet to uncover. His book *Breaking the Spell* was an attempt to elucidate what it is.

His question is: why has "evolution" permitted and even seems invested in forging this incomprehensible extravagance? Religion must somehow confer a *biological advantage* on its adherents; therefore he believes, revealing what that advantage is will contribute to "breaking the spell" with which religion has mystified our minds. Richard Dawkins, in *The God Delusion,* pursues a similar line of argument.

Fundamentally I agree with the overall thrust of that question, but not as Dennett formulates it. I believe he is basically asking, as I am, *does religion have a place in a material universe?* As he asks it, however, the question is overly narrow and, given his perspective, somewhat inconsistent. Despite his awareness of how virtualities function, he seems to assume that social "memes," like religion and its doctrines are stand alone units that correlate to survival under the same conditions as biological traits. They are selected because the individual or the group that uses them thrives. He ignores the fact that survival in the virtual world of society *is itself virtual.* Once things like religion "come to be" in a virtual world, they survive by continuing to function *for that world* in a way that is analogous to but not the same as physical, biological *existence.* The "survival advantage" is not for the biological individual given to it by religion, nor even, as Darwin said, because of religion's value for group survival; it is broader. Group survival is enhanced by the *entire cultural gestalt* of which religion is only a part. The cultural community survives, and so the virtual culture survives, and its religion maintains a virtual existence within it.

I wonder how he missed that? Perhaps it is his reductionist mindset, which underestimates matter's communitarian dynamism — the depth of its power to integrate. Reductionists tend to see "real reality" in the components and not in the composite. Whatever the reason, he seems not to consider the possibility that religion's *existence* is determined by its role as an integral component in the coherence of *a cultural complex* whose sustaining power for collective human survival is due to many factors that function together resulting in something not unlike an organism. (It is so much like an organism that people have been willing to sacrifice their lives for it.) Religion as a cultural artifact is meaningful because the virtual world of which it is a part is meaningful for the group that survives by it. If the group is thriving and the whole culture is strong, it can even absorb an energy-drain in one of its components. So a religion with an obsolete view-of-the-world that perhaps could not stand on its own can be kept artificially alive because of the traditional role it plays in a *gestalt* that *does* stand on its own, for reasons that appear to have nothing to do with religion and perhaps even contrary to it.

Religion under these circumstances can also invert itself if necessary to fit the culture's broader demands. I believe this is what happened to Christianity when it became the state religion of the Roman Empire. It was Caesar's concept of "God" and morality that ruled, not Jesus'.

Not all religious doctrine is altruistic, and reductionists' "biological explanation" has, since Darwin, been traditionally directed solely at accounting for the role of altruism in biological survival. Religion is much more complex than the stereotypes suggest. Dennett's *cui bono* fails to ask why some religious beliefs, like the doctrine of "original sin," which we will examine in chapters 4 and 5, foster an individual self-destructive self-denigration — biological *disadvantage* — yet the religion flourishes. The explanation can only be found in looking at the larger picture — the virtual complex of which religion is only a part. It is significant that the traditional Christian doctrine of original sin was articulated by a member of the Roman upper class a hundred years after Constantine's promotion.

a christian culture

While the Christian religion may have been the dominant factor in our western culture's formation and initial expansive energy, at a certain point historically it humbly took its place as a function of the whole. In our time it has become one piece in a large and complex puzzle, a small gear in a great machine whose survival power is fueled by other interests. And so long as the machine is running well, its religion — no matter how independently irrational and inconsistent it may have become — will be kept running along with it. This kind of overview corresponds to an entirely different paradigm than the simplistic vision that underlies the reductionist perspective which Dennett and Dawkins represent.

The essays in this book work on the background premise that if religion changes, the whole will necessarily change with it, and *vice versa;* for what religion is and what it does is determined by its place in the whole. That *leitmotif* may not be expressed or even immediately apparent in every instance, but it is a guiding notion — one of the big ideas — that hovers over this volume. It suggests that we are not as free of religion as we think we are, nor is our society.

There are some important implications that accompany this broadening of perspective. One is that a change in culture and religion entails a change in our social and political structures. Culture not only produces religion but also the other systems by which we live. Our politics, economics and religion have come to us out of the mists of the past bound together as one organic whole. The call from many believers that authentic response to religious imperatives entails economic and political changes that will eliminate injustice and inequality, is familiar to us all. The cry arises from both sides of the political divide — from individualists and communitarians — each with reference to their own religious vision, and each persuaded that the common good will be poorly served without it.

These demands are valid, predictable and perfectly reasonable on the face of it. They seem to diverge only because they each lay claim to different aspects of the culture's religious value configuration. But the explanation is actually much more complex and works in reverse order as well. There is more than enough evidence to show that those who benefit from the political and socio-economic system will search-and-find (and maybe even create) the ideological justifications necessary to keep things, and themselves, in place. Religion has been made to serve that purpose so often in our history that it has left its mark in the residue of extant doctrines. Where there is no intention of allowing the political and social structures to change, *religion will not be allowed to change either.*

There are those who recognize religion's interactive role in exactly such a resistance. Hence the *rejection of religion* on "political" grounds — one might even say, on "religious" grounds — is a prominent feature of our cultural landscape. The *philosophes* of the enlightenment saw the Church as an irrational opponent of liberty and reason, and worked for its demise. *"Ecrasez l'infame"!* was Voltaire's famous cry, *"crush the beast."* It was a call to a *religious* crusade against the traditional Christian religion for the sake of humankind.

More recently in Latin America where a liberationist Christianity was used to support revolutionary change, religion was attacked by the upper classes with which most Catholic Bishops identify. Today in our own country where a fundamentalist Christianity rejects communitarianism and the economic sharing it implies, that kind of religion is being promoted by the upper classes ... *and the Catholic hierarchy..*

Culture is a unitary phenomenon and its components tend to integrate because the human community lives *necessarily* under its shelter. There is no way to escape it, because humankind is constantly assaulted by *indeterminacy — the void —* and culture with its religions is the imaginary door built to shut it out.

the void

Why is culture so central to humankind's way of life on this planet? We humans are a unique life-form. In our case the evolution of our minds has eliminated the instincts of our animal past, leaving us without a guide for how to live. The clouds parted and we suddenly found ourselves suspended over a vertiginous abyss. How do we live as humans in the indeterminate world our minds have opened for us? Our symbol-making consciousness responded by creating a virtual world that purported to eliminate indeterminacy. Culture reflects the belief that just responding to the natural urges we share with other animals — to provide ourselves with food, clothing, shelter and family — is not enough. What about the rest? But that there is a "rest" is itself a cultural assumption. How have we responded to this assumption in our history up to now?

Culture is our projection of who we think we are — why we are here, and what we should live for. It is a virtual substitution for biological organisms that no longer provide that information for us. Following, then, on our culture's value projections, we construct our societies, our buildings, our machines, our systems of extracting wealth and wielding power ... *and our religions.* Culture tries to make up for what our biological instincts will not tell us.

All cultures are a communitarian enterprise because they are the source and product of our social "selves" whose very identity was created for social interaction. Culture attempts to fill the void — to make clear for us what we should do with our lives. Culture is a work of the collective imagination. One would think the notion of an individualistic culture were a self-contradiction ... but we know well that our individualistic Western European culture is in many ways blind to that insight; and it was our traditional Western European religion — Christianity — that laid the groundwork for it.

Culture's standard bearer has always been religion. For religion's notions and symbols claim to be the naked confrontation with the terror of the void. A particular culture will not go away so long as there are human beings who live by it, *nor will the religion that was born with it.*

Our culture's religion, and our religion's culture, travel with us wherever we go. They are the virtual glider that bears us up over the abyss. Culture and religion are eternally wedded to one another, and we to them, for they are the response of our diaphanous human consciousness to this opaque random world of matter in which we awaken *as if to a dream*: the echo of what we think we hear. *Religion, like all cultural artifacts, is a work of the imagination.* Given the phenomenon we are confronted with — the void — we have no choice. We are blind from birth; and there is no guide. We have to grope in the dark and *imagine* what it is we are feeling ... even the very contours of our own face. The "self" as *solitary individual* is the imaginary product of western culture; so is the religion that nourishes it.

We cannot live without religion; for as human beings we are forced to confront the void. Those who deny religion's traditional form, as I do, or any form, as others do, are really, in my opinion, proposing an alternative religion whether they realize it or not ... *for we cannot live without wrestling with the void.* Dennett, to his chagrin, sees that religion refuses to disappear. But he urges us to ask, why? If the answer we get seems myopic, perhaps it is because we have allowed Dennett's prejudicial reductionist way of asking the question to guide the enquiry. *Cui bono?* What *biological advantage* does religion confer on those who have it, as opposed to those who don't? I contend there is no way to test that *because those whose culture is not built on religion do not exist.* Every culture has a religion embedded in its origins, because every culture is the result of a multi-millennial confrontation with the void. Dennett's reductionist assumptions drive him into a corner. He has no answer because he has a robotic and unhistorical view of the human being and its social elaborations. And if we were to modify the question to reflect the depth, pathos, and historical continuity of the human condition, how should it be asked, and how should we answer it? This book is an attempt to do that.

the metaphors of religion

By now it should be obvious that I am using the word "religion" in two senses. The first refers to religious institutions as they have evolved historically and actually exist today. The other is religion as I believe it must exist — defined by its essential elements. I believe religion in this latter sense will always exist, embedded in the culture functioning perhaps subconsciously and in ways that are not immediately recognizable as religion. We have no choice. The void will not disappear and culture must find ways to deal with it. We are human. It's what we do.

But we don't need religion (and our culture) as we have inherited it. My primary complaint is that western religions insist their doctrines are facts, literally true. To the contrary, I contend, religion has no facts of its own. Its doctrines can only *be poetry, a cultural artifact, a work of the imagination.* Many of the doctrines that have come down to us, if taken *metaphorically, poetically,* can perhaps continue to serve as we seek to face the void made more abysmal for us by modern science; but taken literally as facts they undermine the cultural project, for by standing in complete contradiction of the natural order, they falsify reality. The void cannot be either confronted or embraced, because its reality is being denied; fantasy is put in its place.

The only "facts" there are, are what can be known to all, and examined and expressed by science. Religion interprets those facts for what they *mean* to the human family. Religion is poetry and poetry is a work of art. Some poetry is better than other. Theologians are those who judge *religion* and that means they need to be literary critics. We can only hope that these women and men are in touch with themselves, *for the standard for judgment is humanity*. Religion is to be judged at the bar of humanity, not the other way around, and that necessarily includes common sense. The world, *as it is,* is the reality that religion has to help us embrace. If it doesn't do that, it is of no value. This is a simple enough formula, and it seems to parallel what was said by Jesus, *"... the Sabbath was made for man, not man for the Sabbath."* We ask, in the deepest possible sense, does this religion, this doctrine, this ritual, this morality ... *work for us*? ... or does it make us robots, slaves to something *not us* — *alien?*

the metaphor of death

Death is the principal human phenomenon that all religions address. But death is not only the physical demise of a biological organism; it is also a powerful *metaphor* — a virtual reality. It is *a symbol* that represents our blind-sided relationship to *existence.*

Religion is the traditional tool elaborated by human culture to stand in the breach against death; it defines what death *means* as a metaphor and proposes an appropriate *metaphorical* response. Religion is at the heart of every culture because death is such an apt metaphor for the void — the unfathomable mystery that characterizes *existence* itself. Every culture has some mechanism for dealing with the immobilization produced by the experience of death and its spontaneous contradiction of *existence.* Some cultures, like ours, very directly project an imagined parallel world where the persons who died are said to "have gone" and where we will find them again. "Life is changed," our rituals say, "but not taken away." Thus our traditional religion eliminates the sting of death by *effectively denying it*. The fact that so many simply take for granted that our "souls" will live forever is a testimony to the power of culture. Culture makes us see things that are not visible. We have all been formed in this belief. We can hardly conceive of religion without it.

One would think that death was simply an organic fact, safely beyond the reformulations of culture; but it is as virtual as anything else on our social horizon. The very fact of its denial by traditional Christianity is proof enough of that. Death impacts the "self" which was painstakingly assembled by society over many years of formation. The culturally constructed self *necessarily* perceives death through the lenses provided by this process. The self and its death are both cultural artifacts, two sides of the same virtual coin, and the individual tends to react *as if he/she were following a script prepared in advance by the culture.* For us in the west, two thousand years of Christian indoctrination about the reality, character and significance of the human individual "self" — the "immortal soul" — and what happens to it after death, color our feelings *even after those teachings have receded from public acknowledgement.*

We have internalized them. That's the way culture works. It is not a rational process; it does not have to do with active "belief." The conceptual content may be totally absent, but the affect and attitude remain. "Death" in this case is now a cultural "meme"[8] with a life of its own whose impact on the human psyche is something like what Jung called an "archetype." Death is not just the "demise of the biological organism." It is the demise of an organism *symbolically understood* through the eyes of a multi-millennial virtuality called "western culture" that had been given its fundamental shape by the Roman Empire's version of the Christian religion. There is no way that the uncontested millennial belief in a "particular judgment" for each individual "soul" which will determine whether or not it will be "punished eternally," would not impact how one feels about dying *even after active belief is no longer professed.*

Other cultures, like those inspired by Buddhism, encourage a detachment based on the perception that life and its forms are evanescent — basically illusions, like the "unreality" of the self. That we all disappear, they seem to say, is exactly what one should have expected, *for that is what happens to all living things, from amoebas to elephants.* The "self" they insist, is not "real." These religions, from our point of view, would seem to be less effective in confronting the void, for they offer nothing after death. And yet they flourish. How could a "solution" so diametrically opposed to ours work so well?

---

[8] "meme" is a currently popular term that refers to a cultural unit, like ideas or social values or practices. The way "memes" change and grow in society is similar to living organisms and genes which evolve by natural selection. It was coined by Richard Dawkins in *The Selfish Gene* 1986

The answer is that the hypnotic power of *culture* makes it happen. It's no more impossible for a culture to assure us that life is a temporary cycle for every living thing, than it is to claim, without evidence, that we will all live forever in another world. Western culture created the very notion of an individual "self" and vested it with precious freedom, sacred rights and solemn responsibilities, in large measure due to belief in the eternal existence of the "self." The east has traditionally downplayed the importance of the individual *and the social self is formed by that perception.*

The anguish of death and the individual self are correlates. In the West, belief in the immortality of the self implies an importance that death contradicts. Reduce the importance of the individual self, and you reduce the impact of death. Death, then, ceases to be the catastrophe that western religion needed to make it in order to establish its case for the resurrection of Jesus and the eternal salvation (or damnation) of the individual "soul." And without individual accountability under the threat of "the second death" — eternal punishment — the Christian religion could not have performed the theocratic role the Roman Empire assigned to it. It was the reason it was chosen as the State religion. The fact that the Christian "afterlife" was politicized by its absorption into the state apparatus of Rome, made fear of eternal punishment a priority. This transformed Christianity. What St Paul may have imagined to be a *cosmic communal salvation gratuitously awarded to all with no concern for merit*, as we see in his letters, was reinterpreted after the takeover by Rome to focus on the deserving individual alone. It was almost predictable. The empire wanted compliant behavior, and fear of hell for the individual was the magic formula that guaranteed it. This was quite different from the message of Jesus. That imperial reinvention gave a foundational shape to Christianity that it retains to this day in almost all of its versions, "reformed" or not.

On the other hand, if culture were to emphasize the primacy of the human community — if the principal source of significance was not the "self" but the group — then an individual's life becomes less his/her own, more available and indeed enhanced the more it is at the service of the group. Death is less of a disaster. Notice how this very dynamic, so foreign to us in ordinary circumstances, spontaneously comes into play in times of calamity (like war or natural disaster), when survival itself requires a communal response. At those times it is the individual's contribution to the collective effort to survive that is recognized as important, not personal superiority or the private accumulation of resources or the individual's ability to survive.

But this experience need not be limited to such extraordinary events. Individualism is not grounded in some absolute; it is a cultural preference. We live under its dominance even though we never personally chose it. But individualism is *virtual* and it can be changed. And if it changes it will change the way we live our lives — what we tell ourselves we are, what we have a right to expect for ourselves and what we should strive for during our time under the sun.

religion and trust

Dennett following Dawkins calls the components of culture, "memes" in an analogy with "genes." But unlike biological traits, memes exist only because we create them. And yet they are not illusions. They are the most important issues we deal with throughout our lives; they are as necessary as food, clothing and shelter ... as real as life and death. It's not surprising that sometimes we are willing to die — or kill — rather than see certain memes change or disappear. But at the same time, we have to remember that it is we who create them, and we can change them.

Religion is our primary defense against the potentially immobilizing and humanly mutilating effect of the void whose symbol is death. That makes religion in some form *indispensable*. But the form that it was given in the West in a pre-scientific age is not immutable. Religion's mandate to neutralize the sting of death must be allowed to function *in terms that speak to us in our time as we have become* with the knowledge that modern science has given us. *Who we think we are has changed.* Obeisance to a sacred past has no validity here. *We need religion*, but not as it has come down to us. Religion exists for humankind, not the other way around. *"The Sabbath was made for man ..."*

But applying the formula is not that easy. Those "facts" — those particular traditional religious beliefs, like the immortal soul or an intervening humanoid "God" — were all we ever had. How do we confront the void without them ... *in practice and in detail?* Can we *trust existence,* without our traditional beliefs? These beliefs, we have to remind ourselves, are claimed to be "facts" about reality. Our religion insists they are literally true.

That insistence, in my opinion, is one of the things that drives the new atheists to question whether religion should exist at all. Both sides in the religion debate are completely convinced that what they are fighting for is a matter of life and death. Since culture "saves" us from the corrosive power of death, we cling to our religion because we think that without it we cannot accomplish the task; and its antagonists think that is the very thing that keeps us from the adult adjustment to reality that will alone grant us true peace of mind.

Our pluralistic society tolerates more than one religion ... as well as none. Does that tell us something? Is there a *core insight* at the heart of all these various positions that explains and justifies this tolerance? This gives rise to the question we started with at the beginning of this prologue: Can religion move past its traditional literalism and allow itself to be re-set in another "factual" context? In other words, *can religion evolve*? Right now, in the Christian west, for those trapped by the "infallible" beliefs provided by either their "Pope" or their Scriptures (or both), the answer is *No*. Theocracy nourished by "facts" that do not exist, is as much a serious threat as it ever was. That is enough to explain the intensity of the reaction against it.

religion? ... *doesn't that mean "God"?*

What is this *core insight*? For organisms as complex as ourselves, shaped as we are by the intersubjectivities and virtualities of human society, the question cannot be answered without appreciating what *existence* means to our poor frightened species, the only animal that has to live suspended over the abyss. I believe the *core insight* that drives all versions of religion is that *at the heart and source of all things there exists a living dynamism that is life-giving, benevolent and trustworthy*.

"Benevolence" is not "known" (provable) because there are no unambiguously objective facts that compel its acceptance as a logical proposition. But it responds to a different kind of logic, anyway, because it, and the "trust" it evokes in us "persons," are not definable in any terms other than their own. It's a "person" thing. We either understand it or we don't. But I claim benevolence is *connaturally understood* in a cognitive embrace of *material energy* in its most palpable and undeniable form: *the* **conatus**. We *understand intimately* what *matter's energy* is, in both its potential and actual forms, **in ourselves**. For *we are* what matter is.

So, is this transcendent dynamism, "*matter's energy*," a "person"? I say No, and emphatically. It is *not a separate entity* of any kind outside of its functioning in our human organisms; there is nothing I can point to that acts like what we mean by "person." And we are in a position to know, because we, persons, live immersed in *matter's energy* every day, both inside and outside of ourselves. But it is something that has permitted itself to be "kneaded" into even the most minute element of this universe of which I am a part, and that evokes in me the presence of a massive subjectivity of some kind, too big and too devoid of "self" to be called a "person," that must contain within itself the potential to become me, *because I AM THAT*. This is the key. Without an appreciation of the **significance of the universal presence of matter's existential energy — the conatus** — in every life-form we know, matter is reduced to inert random mechanism, the religious project ceases to be poetry and Dennett's robots rule the earth. The *embrace of existence* that the void seemed to call forth, will never materialize. But that would imply there were no *human beings.*

If what Dennett claims about matter is true and we are no longer *human,* then why do *WE LOVE being ourselves and being here with our people* ... as does every living thing? Even after we hear Dennett's "truth" about ourselves, *why is the spell not broken,* why do we still refuse to disown as illusion this *existence* that we love so passionately, so poetically, so mystically? Explaining this stubborn *obsessive love* of *existence,* is the poetry that is religion. *Celebrating the* **conatus** is religion.

Yes, absolutely, I am talking about *love.* But it's a tough love that embraces the void. This will entail a broad, reality-grounded understanding of "benevolence" that challenges the infantile fantasies, extracted from traditional religion's narratives, that up to now have been the sole descriptors for both sides of the debate. What the "religionists" insist is literal fact and the "anti-religionists" reject, is the same impossible fairy-tale: an anthropomorphic — *humanoid* — "God" of the book who "chose" evolution to do his creating for him, micro-manages the universe from day to day incomprehensibly "permitting" holocausts and home foreclosures, and rewards or punishes each individual in the afterlife.

Once the book's spirit-"God" and "his" physical interventions both before and after death are clearly understood to be *metaphors,* then the poetry of the stories, which are the epic chronicle of our people's attempts to *relate to the void of existence,* can be explored and allowed to evolve. But until then, the "book" and its literalist promoters remain the primary reasons for the well-deserved rejection of religion.

If this literalism can be abandoned, we will actually begin to lay the foundations for a religion that *we need to have exist* ... because the two end-posts of this dialog, **life-fact and death-fact,** the limits where knowing ends and the void reveals itself, are the brackets within which our destiny unfolds. Denying either pole will not be possible. Right now, that is not true, because in the West in the name of revelation, "religion" denies death ... and "atheism," in the name of a reductionist science, denies the reality and significance of life.

PART ONE

faith and religion

Both faith and religion are intrinsic to being human. This may be considered the theme of Part One. I do not present it as an exhortation, but rather as an observation of inevitability. Faith and religion correspond to the human condition. We cannot escape it. In this part I hope to establish the bases for this inevitability and allow its implications to assume a guiding role in our thinking.

The human project goes well beyond food, clothing, shelter and family. There is one principle reason for that: *death.* Both as organic reality and as existential symbol, death stands as the contradiction of the **conatus**, the natural urge to self-preservation which extrapolates to the expectation of endless life. The **conatus** is also responsible for our sense of the sacred.

A contradiction of such intimacy and finality has the potential to jam our circuits. That paralysis has been averted by the virtual world that our culture has conjured for us — a vision that worked for millennia to dispel the emptiness. When the coherence of that world breaks down, as it has for us in the era of modern science, death re-emerges as the ultimate and defining reality. *Being-human* suddenly seems absurd, *and from there, all of existence as well.* Our culture and its religion, our traditional bulwark against the abyss, has failed us. Naked and afraid, we find ourselves facing the void. It is the human condition. The culture must find a new way to deal with death. What we have come up with so far is grotesque.

Our religions lie at the heart of the matter; they are the foundational visions — the interpretations — that determined what direction our cultures would take. If the culture is no longer functional for life, if it no longer deals effectively with the sting of death, much of it can be attributed to the way the religion at its core has evolved (or not evolved) through the millennia. In this first part, I do not want to address the details of that problem, but rather to make an effort to understand the generic phenomenon and why it will never go away. For me it is not a theological question, *it is metaphysical.*

Chapter I

~~Faith~~

F aith is relationship.
There is nothing startlingly new or esoteric in that statement which implies a distinction that we referred to in the prologue. Beliefs — doctrine, dogma — are considered "facts" with a determined cognitive content and claim to be objective *knowledge*. Faith, as used here, does not. It's a relationship: a connection between living things, an intersubjective valence that implies recognition, trust and reliance.

In this chapter I want to elaborate a description of faith that is not derived from established religions of any kind, Christian or not. I will propose a view that is consistent with the conclusions arrived at in *The Mystery of Matter (MM)*. This conception of faith will apply across the board to every human being, of whatever tradition, culture or intellectual persuasion ... and that includes "atheists," whose reverent embrace of *existence* and sense of the sacred, without recourse to anything supernatural or other-worldly demolishes the traditional accusations that their stance somehow implies a disdain for the reality which we *all* respect, love and struggle to understand.

Such attempts at semantic adjustment, however, are still far from adequate. For, even taken in its most subjective sense, the very word "faith" has been fatally robbed of openness by a long association with Christianity's endless disputations about supernatural other-worldly realities. It is virtually impossible to use the word "faith" now without evoking connotations that distract from the simple natural phenomenon I want to elucidate.

There is nothing supernatural in what will be proposed here. So, like the words "God" and "sacred," a radical disclaimer has to be made for the term "faith." I will try to be clear in context and, since the word "faith" is under erasure, from this point forward, you will find it written but crossed out, like this: ~~faith~~.[9] That doesn't mean it's eliminated ... it's simply a reminder that it is no longer being used with its traditional religious "otherworld" significance.

relationship

L et's begin with "relationship," just what does it mean in the context of our discussion?

The word relationship can be used in an *objective* sense referring to the way two or more things are connected by a physical, biological or legal bond. But here I use it in a *subjective* sense implying a conscious mutuality between subjects based on recognition.

We usually use adjectives like "personal" to characterize this phenomenon, which would seem to imply that relationship occurs only at the human level. But clearly, we have relationships, and sometimes very intense ones, with what are not currently defined as "persons" — our house pets and farm animals, for example. We relate to them, and they to us and to one another. Yet they are not "persons." What is this phenomenon? ... *an attitude* assumed by conscious living individual organisms — **subjectivities** — toward one another based on mutual recognition. We often couch it in terms of "knowledge:" we say we *know* them, and they *know* us.

We dealt with the cognitive side of this phenomenon in *The Mystery of Matter,* chapters 8 and 10 on interpretation and recognition. We saw that recognizing an individual as a center of intentionality is not *knowledge* in the conventional sense of the word. It is an *understanding* derived from *interpretation*. It utilizes our time-bound cognitive equipment to assess the *drift* or direction-of-movement of what is really a process (the continually unfolding intentions of another living individual), without the "snap-shot" effect we call abstraction. In order to generate an interpretation of the moving, changing intentionality that I have encountered in the other, I necessarily have recourse to my understanding of myself.

Relationship, then, is a mutual attitude focused on the running interpretation of active intentionality or bearing; it is an *understanding* that prescinds from the "knowledge" of *what* the center of intentionality is. For the interpretation of intentionality to occur, there is no need to have a "what," a

---

[9] This is inspired by a term and procedure used by Jaques Derrida.

"thing," a predicate. *"What" I have encountered is fundamentally irrelevant from a relational point of view.* It doesn't substantially matter if the "other" is a dog or a cat, or a dolphin or an extra-terrestrial. What matters for *relationship* is its conscious bearing ... specifically toward me ... which inspires my bearing toward it. I interpret that bearing and take a stand toward it — that is relationship.

Our relating to other human individuals shows the same features. We all know many people, but we *relate* in different ways to each individual depending, we say, on "who" they are, not "what" they are, meaning whether they are friendly, not just that they are humans. Just being human, as far as relationship is concerned, is not the most relevant factor.

relating to myself

What about myself? Can I relate to myself? We saw in chapter 6 of *MM* that self-awareness is neither innate, nor instantaneous. I come to "know" myself only gradually through the interpretation of my own intentionality like any other center of process. That I love this self that I come to know is usually taken for granted; but as we are unfortunately aware, a self-loathing or lack of self-respect is not beyond the realm of possibility.

Over time I'm really getting to know my body and the impact on it of past experience, which is the organic basis of my personality. It's not something I do once and for all. My sense of "who I am" in society continues to develop throughout my life, open to amended interpretations from new information about my past and my predilections. I recognize my reactions and I either like them and trust them or I don't. And at some point I may decide to *redirect my intentionality in order* to suppress and override or encourage and intensify my reactions as I choose. There is a recognition that my "social-self" is not really "me" in the deepest sense, and that I have the right *and the ability* to change it. This all requires that I "relate" to my "self" almost as if I were another.

The general point is that in all these cases relating is not based on the conceptual or scientific knowledge of a fixed object as we've defined the term in these reflections, but rather on *interpreting and responding to a process* — an activity that results not in knowledge but in *understanding.* And correlatively, knowing something or someone well or even intimately — as with another human being or even *myself* — does not eliminate the need to continue to assess the ongoing events that are the expressions of a possibly changing intentionality.

A relationship, therefore, is fundamentally *non-conceptual.* It is not based on "knowledge" but rather on *understanding,* which we have proposed is *somatically* based — based in the *body. Understanding,* because it is grounded in experience, always involves *organic self*-awareness. It most appropriately eschews the word-labels of conventional language and operates "wordlessly," which can mean, silently, in contemplative realization or, linguistically, in metaphor.

intentionality in the darkness of *existence*

As we approached the encounter with the "darkness" at the core of reality uncovered in chapter 13 of *MM* — "the void" — which terminated our analysis, we realize that with *matter's energy* we are in the presence of something far beyond anything our cognitive apparatus was designed to deal with. *We do not know what it is.* But this is astonishing ... for we are made of it*!* Why don't we know what we ourselves are? As we will see, this defining paradox creates the significance of ~~faith~~ for human life.

Experiencing *existence* is not entirely unlike meeting another life form for the first time. *Material energy,* after all, is a living dynamism. In living things, *existence* is a reflexive self-embrace expressed in the **conatus.** I encounter this vital energy throughout the biota of living things; it is the source and wellspring of their life as well as my own. Everything alive is bursting with the drive to survive derived from *matter's existential energy.* It explains everything: *what* and *that* and *how we* are. It explains *me* ... and everything I am and want and do.

Material energy is observably present and functioning in every life form there is, most of which exercise a relational behavior at their own level, minimally to food sources or enemies or potential mates, and at the human level to intense interpersonal connections. There is a relational potential in matter's energy. Some might interpret this fact to mean that material energy itself can be related to as if it were a separate or individual entity.

But that is not possible for two reasons: first, *it cannot be related to as "other,"* because it is myself. Second, it is not some recognizable delimited entity ... a "thing" much less a conscious living individual, like a "person." In our experience, it is not. It is *all things.* It is never found "by itself;" it is always only *things "other than itself"* (so to speak) and the specific relational intentionalities found in these things are tied to the particular level of emergence (integrative complexity) they've achieved. There is an absolute identity between *material energy* and its many manifestations at all levels ... *one of which is me*. *Material energy* shows no evidence of the kinds of recognition and intentionality that we are familiar with in our *relationships* with other separate living entities, whether animal or human.

Matter's energy is us; for we all, whether humans, bonobos or bacteria, are members of the same family, made of the same "stuff," evolved over eons of time out of the same primitive elements. None of us, at any level or at any time, or in the exercise of any function, is anything other than this *material energy.*

Nevertheless, even though there is no clear evidence of any separate individual living entity called "*matter's energy*" apart from the things I see, I know through observation that matter's energy is a living dynamism, providing to all things, at the most elemental level a non-conscious intentionality, a self-embrace — the **conatus sese conservandi** — the "instinct for self-preservation." It was by this non-conscious intentionality of *existence* ... not thoughts, or "plans" ... but a blind, reflexive, paroxysmal self-embrace — the drive to survive — borne forward through natural selection, that all things came to be ... and to be as they are ... *including me.*

availability

I'm sure you have noticed another paradox. All of us life forms are free to use *material energy* for the construction of our own selves and our continued survival as we choose, each in its own way. Our species' evolution has not been directed solely by forces outside of our selves. In my case, *existence* is encountered with a permissive bearing toward my "person." I have it, in other words, as if it were entirely mine. I was not even aware that I am an emergent form of *matter's energy* until science brought it to light for me. Even now I find it hard to believe that I am constructed of something *that might in any way be other than me*, and so when science confronts me with the reality that I am made of the same materials as a plant or an animal or a brackish wetland, I do not spontaneously absorb it. Following in the tracks of my tradition, I tend to set myself at a distance from *material energy*, claim that I am "spirit" (i.e., other-than-matter), and objectify it as if it were not me. But, of course, matter is *me* ... and it is not only me, it is everything*!* We cannot avoid relating to it ... because *it is our very selves* with which we are in intimate necessary contact. The relationship exists long before we begin thinking about it.

But there is even more paradox. While the *material energy* is "me," the "making it available to me" is not. In other words, it was not "mine" to dispose of for my own *self-origination*. I did not make *existence* available to myself, nor did I plan and generate my body with its organs and brain, cells and vital chemicals. I am aware of the fact that I have no ultimate control or ownership over this material energy which-is-me. The availability, however non-directive and non-personal, implied in my intimate possession of material energy, is due to an initiative, or a "permission," if you will forgive me the allusion, that comes from somewhere else. It is not mine ... and this gives me a sense that there is *an intentionality* here, a bearing ... maybe not one that is directed by personal choice, or to me personally, but certainly one that I am related to in a way that is vital to me, ... because it *is me*, and without it there would be no "me." It might be passively permissive, but matter's energy is not only vitally important to my life, it is the source of my self identity. The **conatus** that is my personal self with its desire to live, is responsible for my self-identity. It comes exclusively from *matter's energy. I AM THAT!*

I cannot downplay the absolutely transcendent importance that this availability has for me. Since I love existing, and I love existing *as myself*, I most naturally *love* that in and by which "I live and move and have my being." How I *relate to it* is necessarily affected by the simple fact that the *relationship* here is not optional. It is not discretionary ... *it is **personally constitutive***. This relationship makes me to be-here and to be me. *I am not self-originating* and so I am necessarily related in a most profound and intimate way to the source of that origination.

existence is not mine? ... the religious experience

In this sketch we recognize the familiar elements of what has traditionally been called "the religious experience." It is the realization that while *existence* (*matter's energy*) is me, it is *not mine*. This experience has classically been cited as the prologue to ~~faith~~. It is traditionally said to occur in an event that generates the awareness of impending death ... for it is then that I realize that what I define as "me" can disappear ... that I did not "possess" my *existence* as I thought. This is something of a disturbing discovery. But consider the paradox — that the recognition of something as commonplace as death should be *so shocking* in my own case as to be aptly described as a "revelation" that has the radical potential to disrupt my life, is an indication of how blindly identified I am with *existence*. Until I realize that *existence* is not *mine*, I take it as if I am it, or own it ... my *knowledge* of the inevitable death of every living thing notwithstanding. This is a stunning anomaly! It is the ultimate *realization* ... and a clear example of the difference between knowledge and *understanding.* My spontaneous sense of total identity with *existence* — my **conatus** — had completely overridden my rationality. I knew *all along* that I would die ... *but I did not realize it — I did not understand it.* And when the somatic realization of death occurs, when my whole organism becomes aware of its significance, it can short-circuit my thinking process altogether and immobilize me.

There is an existential self-embrace at the core of myself — a **conatus** — and I see that it is what drives every life form on the planet. I have no trouble *understanding* this universal identification with *existence* and the desire to continue to *exist.* As a matter of fact it's one thing for which I don't demand any explanation whatsoever. I *understand* it implicitly, con-naturally, in and of itself. But, despite this I *still have no idea what it is.* Why do I need to *be-here*? Nevertheless, everyone understands exactly what I mean, because everyone's self is constituted of this very same empirical dynamic: *the drive to survive.*

I experience matter's energy as my self and only in a later step try to objectify it. But such objectification is a fiction. For by doing so I omit the fact that the "I" that seeks to know is not only the very thing (the "what") I want to know, but *it already understands!*

These paradoxical dimensions of *existence* are universal. The vital features of *matter's energy* that we are exploring — the self-embrace of *existence*, the drive to survive, universal availability, communitarian integration and the primacy of the totality — characterize the entire universe.

existence is a totality

Every living thing is hell-bent on staying alive, and taking care of its young; and in order to do so spends the major portion of its waking life killing and eating other life forms. We humans are no different despite our often declared distaste for it. We cleverly conceal our participation in the general slaughter with our complex division of labor. But make no mistake. If everyday we weren't scarfing down the proteins, carbs, and oils ripped off the dead bodies of our sister species, both plants and animals, we'd be gone. That's what we do, because that's the way *being-here* and staying-here works — there is no other way.

This selfishly focused intentionality is common to all life on earth. Everything treats everything else as potential food. This has been the source of great scandal for humankind since time immemorial. Religious people of our own tradition, for example, have been so offended by the universal predation that very early on, our wise and venerable forebears concluded there must have been a "mistake," a catastrophic "fall" from the original intent of creation. A friend of mine, who obviously shares this point of view, once said to me, "how can there be a 'God' if he created a world where one animal has to kill and eat another in order to live"? Convinced that a good, rational, person-"God" (as our tradition conceived "him") could not possibly countenance such a state of affairs, the Christian tradition, for one, had the audacity to condemn reality in its current form as corrupt — the result of an "original sin" — and claimed to know the way things *really should have been* had the assumed catastrophic transgression not occurred. And so this interpretation was retro-fitted to explain the ancient Hebrew scriptures which said that once things were set right, "the lion will lay down with the lamb."

But this fantasy-interpretation fails to recognize that the biblical passage quoted is poetic hyperbole, a metaphor for justice and peace among humankind. A moment's reflection will remind us that the lion is *not supposed* to lay down with the lamb. It's right for the lion to eat the lamb. We eat lamb, too*!* That's the way it works. Our task is to try to understand reality, and the "sacred" from that *understanding.* Otherwise we distort it, creating fictionalized scenarios to jibe with our projections. Living things kill and eat one another in order to live. That's the way *existence* has evolved on our planet.

But is it really such a disaster? I discern in this phenomenon the **free exchange of constituent elements within a totality.** *Matter's energy* tends to treat itself as one global living thing, and the permissions on which life is built include the mutual availability of everything to everything else within the whole. It seems to be a corollary characteristic of the communitarian nature of *material energy's* self-embrace.

It confirms that as far as *existence* is concerned, the human phenomenon is not the transcendent thing mainstream Western theistic philosophers imagined. There is no special concession given to any individual "person" or species. We are gallingly aware of this. Western culture's stubborn insistence on the separateness of humankind from the rest of "material" creation has always been contradicted by the reality of human vulnerability. We face the same predation, disease, deterioration and death that are endured by all other species in this vale of tears. In the West, that fact was interpreted as the corruption of "matter" caused by "original sin." Unfortunately it encouraged a dualist escapism that only aggravated our anguish. For it meant we suffered the added torment of believing we were unnatural ... "spirits" trapped in cages of matter ... and, because of "original sin," *had no-one to blame but ourselves!*

The ultimate indignity against which we rebelled, of course, was *death*. But upon further reflection death will be seen, similarly, to conform closely to *existence as a totality* that we are uncovering here. The keynote is **universal availability.** Since every *thing* is made of *matter's energy*, their constituent elements are always potentially available for use and re-use by others. The experiments are not ours ... they are functions of the Whole. When we die our *material energy* is re-cycled for use by a multitude of other species right up the food chain. We might be less offended by death if we could identify our own *existence* with *matter's energy as a whole. Existence,* not unlike *esse,* "being" for the scholastics, is *one thing,* and we are part of it. We belong*!* That is our reality, our torment, as well as our guarantee of endless community. What we are, *matter's energy,* will always belong, for it will always *be-here.*

So, despite our habitual indignation at being subject to the same travesties as everything else in our universe, *existence* appears blithely impervious to the exchanges going on within the walls of its house. This subjection of the individual members to the agenda of the whole, I see as the inevitable expression of the communitarian nature of *existence.*

existence's absolute availability

The availability of *existence* is a corollary of the metaphysical primacy of the Totality, the homogeneity of the substrate. It is entirely consistent with this focus on the Whole to accept death as our participation in the "project." It is simply another manifestation of *the profound availability of everything to everything else,* the sharing that constitutes the self-embrace which, from my point of view as a recipient, becomes the bottomless generosity that is the *intentionality of existence.* Death is our logical destiny, the ultimate confirmation that we are *matter's energy*, a part of the main, for it is the individual's participation in the universal availability of the substrate of which we (and all things) are constituted. By actively embracing death as an indispensable phase of our membership in this totality, we ratify with our own chosen intentionality the attitude of *existence*. By making our own substance a donation, we consciously "join the program," as it were. We intentionally become ... and thus come to *understand* ... what *existence does* — its bearing, its intentionality, *which is total availability.*

There is nothing to indicate that *matter's energy* wants anything for us or from us *whatsoever*. The availability and the permissions that go with *existence* are absolute. Everything we pursue in life has been chosen by humankind itself. The complex moral and ritual codes that people of our tradition have followed for millennia as *"religion,"* claiming that they were the "will and word of God," we realize now were metaphorical assignments designed to encourage compliance with our community's chosen values. These are *our choices*. *Existence* commands nothing. It has only one "goal," to *exist* in us as it does in all things. It is as naturally and fully present in one form as in another, and that is precisely why our experience is that all things manifest the same *univocal* "presence." If we were to try to characterize *existence* in *personal terms* (metaphorically speaking, of course), we could say that *existence's* intentionality toward all the things that are made of it, which of course includes us, is *self-emptying*.

But even that statement is misleading. It tends to treat *existence* as if it were a *separate entity* to which we can relate *as if it were an individual*. In fact, as we experience it, it is no such thing. For it is never encountered separate from the things it has become. Even at the most primitive level, existence is always something that it has become — a quark, a gluon, a neutrino bound into the hadrons of the atom. *Existence* is only seen in some combined form; it is a communitarian phenomenon.

One unavoidable fact that keeps tripping up any attempt to conceive of existence as a separate, objectifiable entity to which I can relate (as, for example, to the traditional "God-entity,"[10]) is that *I exist*. I am a "concrescence"[11] of matter's energy. My most immediate and revealing under-

---

[10] The scholastics proposed to explain the presence of "being" in all things as "participation in "God's" being." It is now called pan-emtheism.. Here I am referring to the popular "theist" image that pictures "God" as an entity quite distinct from the rest of reality. It is something the schoolmen, in fact, did not hold.

standing of the intentionality of *existence* is had with and within my own self. Ultimately, it means *I cannot objectify existence.* So I cannot relate to it the way I relate to entities that are other than me. *I am not-other than existence.*[12] I am inescapably an intimate part of what matter's energy is and does. No matter how I try to set it "out there" over against myself and look at it "in itself," and relate to it as to another, the "I" that's doing the looking is also always and only *matter's energy.* I am always within the circle of the existence I'm trying to objectify, look at and relate to.

I am matter's energy. I understand it intimately — connaturally, somatically, non-conceptually — even though I do not *know* what it is. ... So, where can I go from here? I embrace being-here and being myself. Anything else would border on the pathological. *I trust* the nature and character of matter's energy ... which is, after all, *me.*

And that is what I mean by faith.

faith

Someone might say, so, what's the big deal? Who doesn't do this? There's nothing arcane or esoteric here. Is this what you mean by faith ... something this common?

Yes, yes! ... exactly this common. I want to focus attention on the sheer simplicity of the phenomenon. This faith does not require revelation; it comes quite naturally, in fact it long precedes analysis ... and it seems to *tell us nothing.* It is **not supernatural** in any way. It is not itself knowledge and no new *knowledge* can be inferred from it. It doesn't give us any of the traditional information that we have been accustomed to expect from religion's "beliefs":

... it doesn't tell us how we should live;

... it doesn't guarantee that the human species will survive, much less, as Faulkner claimed, "prevail;"

... it doesn't tell us of a continued experience-as-self after death;

... and it suggests that our traditional western religions are metaphoric attempts to objectify existence, mystify socially prescribed behavior and defuse (or exploit) our fear of death with an imagined contractual connection with an other-worldly "God."

---

[11] This is Whitehead's term for a "thing."

[12] Nicholas of Cusa used the term *non aliud* as a characterization of "God."

Existence is so amorphous and un-focused as to be available to become anything and everything ... suggesting, paradoxically, that *in itself it is nothing*.[13] Use of that word brings us back to the "darkness we encountered in chapter 13 of *MM* and cited in our prologue. Faith does not dispel the darkness because it gives us no new *knowledge*.

This "darkness," which from another angle the Buddhists call *sunyata,* emptiness, is the metaphorical corollary of the very same austere foundational teleology we have called a self-embrace. It is a passive, undemanding availability that is so absolutely without limits as to what it can become as to appear to us to be *no-thing* whatsoever. And yet we know that it is pure energy, the power of infinite potential, the source of all the energy we see in our roiling universe and teeming planet. This I internally and connaturally *understand.* This "darkness" is the raw energy out of which everything congeals and one of whose forms *is me.* I am in intimate touch with that energy; for it is my very self. It gives me no information but it tells me something very important. It says that I am part of a self-donation so unimaginably immense that it has allowed its own energy to be harnessed to become *only* what *we* are. It is precisely its utter *emptiness* of all "self-ness" that reveals its character and its unique bearing.[14] *Existence* simultaneously is no-thing, ... wants nothing ... and makes everything *be.* And it is that "maternal" character, allowing us to be born of and feed off its own substance, that impels us to find transcendent metaphors like "Mother" or "Father" to express the obsessive self-embrace — *the* **conatus** — that we find at the core of ourselves, a reprise of the primordial intentionality of *existence,* making us to be and to be us. We are the way we are, because we are made of *material energy* ... everything made of it reactivates its dynamism: an irrepressible drive to survive ... and a self-embracing communitarianism which is gestating a yet-to-be realized total availability to others. We touch it intimately when we are in intimate touch with ourselves. We ourselves, apparently, are that very

---

[13] We are reminded that Pseudo-Dionysius spoke of "God" as "non-being."

[14] The Greek word *kenosis* which means "emptiness" is used to great poetic effect in Paul's letter to the Philippians, chapter 2, referring to Christ's "emptying himself." Christian theologian Nancey Murphy speaks of the *kenotic* nature of God. It's not surprising that these images should occur across the traditions ... people have eyes to see. Cf Nancey Murphy, *The Moral Nature of the universe,* Fortress Pr., Minneapolis, 1996

"face of 'God'" our tradition has been so avidly searching for through the millennia ... and, I believe, the only one we will ever see.

trust: identity with *existence*

I begin to *understand* myself and my relationship to reality in the same way I come to *understand* any other living phenomenon — through the interpretation of its intentionality. In this case it's my own. Once I begin to surrender to my complete identity with *matter's energy,* to embrace *existence* as a common substrate available to all, and myself for what I am — a part of its very substance — I begin to develop a new cognitive relationship to myself; for I am both subject and object of this *understanding.*

The key is that in coming to *understand* myself I am simultaneously *understanding matter's energy* for we are one and the same thing. In understanding myself I am in touch with existence itself, for mine is the same self-embrace and availability (both passive and active) that characterizes everything in the universe.

Other species of living things express their drive to survive each according to their capacities and, it seems, automatically. For them, there is apparently no possibility of *not* identifying with the community of *existence.* So for them there is no need for faith. But as we well know, we *humans* are quite capable of imagining an abysmal and bitter disconnect between our own *selves* and the existence of the substrate because of what we perceive as the incomprehensible contradiction of death. Death suggests the disappearance of existence, and from that, our non-identity with *existence* — *that we don't belong.*

Therefore we need faith. *Faith is the personal appropriation of the* **constitutive identity** *of my "self" with matter's energy.* I acknowledge my reality as an organism made of the substrate and part of a living totality whose extent in depth and breadth is beyond my ken. Faith is an affirmation (surrender) that overrides existential doubt and cognitive darkness. With faith I do not need to *know existence* as "other," for I *understand* it as myself — organically, connaturally, intimately.

Faith reaffirms identity with *matter's energy* and the universal community it has spawned. With faith I ratify my intimate relationship to *existence;* I embrace *matter's energy* for what it is. I belong here, for what it is, is what I am. I love it, because I love myself. I call its benevolence, metaphorically, "love," because my only experience of benevolence has been exclusively from other human persons who love. But clearly, the word "love" as I understand it, can hardly be applied to a benevolence of this magnitude, intimacy and universality. Frankly I have no idea what I am dealing with. All I know is that this whole universe in which I am immersed and sustained is its beneficiary.

Faith is an attitude that surrenders and commits to the project of universal availability and endless existence embarked on by the totality. In its surrender, faith recapitulates the living self-embrace of being.

The very act of faith then, paradoxically, becomes a datum in the confirmation of the interpretation of the intentionality of existence. ***Faith is human existence in the act of self-embrace*** — in my case as a human being, an act of quiet and grateful self-acceptance of myself and the universal family that has spawned me.

I belong here, for better or worse.

Chapter II

religion

For me, the point of *The Mystery of Matter (MM)* was to update the traditional metaphysics that I was formed in. That meant, effectively, to make a philosophical attempt at plumbing *the nature of reality.* This daunting assignment was not entirely my choice. I was driven to it by a tradition that had filled my brain not just with religious beliefs, but with a vision of *what it means to exist.* It was a vision that no longer corresponded to the real world. If I was going to re-evaluate my religious tradition and separate the baby from the bathwater, I would have to do it on all fronts. That required dealing with the questions metaphysics proposed to answer. You may not agree with my conclusions, but, if you are from my tradition, I'll wager that you understand why I had to do it.

What came of all that? *MM* concluded that *existence* is a homogeneous *material energy* whose self-embrace and communitarian elaborations have grown into everything there is in the universe, like an immense tree. The religion in which I was educated, however, was synchronized to a high degree with traditional Greco-mediaeval essentialist-dualist metaphysics — setting spirit against matter — which I described *ad nauseam* in those pages. I do not need to repeat its elements and the baleful effects of that artificial division for us. This chapter will explore the impact the shift from traditional metaphysics to the process cosmo-ontology presented in *MM* will have on the kind of religion that the traditional philosophy was conjured to support.

religion and "the other world"

Classic Greek Platonic dualism was responsible for giving western religion, and ultimately Western culture, its basic orientation. The religion we inherited was focused on another world — a world of living "spirit" — and demeaned this one supposedly made of dead, inert, dying matter. Much of what is destructive and pathological about us can find its roots there. Our new understanding is that there is no such other world populated by entities not made of *material energy.* Whatever it was that we thought was exclusive to that other world, and hence, excluded from this one, we now know is simply an aspect of the apparently infinite potential of matter. What does that mean for religion? Must religion disappear? Partial answers to that question appeared as "asides" scattered throughout *MM* and I want to try to pull them together here.

First, there's a *starting point*: Human life is permeated by what I have been calling a "sense of the sacred" which may be reasonably claimed as religion's perennial source. Religion has declared this human feeling to be implanted by "God," and therefore its own exclusive domain. As a matter of observable fact, however, the sense of the sacred is a phenomenon that is found universally among humankind, directed at a variety of revered objects and practices that differ among cultures to such a extent that they appear to have almost nothing in common except the dynamism itself. It's also important to emphasize that much of what is considered "sacred" is not directly connected with "God" or religion. But the phenomenon, even though it is virtually universal, remains unexplained. Any proposal that there is an initially obvious *objective* numinous source that accounts for this sense is routinely denied by analysts, even religious ones:

> Let us first of all delimit the significance of the term "sacred." ... the experience of the sacred bears upon a zone that is intermediate between "God" and the profane in the everyday sense. The sacred is that which an individual experiences as being in the depths of his or her own existence ...[15]

Without repeating the multitude of suggestions made in the last two hundred years to account for it, the position taken in *MM* is that "the sense of the sacred" is the resonance of the **conatus sese conservandi**. The *conatus* is the urge to self preservation, the constitutive self embrace of *existence*. This irrepressible hunger to survive is necessarily accompanied by an intense love of one's own existence. The *conatus* is innate in us, and by all evidence in animal life as well, even in its most primitive forms. In our case, from the moment of birth, the love that emanates from "self-love" is at first directed toward our immediate caregivers, parents and families. And then, in varying degrees of intensity it radiates out to all those things — people, forces, substances, practices, social constructions — that are perceived to protect and promote that *existence*. There is no "God" immediately evoked by the "sense of the sacred."

---

[15] Antoine Vergote, *In Search of a Philosophical Anthropology*, tr Muldoon, Louvain, Louvain U. Press 1996, p. 206.

The *"drive to survive"* in humans is also accompanied by a connatural **cooperative disposition** called altruism by Darwin, necessary for community to exist. Recent discoveries have shown that there is an innate empathic disposition in humans (and other higher animals) that can be traced to "mirror neurons" which evolved in the mammalian brain more than 100 million years ago.[16] Empathy only appears to run counter to the self-preserving dynamism of an individual *conatus*. The connection is straightforward: community is essential to individual survival. Hence love of the community — making the community "sacred" — is easily understood as the recognition of what is necessary for individual survival. These are the building blocks of what we call religion.

The self-embrace of existence, — the *conatus* — achieves its survival goal by collectivizing. This communitarian strategy, constitutive of even the most primitive elements of matter, was repeated again and again throughout cosmic history, in fact on each and every occasion in which *material energy* produced a new emergent form. This existential self-embrace operating through cumulative collectivization is a fundamental dynamic in all constructions of material energy. It was naturally selected because it enhances survival. It accounts for cooperation in living organisms — and cooperation is the *foundation stone* for the formation of human society beyond the level of family and clan.

The interdependence of individual and group survival is on display even in the earliest experiences of the human organism. Like other species that have a long period of infant and youth dependency, humans are reared in a context where the inability of the individual to survive on his/her own is an essential element of psychological identity. Even after the achievement of maturity, the necessary role of the community in human survival remains paramount and serves to confirm society's centrality in human life. The community shapes the individual. Society remains sacred.

The proximate social unit, family and clan, takes the individuals' *conatus* and its "sense of the sacred" and gives it a communal dimension through religion. Religion is the local community's metaphorical vehicle of group survival. The local human community is the ultimate guarantor of

---

[16] Mirror neurons allow for the simultaneous reverberation of the feelings observed occurring in another organism. *The Mystery of Matter*, p.223-224

individual survival, and therefore a necessary locus of the sense of the sacred. It projects its needs as sacred responsibilities onto its individual members *through religion*. In our tradition, ethical demands are promulgated to the members in the form of commandments given by "God" who is imagined as a human person. Religion, then, is the attribution of existential significance to particular myths, rituals and moral codes that elicit behavior of believed expediency to the survival community. In this respect, religions are similar the world over. They imagine that personal deities give commands and reward or punish socially important behavior. These relationships are expressed in myth. The central "myth" is that there are personal gods. Religion and a personal "God," at least in the West, are inseparable.

"God" and religion

What does the study made in *MM* tell us about "God" ... and how important is "God" to religion?

The first problem in dealing with this question has to do with words — specifically the word *"God."* If I ask, "is there a 'God'"? just by using the word I have already predefined what I am looking for, because in our culture that word comes already loaded with imagery and associated descriptors. That imagery, it hardly needs to be emphasized, is completely anthropomorphic. It projects human characteristics onto "God."

As a way of avoiding the pre-emptions lurking in the term, therefore, I have chosen to begin with the commonly observed phenomenon of the "sense of the sacred" and work backward to the source, "necessary and sufficient" to explain it, *whatever it may be.* Whether that source should have the word "God" applied to it is a second issue and requires further discussion. Any other procedure, to my mind, runs the risk of begging the question. But notice. "God," as a heuristic notion, does not survive being reduced from a premise to a conclusion. For once it is recognized that "God" is, logically speaking, derived from and subordinate to some more fundamental human experience, the concept "God" changes character and takes on the features of its conceptual mentor. "God," in a universe of matter, derives from a "sense of the sacred" that is itself the echo of a material drive. It suggests that whatever "God" there is, is material.

In *MM* we discovered that our impulse for self-preservation springs from the very nature of the *material elements* of which we are constructed. *Matter's energy*, the homogeneous substrate of the entire universe — that "stuff" from which all forces, energies, valences, properties, particles, as well as their composites have sprung — is *existence.* It can be validly described as *that in which we live and move and have our being.*

I am well aware that *that* phrase was used by Paul in his speech on an "Unknown God" at the Areopagus in Athens.[17] Be that as it may, the description, according to *MM,* is scientifically valid. Some may personally decide to accept the identity with Paul's traditional description and call it "God." But that is their choice, and they must accept full responsibility for the use of a term that comes pre-loaded with spiritual and humanoid connotations that we know are not true. *MM* does *not* conclude that *material energy* is "God." But it *does* recognize that *material energy* has characteristics that have been traditionally associated with divinity: Matter is (1) neither created nor destroyed, (2) the transcendently creative source of every construction and organism in the universe, (3) the matrix in which all things "live and move and have their being," (4) the **source of the sense of the sacred ...** and (5) something we can *relate* to with trust (that was the burden of the previous chapter). The free decision to conflate *material energy and* the *traditional language* surrounding "God" is a choice, not a conclusion.

Making that choice involves some *caveats.* Our traditional religious "doctrines" are imbued with the archaic scientific world-view in which they were born. They believed that "God" fashioned the universe and manages all the events that occur in it. That world-view is factually erroneous and its projections about "God" anthropomorphic; they are scientifically false and philosophically untenable. The scientific facts are primary and must remain primary. I limit myself to saying that the traditional poetic descriptors may validly be applied to *matter's energy* **as metaphor** if done with due regard to the controlling data. The fundamental facts must always be respected: I am related to *matter's energy* as to the source of my *existence;* that relationship is reflected in my *conatus,* and from there in my sense of the sacred — separately from the religious poetry traditionally used to evoke it. I have no knowledge of "God" that is independent of the religious traditions in which I was formed.

---

[17] Acts 17:28. *The Jerusalem Bible,* Garden City, Doubleday, 1966, fn "*f*" on page 231 of the NT in referring to that particular phrase says: "Expression suggested by the poet Epimenides of Cnossos (6th c. BC)." The origin of the phrase is not "Christian."

There is no problem with religion as *metaphor* (although some religious metaphors may require serious disclaimers). In fact the poetry that is religion may be essential if our sense of the sacred is to have its full creative effect. The major problem is that religion generally does not project its constructions as poetic metaphor but rather as *scientific fact.* Such an insistence is destructive not only of science, but also of the power of religious expression. A religion that calls its mythic constructions "fact" stifles thought and opens itself — deservedly, in my opinion — to ridicule and rejection. But, just as important, it simultaneously robs "myth" of its power to bring light and life to our existential experience. In our "modern" era, the combination of an arrogant reductionist scientism and a religion that offers a set of parallel "facts" whose existence it pontificates by pure ungrounded *fiat*, has been fatal. We in the west live in a state of spiritual impoverishment because, in the main, religion refuses to apply its sacred song to *reality as science has discovered it to be.*

Let me be clear: that there is a personal "God"-entity who designed and created the universe and all its forms and features *by rational choice*, is *not a fact;* ... that there was an "original sin" responsible for human "concupiscence" and the loss of a natural immortality, is *not a fact;* ... that the man Jesus was the "God"-entity defined by traditional western notions, biblical imagery and perennial philosophy, *is not a fact.* To claim anything else, in my opinion, is to feed the pathologies of religious bigotry, disdain for the "flesh," disregard for rationality, ethnic self-aggrandizement and a world where genocidal plunder has always been justified in the name of someone's ersatz religious "facts." **Religion has no "facts."** What it has (and can lose) is the poetic power to make richly human our relationship to that in which "we live and move and have our being" — transcendently creative reality as uncovered and articulated by the science of our times.

anthropomorphism

In order to sustain the premise of a "personal" deity, western religion has always presented "God" in anthropomorphic terms. What does that mean? Anthropomorphism translates to "human form" and states that, "God" thinks, sees, hears, wills, commands, judges, provides, is insulted, gets angry, rewards and punishes, loves and forgives, similar to human beings. Like any one of us, "God's" day is made up of a sequence of thoughts, feelings, decisions and actions. Such a way of imagining "God" seems to be confirmed by the Jewish scriptures which describe "God" with exactly these kinds of images. All the religions of our region of the world are built on that tradition.

Who is to say that this isn't true? Well, in fact, the entire Christian theological tradition — at least from the second century of the common era — has always maintained that it isn't true. The theologians based their opinion on what came to be called the *philosophía perennis,* "the perennial philosophy" which was in broad terms, some version of the thought of Plato, or later in the middle ages, Plato and Aristotle. They challenged the imagery of the scriptures because they believed their philosophy was *science* and it told them what "God" was really like.

Even before the common era, Jewish theologians in Alexandria made an attempt to connect Plato's philosophical vision with the imagery of the Jewish scriptures. Philo is the one best known to us. Christianity has tacitly acknowledged his influence, and the reason we know that is that his writings have been preserved.

Christian Platonists' basic tenet was that "God" was "being itself," the source and repository of everything that is. And since "God" was "being" they thought you could know what "God" was like by examining the characteristics of the "concept of being." In effect they "reified" the *idea of "being,"* used *logic* to elaborate its characteristics and applied it to "God."

"God" was "being itself," and thus utterly perfect. "He" was complete and fulfilled; he had to be pure "spirit" (for matter was subject to change and possible diminution); he lived in an immutable and impassive state of unalloyed bliss. Since "God" was not matter he could not change; *not even his thoughts could change.* This is not easy to imagine.

But there is more. Since the concept, "being," logically contains within itself everything that is, they thought "God" must contain within "him"self everything that exists. Now "God" is pure spirit, therefore "all things" must be in the form of *ideas, which are immaterial.* According to classic philosophical theology, then, we are **part of** "God" by being "thought" by "God." But, because "God" *is* his thought, it means we exist *in God.* "God" "thinks" us in the very same thought in which he contemplates himself. We are *not other* than "God."

What they drew from this was truly extraordinary: for "God" to know us *as other* would mean his having two different concepts; and that, according to traditional theology, is impossible. "God," like the concept of "being," is utterly simple. "He" eternally thinks and wills only one thing — himself.

If he "knows" us, it can only be as part of himself. Please note: this is totally beyond anything we have ever experienced. Even philosophers have a difficult time wrestling with these abstractions, and throughout the centuries, pastors with responsibility for teaching the "ordinary people" did not even try. In practice, they fell back on the anthropomorphic "God" presented by the myths and metaphors of the "Book" and offered them as literal. But it was false *by the scientific standards of the time*, and the educated knew it. Hence, the humanoid character and behavior of "God" as presented in scripture has always been considered *metaphor* by the theologians since almost the very dawn of Christianity, and the abstract concept of being, *the literal truth.*

You may not like it, and it is no longer universally accepted, but this is the classic perennial philosophical theology. Most people are not aware of it because it was effectively ignored. Anthropomorphism was encouraged and actually turned out to be extremely effective in running the Empire's official Church. The potential mysticism embedded in a vision of "God" who was *not other* than us was never made available to the people. It was bypassed in favor of a simple formula of eternal reward or punishment after death, meted out by the "God of the Book" who commanded correct behavior, *which of course included submission to the authorities.*

God as "person"

The turning point for me in my theological journey was when I realized that there is no "divine providence" in any normal sense of that word. The analysis of that realization was the burden of chapter III of *An Unknown God.* "God" does not react to human need, nor does "he" intervene in human events whether they are due to human freedom or the mechanical forces of nature. "He" does not act like what we mean by "person," so I say it is improper to use that word of "God."

The reader should be aware, this is not a new problem. It has been a traditional point of tension in western religious thought since before the advent of Christianity. Plato's "One" was immutable and beyond time. For the world to be created by this changeless "God," it was first necessary for "God" to emanate another godlike being who was not "God," and who could therefore interact with the world of matter in time, and carry out the tasks of crafting the heavens and the earth. That intermediary, "the first-born of all creation," was given various names at various times: *Demiourgos* by Plato, and then later the word *"Logos"* taken from Heraclitus and the stoics was used by Philo and applied to this "second god" whom Philo identified as the personification of "God's" word and wisdom. Christians became convinced that Jesus himself was the *Logos* come to earth to rectify a creation that had gone bad ... to create the world anew, as it were.

This *Logos*, then, was originally conceived as a *mediator* between an utterly transcendent "God" who lives in the timeless rapture of self-contemplation, and the grubby world of space, time and matter. According to this view, anything in the scriptures that even hinted that "God" himself personally interacted with us in our world was necessarily a metaphor.

The "God" of the Jewish "Book," as we all know, was very different; "he" was painted simply as a larger-than-life human person. "God" created the world with no help from anyone and was said to intervene in human history in ways that corresponded to the sequences and modulations of existence in time. Aristotle would have called it anthropomorphic. That put traditional philosophy in a dilemma because it eschews anthropomorphism. Thomas claimed to follow Aristotle and yet *insisted that* "God" is a person. How did he pull that off?

Aquinas used the *analogy of being* to support his claim. His reasoning went like this: because we, finite spirits, are persons by reason of our "immaterial" souls with the powers of **intellect and will,** "God," an infinite spirit who created us must have those *ideas* as part of his nature. "He" could not be anything less; "God" must have intellect and will and therefore is a "person."

These were the conclusions of an abstract reasoning process and the kind of entity they describe was a "person" only by abstract definition, not by personal experience. "God" does not interact in spacetime or with matter. But, here's the rub. Once you tell people "God" is a "person" they don't imagine "him" in terms of Aquinas' abstract definitions (*they can't ... no one can!*), but of what the word "person" *means to them*. "God" was imagined anthropomorphically. Aquinas' philosophical accommodation to Christian tradition helped set anthropomorphism in stone. The official use of the word "person," in other words, evokes an image that completely neutralizes the philosophically nuanced reality and there is no way to correct it *for the philosophical version of God-as-"person" is simply not thinkable. You cannot use the word "person" and NOT think in humanoid terms.* To claim that Christians do not *imagine "God" anthropomorphically* is absurd.

For mediaeval theologians, philosophical thinking not only did not permit "God" any interactivity with humankind, it also meant that *"God," as "being," was not an entity* definable and delimited over against other entities, and therefore **not an individual** in the normal sense of that word. If "God" is not a separate entity, how could "he" possibly be a "person" as we understand it? For the ordinary Christian untrained in theology, to understand what the schoolmen really meant, therefore, it would be better to say that "God" is NOT a person, than that "he" is. Theology, by insisting on calling "God" a person was necessarily (if not intentionally) misleading the ordinary people. If, to this day, anthropomorphism is ineradicable in all versions of western Christianity, it can be traced to this.

For mediaeval theology, calling "God" a person is a **mere formality**. We can relate to "God," but we have absolutely no idea what it might mean for "God" to relate to us. The only thing we know is the one-dimensional benevolence of our own *participation in existence*, and I suspect that is all there is. It's not a lot of information, but it is something we know for sure. Whatever "God" there is, sustains us in *existence* here and now. *We know that because we are here.*

The upshot is, the perennial philosophy provides no more support for the imagined interventions of a creating, micro-managing, providential "God" of the "Book" than does the cosmo-ontology we have elaborated in *MM*. Whatever modern science knows of "creation" and "providence," is sufficiently and necessarily explained as the evolutionary dynamism of *matter's energy*. There is no need for any other agency. What this means is that to take "God" as *material energy,* sets up the same austere, *exclusively existential relationship* between the human organism and "God" as the identification of "God" with the scholastic concept of "Spirit-Being." In each case, when the analysis is complete, it turns out that "God" is not a "person" *as far as we are concerned*. If the term is used without the clarifications that effectively neutralize it in the practical order, it will necessarily create a profound misunderstanding and false expectations.

Historically the Catholic Church — which dominated Western Europe for millennia and is the single source of the beliefs of *all* Christian denominations — made no effort to correct this anthropomorphism and in fact fostered it. It was understandable. The rituals provided exclusively by the hierarchy lived on the power to assuage, cajole and in other ways control God. But, it is only a "God" who changes his mind and can be placated and prayed to that could keep the Church in "business." And its only a "God" who gives commands and expects to be obeyed or will punish the disobedient, that can be an effective whip for social stability. Such a relational, changeable, anthropomorphic "God," however, every bit as much for traditional philosophy as for the cosmo-ontology presented in *MM*, *does not exist*. Let me repeat: *that "God" does not exist any more for Thomas Aquinas than for me.* Both systems insist: as far as human experience is concerned, "God" is, *practically speaking*, impersonal; all claims to the contrary are products of human imagination.

The empirical absence of any verifiable interaction with "God" even in the experience of believers, corroborates the drift of this discussion: *"God" does not act like a person.* One might think that the mystics who claim to have experienced "God" directly would oppose that statement, but they confirm it. The "God" they experienced was not an interacting entity.

the mystics and a "personal" God

Contrary to common opinion, this "impersonal" feature is confirmed in practice by the mystics of all traditions. This seems counterintuitive; so let's look at it.

The pursuit of mystical experience has always been considered something of an elite, esoteric or even parallel religious project. It went beyond mere religious practice. The original goal of the mystics in the West at least, was to make *direct personal contact* with the very source of the sacred itself. If "God" were a "person" the mystics would be the first to tell us about it. What, in fact, do they say?

The mystics' advice, according to the most developed and articulate practitioners, was to avoid relating to "God" as a person. In the **east**, that advice was explicitly non-theist; the Buddhists rejected belief in personal gods. They said a personal "God," even if one were to exist, was irrelevant to human liberation and self-appropriation, and speculation about it was a waste of time.

Contemplative practice was expressly defined by the Buddha from the start as a non-theist and even anti-theist endeavor. The Buddha taught that it was the illusory belief in the ability to achieve a *personal existential permanence* that was responsible for the unnecessary anthropogenic aggravation of the suffering that is endemic to existence. Belief in the gods, with the reward and punishment, eternal life and happiness alleged-ly promised by them, was a prime symptom of this illusion:

> ...the immortality of the soul through appeasement of the gods by prayer and ritual ... has no place in the Buddha's teaching. ...[18]

> Absent from all these [Buddhist] systems is any notion corresponding to the "God" of the monotheistic religions ... the idea of a personal relationship with an ab-solute being in another, transcendent world is foreign to Buddhism.[19]

In the **West**, the Abrahamic religions, in contrast, presented the source of the sacred as a personal "God" whose anthropomorphic characteristics were initially brought over from the "Book" to the contemplative practice pursued by the desert hermits and in the first monasteries. The relation-ship was first conceived in "personal" terms as between two lovers (The Song of Solomon, John of the Cross, Jalal-al-din Rumi) tending historically in Christianity to focus on the personality of Jesus as "God" (Thomas à Kempis).

In the case of **Christianity**, the overwhelming influence of the person-alist anthropomorphic imagery and rigid doctrinal formulas about "God," imposed with terrifying severity by an inquisitorial church, prevented any open rejection of the *doctrine* of a personal "God" as Buddhism did. But, within the range of possibilities available, adept contemplatives *without challenging the doctrine,* separated themselves from the imagery and pursuit of a *personal relationship* with "God." Regardless of how laden with expressions of "personal love" their journey may have begun, Chris-tian mystics eventually came around to describing a relationship in which the interactive dimension was muted, relegated to superfluous status and eventually ignored altogether. Often the very "stages" of growth in "perfec-tion" reflected the increasing realization of the absence of interaction with "God."

As with the Buddhists, most of these ascetics were focused on practice and did not make doctrinal comments on their experience. They tended to find "God" in the simple acceptance of the "divine" depths of their own existence and the uneventful routines of everyday life. Some few, howev-er, did have "theological" interests and attempted to translate their experi-

---

[18] Takeuchi Yoshinori, ed., *Buddhist Spirituality*, Crossroads, NY, 1997, p.10.
[19] *ibid.* p.xxiii.

ence into philosophical terms. Given the nature of what they were discovering, this effort sometimes got them into serious trouble.

Christian mysticism as proposed by **John Scotus Eriúgena** (d. 877), followed in the footsteps of the 4th century Gregory of Nyssa, 6th century Maximus the Confessor and Pseudo-Dionysius. Eriúgena called "God" *natura naturans* and the cosmic order *natura naturata*, "God's" "theophany." This identification of "God" with "nature" infuriated the authorities 350 years after his death and he was condemned along with other more contemporary theologians whom the IV Lateran Council (1215) called "pantheists." There seemed to be no "statute of limitations" for the Inquisition: their bones were ordered dug up and burned.

Christian mystical writers of the early 14th century, **Marguerite Porete and Johannes Eckhart,** both speak about "transcending religion." Marguerite was the inheritor of the mystical tradition of the feminist Beguines. She says she came to see that the scriptural "commandments" and growth in ascetical practice were "obstacles" in the sense of being *early partial goals that must be transcended.* The mature mystic, she says, has no goals whatsoever, no aspirations, no ascetical or prayer practices because she is no longer "traveling toward God;" she has arrived. She exists in a state of complete union, and all imagined interaction has ceased.

> The soul ... no longer seeks God through penitence, nor through any sacrament of Holy Church; not through thoughts, nor through words, nor through works; ... not through justice nor through mercy ...
>
> ... such a soul neither desires nor despises poverty nor tribulation, neither mass nor sermon, neither fast nor prayer, and gives to nature all that is necessary without remorse of conscience. But such a nature is so well ordered through the transformation of the unity of Love, to whom the will of the soul is conjoined, that nature demands nothing that is prohibited.[20]

That a human being, body and soul, especially a woman, should consider itself "part of God" and therefore beyond obedience was more than the inquisition would tolerate. When she refused to retract her book, *The Mirror of Simple Souls*, she was burned at the stake in Paris in 1310, for "pantheism," naturally.

Johannes Eckhart, a renowned Dominican theologian, the successor in Aquinas' chair at the university of Paris, and venerable elder of his or-

---

[20] Marguerite Porete, *The Mirror of Simple Souls*, tr Babinsky, NY Paulist Press 1993, ch 9 & 85

der in Germany, was probably a correspondent of Marguerite. He taught that the soul has to "get beyond God, to the Godhead beyond the Trinity" — unconditioned being. "God," he said, and "Trinity" were terms of religion. They are human terms that represent our projections and do not denote the "Godhead."

> The authorities say that "God" is a being, an intelligent being who knows everything. But I say that God is neither a being, nor intelligent and he does not know either this or that. ... Therefore we pray that we may be rid of God, for unconditioned being is above "God" and all distinctions.[21]

The "Godhead," he says, is pure simple limpid "being," the goal of a "breakthrough" that marks the realization of an identity with "the Godhead." The "soul" realizes that it is an intimate part of "being," and that it is as it was before birth when "it wanted what it was, and it was what it wanted." Contact with "God" is had in the depths of the soul in a pre-existing and unearned unity where the "being" of each is meshed and indistinguishable. This contact is *not ecstatic*. It is the simple experience of oneself, but *understood* as absorbed in the "being" of "the Godhead." Eckhart was condemned in 1329 two years after he had died of natural causes, thus deftly avoiding the fate of his Beguine mentor.

Spanish Carmelite mystics of the 16th century, **John of the Cross and Teresa of Avila** produced writings that claim to lead to a unity with "God" that goes beyond visions, feelings or interest in a supernatural world.

For John the goal is simply the darkness of "faith." Search for "supernatural" experience is explicitly rejected because:

> "[God] has laid down rational and natural limits for man's governance; wherefore to desire to pass beyond them is not lawful, and to seek out and attain to anything by supernatural means is to go beyond these natural limits." "They are unnecessary" ... "To desire to commune with "God" by such means is a most perilous thing. ... the soul must conduct itself in a purely negative way concerning [visions] ... in order that it may progress by the proximate means — namely, by faith. Therefore a person should not store up as treasures these visions, nor have the desire to cling to them.[22]

These individuals are thoroughly immersed in the ordinary routines of life and, by their own assessment, completely uninterested in any ecstatic

---

[21] Johannes Eckhart, sermon: *Blessed are the Poor in Spirit, in* Walshe, *Eckhart, German Sermons*, London, Watkiins, 1979 vol 2, p.275
[22] John of the Cross, *Ascent of Mount Carmel*, tr. Peers, NY, Image, 1958, Bk II, ch 21,#1 p.189; #7, p.193; Ch. 24., #8 p.222

condition, visions, feelings, "mystical experiences," or consolations. In fact, their emphatic counsel was that one had absolutely to avoid pursuing any such extraordinary experiences. And the point was not "achievement by non-pursuit." They were very clear about it: *"God" was not to be found there*. Their advice is that "perfection" consists in the awareness of the presence of "God" in all things and at all moments. One touches "God" through the darkness of faith alone. Neither knowledge nor extraordinary experience is sought. Nothing supernatural or "other-worldly" is required.

St Teresa for her part was unambiguous: even the afterlife becomes unimportant, since immersion in "God" will be no greater then than it is here and now.[23]

Most Christians are unaware of this feature of these great mystics. Most have never read what they wrote.

The perspective of the mystics stands in stark contrast with the world-view promoted by conventional religion which is quintessentially "other worldly." It is "theist," which means based on the interventionist power of a personal humanoid deity who dwells in that "other world." In the western versions, any happiness experienced on earth, "this world," is ephemeral, vanishing. The only true happiness is to be found *after death* in that other world where the human being really belongs. For the partisans of this kind of religion, the existence of that other world is critical. For if there were no fear of reward or punishment after death, what could possibly motivate moral behavior? And besides, if there were no other world, where would "God" reside? According to them, he is clearly not present in ours.

The mystics saw things very differently. "God" was *right here* and they needed no incentive to love "him" for he was *not other* than themselves, so behavior was not an issue. What they all agreed on is that, by whatever long and circuitous journey, they all eventually arrived at a vision of "God" characterized by a quiet familial embrace of themselves and everything around them ... because everything is immersed in the suffusive presence of "God." Their "doctrine" — effectively a pan-entheism — would be completely compatible with our cosmo-ontology and a transcendent *material energy.* Their sense of intimate union with "God," which their ascetical practices revealed to have been there all along, led them away

---

[23] Teresa of Avila, *Interior Castle*, Seventh Mansion, chapter III.

from seeking or expecting any personal interaction with "God." Against the background of the two-world theist assumptions of their day, this "discovery" about **the already existing union of "God" and creation** was mind-blowing; it was so counter-intuitive to their religious expectations that they felt compelled to tell others about it, and so produced some of the world's great mystical literature. For me the importance of their writings is not as spiritual inspiration but as theological testimony. It runs counter to the general drift of conventional religiosity. No wonder the Church discouraged people from reading them. Religion does not need "theism" to function; and Christianity's most revered practitioners saw "God," as I do, as that "in which we live and move and have our being."

metaphor and relationship

The mystics who claimed to "know" "God" from personal experience, spoke in metaphor. Only the outdated perennial philosophy — generically, Thomism — dares to say something *conceptually factual and literal* about "God." While few theologians today subscribe to Plato's vision, they almost all continue to hold to a spirit-matter dualism. This is an anomaly, for there is neither evidence nor proof for the existence of spirit separate from matter. How theology *knows* that there is such a thing as "spirit" is not an insignificant question, for religion's very existence — as it has come to be — would seem to hinge on the answer. The mystics don't have that problem because they don't speak literally, *they speak in metaphor*.

Metaphor *does not claim to know*. Instead, it offers a symbol that *encourages the direction of* **our relationship** *to "God" from our side only*.

Metaphor is a symbol as "myth" is a symbol. Myth is not a literal, scientific, historical narrative. It is poetry: at first a story, a legend; then derived from that, a song, a ritual, an icon, a building, a moral code, designed to evoke and express a human response to the interpreted intentionality of the *mysterium tremendum* — the mystery of *existence.*

Now, once I restrict myself to speaking about existence *from our side only* (which is the only side we know anything about), there is one inescapable fact that *I* **have to** *relate to*: I am not self-originating ... I exist by dint of things and forces that are other than me, *whether I know what they are or not.* I owe my *existence* first, to the reproductive choices of my parents, and then more remotely to the entire process by which biological life evolved and reproduced itself on our planet. Since I appreciate *being-here* and being myself, it is very difficult for me to ignore *whatever it is* that made all this happen even though I do not know what it is.

That *relationship-to-source* is the ground of religion. "God," then, is a metaphor, the traditional symbol for the source of that *existence — whatever that source might be* — and the fact that I am really here, puts me in a very humble position with regard to it. There is an unavoidable ecstatic gratitude that arises within me driven by nothing else than the love I have for being here and being *me.* A poet-friend once said:

> If I believed in god, I would consider life a gift. As it is, I think life is an amazing, mysterious stroke of luck!

This is what I mean by the sense of the sacred. I cannot celebrate my *being-here* without celebrating how I got here — *whatever it is that made it happen.*

So whether there is a "God" or not in the traditional sense, there is an unavoidable poetry that is called forth from me *just because I exist.* That poetry and the feelings that compel its composition is what I call "religion." There may not be a "God," *but there must be religion.* Since we do not know "God," religion is the celebration of *existence* through metaphors that evoke its source. But the religious metaphor's target is *the relationship,* not the "thing;" for what is known is the relationship, *not the thing.* Metaphor does not need to know **what** *the source of existence is.* The "theology" of the mystics focused on exactly that ... the fact that they did not "know" was not a problem for them; just the opposite: it was the very doorway to ~~faith~~. *They called it "unknowing."*

metaphors change

One of the results of understanding our speech about "God" as we are proposing it is that metaphors change as required by how the relationship is perceived. Those who use metaphor are not bound by the word and concept because they know its purpose is *to describe the relationship* not the unknown object.

This is important. Take a common metaphor for "God" — father. Since the word is a metaphor, no one can say, "you *have* to use that word." For many the word "father" may no longer work. The word is only a tool ... and as with any tool that no longer works, you put it down and pick up another. "God" as the source of *existence* is every bit as clearly and adequately (and inadequately and unclearly) denoted by "mother" or "brother" or "self-subsistent being," or "principle of organization of the cosmos," or *the living transcendent dynamism of material energy*" as by "father." These are all metaphors, and each of them captures something unique in our *relationship* to the source of our *existence, whatever that source might be.* The reality in question, at this point at least, is not an identifiable "knowable" entity ... *or we would know it.* The metaphors do not tell us *what* the source is, only *how* we are related to it. They are created to express and maintain the focus of the relationship, each in its own way. The mystics had a series of favorite metaphors of their own. They are intriguing for what they both say and do not say: *"cloud of unknowing," "emptiness," "dark night," "nothing."* They evoke the void; but the void is not something the mystics fear; *it is something they are in love with.*

Knowing the thrust and bearing of the relationship does not imply that we "know" "God." By the distinctions we worked hard to establish in *MM* chapters 8 and 10, a relationship is not the object of knowledge but of a sophisticated guesswork we call the *interpretation of intentionality*[24] which utilizes our *somatically driven connatural understanding* to assess reality. Interpretation means we *understand* another's intentionality through *understanding* our own ... and to speak about objectifying our own subjective selves is an attempt to turn a tautology into "knowledge." It is senseless. Without an object there is no "knowledge" but there can be *understanding.* We saw how this functioned for ~~faith~~ in the previous chapter.

This is the sufficient and necessary ground for a sincere mutual respect among *all* religious traditions. Official Catholicism cannot accept that, because it takes its descriptors of "God" as *fact, not metaphor.* And that is the problem: taking metaphor literally. It makes us think we know God, *when all we really know is that we are not self-originating.*

The "thing" — in this case "God" — is unknown ... what is central and guiding is *the relationship.* The existential relationship is *understood connaturally,* from within, because we experience existence, our bodies, our selves, our *conatus.* But "what" we are related to (the source of our existence), and even "what" *existence* is (the self-embrace, the *conatus* itself), is not clearly "known" even though it is my very self*!* I do not "know" any-

---

[24] *The Mystery of Matter,* Chapter 8, "Interpretation."

thing about it but *I understand it intimately. I understand "being-here" the way I understand any tautology, ... the way I understand* 2 + 2 = 4. To call it "knowledge" is nonsense ... *nevertheless, it is self-explanatory.*[25]

understanding

Understanding as opposed to "knowledge" is a characteristic of relationships. When I say I "know" my wife, for example, I don't mean conceptual knowledge ... some sort of scientific or literal definition. I mean I know "what she's like." It is *in and through the relationship* that I *understand* her ... not through scientific, psychological or medical data. For words to describe the person as apprehended in the *relationship*, I have recourse to poetry and poetic symbols — *metaphor*.

I may write one poem in which I call her a *butterfly* ... and then in another *a soaring eagle.* As a matter of literal fact, she is neither. The relationship is *clearly understood* without words but it creates words — *metaphors* — to express itself ... and to express itself ever *anew* because of new circumstances, or new depths of the relationship ... or new insights into the significance of words and images.

Now let's apply that analogy to religion. The relationship in this case is to "God" ... but really ... *what is "God"?* We don't know. "God" is the symbol for the source of our *existence. We only know how we are related, and I know that because I know I am not self-originating.* I express the relationship in metaphor. The metaphors are chosen to express my *connatural understanding* of the relationship which is derived from an intimate *experience of existence.*

Religions are community poems, stories, legends, myths, about an unknown reality whose *existential self-donation is our very selves.* This relationship is rightly called *apophatic,* meaning that *there are no words that literally apply* ... not because the thing we're talking about is not real (I'm real, so the source of my existence must be real as well), ... or that we are not in touch or not aware of it, but because *it is not a "thing out there." It is a relationship I connaturally experience **as myself!*** In this particular relationship, the common transactional element — the "what" that "God" and I

---

[25] The point being made here was, I believe, the focus of Ludwig Wittgenstein's groping in his later work *Philosophical Investigations, On Certitude,* and others. It was the exploration of what he called "nonsense" or "senseless" in the *Tractatus* ... "truth" that was not "knowledge."

hold in common — is *the particular configuration of material energy that is me.*[26] ***My being-here, my hungry presence in the world is, for me, the primary ground for my generating the metaphor: "God."***

We should not be surprised that something as intimate and all embracing as *our relationship to our very own existence* should have been mythicized and poetized and ritualized and celebrated through the millennia in thousands of different ways around the globe. Paul said "all the peoples *grope after* this unknown God." But he adds, we don't have to look very far, it's near to each of us, for it *is what we live in ... and move in ... and have our being in.* You just can't get any nearer than that.

matter's energy and the words of religion

The unknown "thing" humankind means by "God" is revealed through an *existential relationship* that objectively sustains us. What, then, in our experience, actually provides us with our *existence* and our sense of the sacred? That "thing," I submit, is not a thing at all, but the *survival drive* of universal *material energy*; and we *understand* it quite well for we are an integral part of its reproductive activity. We fight to survive and reproduce because *matter's energy* is driven to survive. *Material energy's* evolutionary self-extrusion accounts for our *existence* and character as well as the existence and character of everything in the universe, its associated *conatus* (persistence in being) and our sense of the sacred. I can say that because, even without knowing *exactly what* material energy is, I am in touch with myself and my world ... *and I understand it intimately.*

At the risk of blurring a clarity of expression that I have worked hard to establish in this study, let me say once and for all for those who are confused about my position: it's not that there is no "God" ... it's that *"God" is a symbol for what we do not know — the source of our existence.* This is so utterly different from the way our tradition has encouraged us to think of "God," that we cannot easily make the adjustments necessary to accommodate what we are learning. And I want immediately to suggest that the first adjustment may be to **stop using the word "God"** because it evokes something that *is* not and *cannot be.* I am referring, of course, to the anthropomorphic imagery taken from the "Book."

---

[26] ... not because of "creation" in the traditional sense, but because my *existence* is directly due to sharing a substrate in which I live and move and have my being.

I am related to *material energy* as to "God." This "God" is not a rational person who acts for "reasons." "He" is exactly as you see "him," like the sun that shines equally on the just and the unjust ... enlivening our bodies even as "he" enlivens the viruses and cancers, the seismic forces and weather cycles that may kill us. *Material energy* has no form of its own. There is a universal self-less-ness, a kind of a helpless unremitting avail-ability, a *generosity that seems to have no end and no need for explana-tion ... it is senseless to us* even though we *understand it intimately — we are it* and live immersed in it and celebrate it with great enthusiasm. *Ex-istence! It* is a great stroke of luck!

"Senseless" is perhaps too strong a word, for while I am not logically constrained, there is a way I feel drawn to *understand* it. I sense in my own existence and the intensity of my own personal *conatus* that I am the result of a *benevolent vitality* that transcends my personal possession of it. It is that very austere and apparently non-personal benevolence that characterizes the relationship for me. But all through this analysis, I have to insist, I *understand* the relationship as recipient, but *I do not know "what"* the donor, material energy, is.

I believe that all along, throughout our entire intellectual history, all we have ever "known" is our relationship of existential dependency on and participation in *material energy* ... and essentialist metaphysics with its "God" as "self-subsistent being" was the attempt to translate that experi-ence into ancient Greek and late Latin. It is not just a coincidence that the traditional essentialist "equations" parallel those of cosmo-ontology. They called *matter's energy*, "being," and mis-took it for rational thought and *idea*. But there was nothing else but *material energy* that those erroneous scholastic categories could possibly have been attempting to describe ... *because it's the only thing out there!*

"our" metaphors

But daring to say that, doesn't entirely solve our problem. We still have to decide what to do with these ancient words. Can we use them any more? They are our tradition, the tracks of our people as they groped for the fountain that wells up our life. We cherish them *as* symbols of our journey even though we cannot allow them to dominate the *facts*. We cannot ignore the skewing effect the word "God" with its anthropomor-phism will have on our vision of reality. "God" used poetically, is one thing. But the word should not be used, even as a metaphor, in objective discourse unless it is accompanied by unambiguous clarifications. If even for the schoolmen, "God" is *not* the way we have been encouraged to imagine "him," it will be even more so for those who embrace the philosophy proposed in *MM*. For cosmo-ontology allows us to go only so far: "the source of the sense of the sacred" is the transcendent living dynamism of *material energy*, possessed by and activated in all things. The rest is unknown.

To the suggestion that *matter's energy* may be itself *only a metaphor* for something unknowable that lies beyond it (didn't Eriugena called nature the "mask of God"?) I have only this comment. As poetry it is powerful, but as a literal concept it is redundant. For unless you are using it to reconstruct *an anthropomorphic spirit-"God" and a separate world where "God" resides,* it can only be standing for another, possibly more foundational, *material energy.* And in that case it offers no new information.

So, religion and our "transcendent materialism" are ultimately compatible ... although it will be a religion purified of those elements that are incompatible with the *facts.* "God" has a right to be whatever "he" is. And even though we don't know exactly what that might be, the *relationship* is real, for we are real ... and we have the right to extol the relationship with the poetry of our choice. But, given the personal importance of what is involved in this *relationship — our existence itself —* it's hard to call it a choice, *for it's hard to imagine being human without extoling it.*

theology and "spirituality"

I also want to be careful here to separate theology from "spirituality." The very word "spirituality" carries a connotation I am not comfortable with. It obviously reflects the historical belief in the superiority of an alleged "spirit" over the "flesh" which meant that nourishing the sense of the sacred is a work of the spirit and not the body. I mean no such thing. But it's a traditional word and I believe as a metaphor it can be applied to our new understanding.

Spirituality, then, is the *affective relational attitude assumed* toward the source of existence — *whatever it may be* — and from there the term refers to the program of personal development that one may use for focusing that affect. It's clearly a work of the imagination because we do not "know" what the source of our existence *is.* But all good poetry is a work of the imagination ... it is not "inaccurate" for all that. Good poetry is quite precise in what it sets out to express — *relationship*; and communal poetry like religion should be refined and modified over time under the *heuristic* influence of reality as the scientific community discovers it.

Spirituality will naturally have an "objective" or scientific side. And the objective side is what I mean by *theology*. Theology uses our knowledge of reality — provided in part by science — *to evaluate the metaphors* that guide our *relational energies* toward that in which "we live and move and have our being." *Theology must deal in facts, and the facts are as known to all. Theology is the interface between those facts and our religious poetry (doctrine).* Some will prefer to *eschew all metaphors* in the pursuit of a relationship that they realize has been severely distorted in the past by being wedded to religion's dubious scientific pretentions and political dalliances. But theology functions here as well. In this case it would ground and encourage contemplative *silence.*

Whether spirituality is expressed in the metaphors of our tradition ... or left to the spontaneous poetry that emerges in the crash of events ... or with contemplative silence ... is *ad libitum.* I would insist, however, that in all cases the "theological" or objective side be grounded in science and with a philosophical interpretative tool, like cosmo-ontology, germane to science. Religious imagery that alludes to other "facts" may be used metaphorically for spirituality but not for theology, and certainly not, as in our traditional theisms, in place of science.

The Mystery of Matter was *not* about spirituality. It was about philosophy and the hints that analysis has given us about *theology.* Theology has to do with clarifying words and imagery, and what I challenge are the anthropomorphisms that are used, not for spirituality, but as religious "facts" whose *non-reality* makes them dysfunctional for faith. There are no realities that exist in another world. There is no other world.

There have been some thinkers throughout western history who proposed imagery about "God" different from our inherited anthropomorphisms. People like Nicolas of Cusa, Baruch Spinoza, and even Thomas Aquinas have supported a pan-en-theist vision of reality, and I have mentioned them many times. But, as much as I am guided by their insights, I believe it is dangerous simply to accept that "God exists" on their terms, for their understanding of reality omits the perspectives of modern science. Besides, their naïve use of the word "God" runs the risk of re-establishing the *same anthropomorphic imagery, managed and manipulated by the same self-serving ethnocentric religions, feeding the same personal pathologies, prolonging the same political and social inequities as always.*

Our traditional western religions stemming from the anthropomorphisms of the "Book," and the Christian doctrinal modifications imposed in ancient times by the power requirements of the Roman Empire, have been individualistic, authoritarian, elitist, ethnocentric, male-dominated, anti-somatic, guilt-mongering, self-denigrating, self-destructive and violently intolerant of other traditions. They have presided over the colonial plunder of the globe and an environmental degradation that may destroy us. They have tended to produce individuals in their own image and likeness. We must realize that our tradition does not necessarily challenge these attitudes and can often been cited in support of them. Unless spirituality changes on its theological side guided by science, nothing will change, and ultimately we will be "like those who look into a mirror and then turn away and forget what they saw."

un-knowing: ~~faith~~ is not belief

The word "God" and its entourage of associated notions has been expropriated by "religion," and unless religion's erroneous definitions are detoxified by being taken as *metaphor*, they will poison our thinking and make a healthy relationship to the sacred matrix impossible. This, I am sure, will draw a line in the sand separating "believers" from non-believers. But the valid religious quest, I have insisted all along, is not belief, but, ~~faith~~ — *relationship*. Belief projects a multitude of "facts" that are just not there. It pretends to have a "knowledge" of "God." But no such knowledge exists, because no such *separate entity* exists.[27] Our "God" is not *other than* us and the material matrix from which we emerged.[28] We cannot objectify it, and so we cannot "know" it. I claim we have an intimate and absolutely certain *understanding* of *existence* because it is what we are, and therefore we can *relate* to it. Our very bodies were spawned by it and function on its energies. Science gives us knowledge of it, but what it *means* to us is something we already *understand and express in poetry, religious poetry. Existence — the material energy* of which our flesh is a

---

[27] In scholastic terms, "God" is not a "substance" meaning a "thing," a *res* with a *quiddity. Cf* Aquinas, *SCG,* I ,25, 10; nor an *Individual, ST,* I, 29, 3, ad 4.

[28] Nicholas of Cusa used the phrase, *"non aliud"* to describe the relationship. Cf Jasper Hopkins, *Nicholas of Cusa on "God" as not-other,* Minneapolis, U. of MN press, 1979.

part — is "God" for us. This understanding challenges our archaic beliefs, but not ~~faith~~. ~~Faith~~ offers no new facts to mystify and delude us. ~~Faith~~ "un-knows" because it cannot objectify existence. But it *understands that existence* is *not-other* and cannot be lost. It functions on the facts as our science and intelligence reveal them. ~~Faith~~ does not know something unknown to science but it *understands* those facts in a way that opens to a loving reliance on existence as it really is. *Existence* is called in this study "the energy of matter," and in other places by other people with **other metaphors** like "*natura naturans,*" "the Mask of God," "the Cloud of Unknowing," "The Dark Night," "*sunyata*-emptiness" or even "non-being."

There are many who have little respect for the *understanding* that comes through somatic experience. Rather than *understand* that they belong to *existence* and surrender to the maddening passionate entanglements and sweet sorrow that material belonging entails, they would prefer to "believe," on the authority of others, questionable "facts" which promise to "save" them from having to embrace this turbid raucous "Mother-of-Matter" that gave them birth and recalls them in death for re-use. They cling to those "beliefs" as if they were a sacred currency allowing them to buy their way out of this world without actually dying. It lets them harbor the illusion that they will *exist* eternally as individuals *somewhere else,* unencumbered by an ancestry of bumbling, tormented, entropy-ridden *matter.*

On the other hand entirely there are those who would eschew the sacred altogether simply because they have discovered that the literalisms of their childhood religion do not harmonize with scientific facts. Some even go so far as to deny their sense of the sacred — their very love of life — in a futile effort to dodge the overpowering impact of the numinous that is right before their eyes ... *terrible as an army set in battle array*.

We carry a sacred treasure in vessels of clay ... It is *the mystery of matter ... our matter.* This treasure needs to be cherished for what it is and not what our ancient fantasies imagined. It is the surrender to our integral place in the living dynamism of groping *existence, the **groaning Mother** whose* creative emptiness endlessly gives birth to this astonishing universe ... our bodies ... our home.

Chapter III

is religion "hard wired"?

The goal of the reflections in *The Mystery of Matter* was to *understand existence*. We concluded that *existence is matter's existential energy*. Its an energy that drives an irrepressible thrust in all matter to continue existing and, for us and other animals, the palpable love our own life. We have argued that it is from there — what Spinoza called the **conatus** — that our sense of the sacred springs. We love our life, therefore it is sacred to us. Everything that produces and supports our existence ... going back to the very root source of the energies that generated organic evolution itself ... are also sacred.

From this apparently simple identity comes an insightful paradox: there is no value perception that springs from anywhere other than the organic base of our bodies. The sense of the sacredness of *existence* comes *from what we are*. The perception of "objective value" which was thought to transcend animal self-interest and derive from an imagined altruistic "spirit" from another world, is in fact simply a function of our bodies. It is the organically grounded instinct for self preservation that radiates its appreciation outward to everything on which the survival of the organism depends. It is necessarily communitarian, for everything reaches out to survive. It is not a choice. It is the very *nature* of the material substrate of the universe.

There is no need to have recourse to two different sources of explanation for the religious phenomenon, because there are not two different "kinds" of reality out there, one spiritual and altruistic needing to grow, and the other material and selfish needing to be eradicated. There is nothing besides *material energy*; and it is sufficient to explain everything we are, everything we want and everything we do. The sense of the sacred is nothing more than the echo of the **conatus**.

Human beings are not blind. We know the universal matrix that extruded and sustains us and we know the extent of the community that we rely on to survive. We hold as **sacred** *all those things* on which our existence and survival depend ... past, present, future, universal and terrestrial, near and far.

religion

In this chapter I want to delve deeper into the traditional way humankind has related to the sacred — religion. Toward this end, I want to examine religion under **three** aspects that we may have thought made it *optional*, but in fact make it necessary. Because it is rooted in the **conatus** itself, religion is *not* an option for humankind. The corollary of this is extremely important: Since religion is so central to the human project, *the determination of its legitimate role is a collective responsibility.* Religion is not optional therefore it cannot be ignored.

In this chapter, then, we reflect **first** that we are not self-originating or self-sustaining, *and we die.* Our unavoidable existential vulnerability is the necessary limit-phenomenon of the human landscape; therefore the individual human being cannot escape "religious experience." The awareness of death in the context of the **conatus sese conservandi** creates an insuperable tension that defines the human condition. Death connotes annihilation. Since the response to this negative experience has traditionally been borne by religion, the experience itself has been called "religious." But it is more fundamentally a reaction rooted in the existentially driven character of *matter's energy.* Because of the thrust of the **conatus**, the human organism lives with a background sense of *anguish and hopelessness* which is always ready to assert itself. Death directly contradicts the instincts and expectations of the **conatus.**

Second, we look at the **necessary role of the community,** family and clan. They are the key to the survival of the individual organism and the primary interpreter of the experience of *existential anguish.* That local interpretation and resolution is traditionally called *religion.* I claim it has functioned for so long that it has created **modifications to the human genome** which include a *genetic pre-disposition* to seek the resolution of existential insecurity in the local community. Effectively, it means religion as a clan phenomenon is "hard-wired."

Third, in the context of these two socially grounded determinants, we examine the potential phenomenon of *faith,* understood as we have offered it here in Chapter I. Faith is traditionally assumed to be a religious activity but as I conceive it, it is actually an alternative to traditional religion and a direct response to the unmistakable message embedded in the insistence of the **conatus.** *The conatus is an unconditional organic expectation of endless life.* ~~Faith~~ voluntarily embraces that intentionality. So, since people are inclined to obey the dictates of the **conatus,** ~~faith~~ is inevitably a majority occurrence within a population, and an authentic answer to existential anguish. Very simply, most people, even those who eschew religion, find a way to deal with death by *trusting existence.* The alternative is hardly imaginable; everyday life would be impossible without it. *Trusting existence* is what I mean by ~~faith~~; it does not necessarily conflate with traditional religion.

Each of these three features will be analyzed from its own appropriate perspective in relationship to the other two. This means we will cover the same ground three different times, each time from a point of view proper to the respective issue. I'm hoping that the sheer thoroughness of it all will make up for the possible confusions the overlapping entails.

the persistence of religion

For these reasons I believe "religion" in some form will always be with us. But, our analysis suggests, not necessarily in the way our dualist traditions have handed it on. What form religion might or should take is not the subject of this chapter. Here we are interested in understanding the persistence of the phenomenon, and the collective responsibility that derives from it.

Stated simply: since religion will always be with us, it behooves us all to work for its sanity and humanity. The reform of religion is not a "religious" project, *it is a socio-political-ethical imperative.* It belongs to the whole of humankind, because grappling with the meaning of the **conatus-***threatened-with-death* — the void — is the universal condition of our species. It is of interest to all of us that some large numbers among us might have become ensnared by solutions to our existential dilemma that threaten the rest of us.

Besides searching for effective ways to assuage our own anguish, to my mind we should turn our attention to the "naturalization" of traditional religion. Religion is poorly served by a "supernatural" dualism that insists that the only thing sacred resides somewhere else, in another world, and that we have to go there to make our unholy world holy. Such a fallacy alienates humanity from itself. It eviscerates our love of life and may encourage us to escape our responsibilities or even become bitter, punitive and despairing. The sacred depths of nature itself, the mystery of *matter's existential energy,* should rather be the focus of religion's celebrations and its encouragement to social responsibility. The burden of this message belongs to us all.

We should be disabused of any illusion that would allow us to walk away from religion, either for ourselves or for others. The "secular" luxury of thinking we have the right to ignore the problem, or that we can leave it to "religionists" and their hierarchs to deal with it, is wrong. The reform of religion is a problem for the whole human race; the survival of our species hangs in the balance. Religion can destroy us, in whole or in part.

It is no less insane to think we can destroy religion than to think that we can ignore it and that it will go away. *Religion is not going anywhere,* neither by annihilation nor neglect. There is no option. We have to come up with a sane alternative to the insanities we have inherited.

A. religious experience is inevitable

The root source of both *religion* and ~~faith~~ is what has been traditionally called *"religious" experience.* This experience is a natural phenomenon. It is rooted in the **conatus.**

It unfolds in a sequence of "realizations." The **first** is innate and characterizes all organisms in their youth. It is the serene unquestioning identification of the individual with *existence* itself. *Material energy* is programmed to live endlessly. This sense, *that to be oneself is to exist,* is as revealing as it is unobtrusive. *Existence* is taken for granted. The joy of its possession is implied but lies dormant until a **second** moment occurs: the perplexity, anguish and perhaps even defensive violence generated when *the certainty of death* penetrates consciousness. It is at that moment that the human organism awakens to the full significance of *being-here.* That, in turn, leads to a **third:** the *"religious" resolution of existential insecurity* by a reassurance of the permanence of *existence* — the reassertion of the assumptions of the **conatus.**

So by religious experience I mean this entire sequence. Fundamentally, existential vulnerability yields to a realization of the transcendent significance of and ultimate solidity of *existence.* This "resolution" has traditionally been provided by religion and so the experience has been called "religious," but it may, alternatively, result in ~~faith~~ which need not be religious at all. This may sound contradictory. Let me explain.

"Existential vulnerability" is the catalyzing factor. It refers to the bewilderment over the impermanence of *existence* caused by an experience of death or its equivalent that entails the undeniable contradiction of the **conatus**. Death is spontaneously interpreted as the end of *existence* and that produces an intense anxiety in us.

This sense of doom appears to be unique to human beings. An animal's terror at a threat to its life ends abruptly when the threat is neutralized. We humans *understand the significance* of death for ourselves. We absolutely identify with *existence* and we are shocked to discover that we do not *own* it for someday we will die. To the disillusioned, *existence* now seems to be only a temporary conquest over nothingness. Once this tragic fact emerges into awareness, it is immobilizing, and if life is to go on, it must be dispelled.

Given the nature of the **conatus,** this is inevitable; death is a shock. *Anguish* springs from the same ground as the sense of the sacred. They are two sides of the same phenomenon. The "sense of the sacred," broadly speaking, springs from the positive side of the **conatus** and coincides with the *resolution* of anguish. It is similarly inevitable because there is a connatural sense of the sheer solidity of *being-here.* The self-sustaining nature of *existence-in-time*, reinforced by our community-based abilities to meet the threats to survival, re-establishes the foundational intuition that *I am identical with existence and have permanent possession of it.* I realize, in other words, that life will go on.

It is the **conatus,** then, in its various manifestations, positive and negative, that is **constitutive** of religious experience. And the experience is given concrete expression in religion. Since none of these factors will ever disappear, we can expect that religion will never disappear, though its forms may change.

religion and religious experience

Religion has taken many forms in the course of history. In its earliest manifestations it was expressed in metaphor (myth and symbol) and ritual (sacrifice, symbolic re-enactments etc.). In the West as it evolved, it increasingly assumed a rational form that codified orthodox beliefs and requisite moral and ritual practice. In general terms, it performed the function of the *"answer"* to existential insecurity. In the west, "God" guaranteed *existence.* But in return, "God" imposed ritual and behavioral conditions, made known to us through "God's" agent, *the religious institution.*

But we are aware that the reassurance comes from the **conatus** itself with or without the interventions of religion. It is based on the organism's intrinsic relationship to *matter's energy,* which is *existence. Existence,* in other words, as experienced in the **conatus**, tends to carry its own reassurance. We totally identify with it and we cannot imagine not *being-here.* The experience of *existence* is so familiar, intimate and all-embracing that nothing, it seems, could be more solid or permanent. So when we are confronted with this unexpected perplexing "disappearing act" — death — the natural reaction is denial. Eventually, after the initial shock and period of grief, normalcy nudges death once again into the background. We are quickly lulled into unpreparedness. Hence, repeated experiences of death can be as traumatic as the first. It seems we never "get it," and it's because of what we are made of. The **conatus** is blind. It cannot *understand* death.

I'm speaking here in general, but not hypothetical, terms. We are programmed to live in this material universe, and so we are readily reassured. I am not specifying the practical agent, the broker of this reassurance. It may be *religion* in one of its many forms — or it may be ~~faith~~, either in conjunction with or separate from *religion.* But in any case, *resolution,* meaning a reversal of the anxiety and the re-establishment of a sense of security in existence is a natural outcome. *The human organism tends naturally to take existence for granted* and becomes immobile without it. The experience of war, a case where one's impending death never recedes from view, causes severe and often irreversible psychological damage. *The constant acute awareness of death is not tolerable.*

Based on the assumed character of "God," western religion assures us that *existence will not* be taken away. That means, fundamentally, that death is an illusion; belief in life after death is a form of the denial of death. In the West, it conjured the existence of the "immortal soul;" in the East it evoked the doctrine of *anatman,* the negation of the permanent reality of the self — what is not really there cannot really disappear. But in each case death is denied and, psychologically speaking, transcended.

Religious experience is fed by our existential helplessness. In traditional Western terms, its resolution is religion's "God." "God" as "being" is the symbol that has been used to answer the *uncritical* questions about *existence* — why is there "being," and why does it disappear. A personal "God," as defined in the West, answers both questions; "God" gives "being" as a personal gift. Hence, in this conception, "God" explains life and death is explained as a withdrawal of "God's" personal gift.

fear and trembling

Religious experience is intense. It's what the classic existentialists said was accompanied by "anguish," or "dread." Kierkegaard described the human reactions as "fear and trembling." It is the quintessential instance of the confrontation with the *void*. There are no "facts" that add or subtract anything from this experience. It is very simply the *realization* of the terminal nature human life in the context of the expectations of the **conatus** for endless existence.

Since there are no "supernatural facts" that literally "save" us from death, in reality death can only be transcended by ~~faith~~, a "relationship" of trust. Contrary to this, religious concepts — *dogmas, beliefs* — refer to supernatural entities and facts, like a humanoid "God" who raises people from the dead, the immortal soul or the unique sacramental power of the Church, to explain and resolve religious experience. Based on these "facts" the Church claims to have been granted control over life in another world and therefore is in a unique position to assuage the torments of the confused **conatus.** "Life will be changed," we are assured, "not taken away." Ritual mediations are accepted as definitive solutions that allow the individual to sidestep the surrender of ~~faith~~. In this case the only faith involved is faith in the Church. The individual's personal appropriation of *existence-as-void* never really occurs. "God," as the symbol of the benevolence of *existence,* is not the object of a relationship, but rather has been turned into a cosmic agent mollified and controlled by the rituals of the Church. The Church's magical incantations are not ~~faith~~ and they do not produce *understanding.* They are justified by dogma, a pseudo-knowledge of imaginary entities that has the effect of denying death. They do not work because they are a denial of reality, and sooner or later they show themselves to be the fiction they really are.

Traditional western religion has been the institutionalized recognition of existential confusion and then its *standardized resolution*, generally achieved by a persuasive re-assurance of the literal acquiescence of "God," in response to Church rituals, to continue the donation of *existence* in another life. The perplexed individual asks the questions, and religion provides the "answers." But these answers are an ersatz "knowledge" that is neither fact nor ~~faith.~~

the religious community

Religion is a local phenomenon. Its myths and mythic re-enactments are performed *in community at the clan-level.* Primitive religion answered experienced insecurity with an *experienced reassurance* (in myth and ritual) often involving dramatic actions, like sacrifice, animal or human (death ritualized and thus "dominated"), of equal or greater intensity as the anxiety. The resulting behavioral modifications elicited from the individual stabilize and solidify the social political entity — the parish-village, the Church-nation, the "holy" Empire — and the individual's integration into it.

Such rituals were clearly intended to precipitate the type of *understanding* I call a *realization.* For this purpose, religion does not wait for the moment of existential crisis. As the custodian of the religious experience, religion often takes it upon itself to actually provoke existential panic, or at least to anticipate the moment of anguish as part of its assignment. Thus under religion's tutelage, fear and insecurity may be precipitated for the first time in the individual in a form pre-determined by religious beliefs. The evocation of "hellfire," the reminder of the evanescence of life and the ever-present possibility of death and an eternal punishment to follow, for example, shows religion in action, creating in its constituency exactly those feelings that religion alone claims the power to resolve.

As we know it in its modern form, however, religion uses abstract concepts and conventional modes of expression in order to respond to this existential helplessness which has most often been re-cast in rational conceptual terms. But the thrust is the same: to guarantee, now more by reasoned explanation relying on new information (dogma) rather than ritual re-enactment and participation, that a personal "God" will continue to provide an *existence* perceived to be intrinsically threatened. Religion takes the form of *knowledge* that is an answer to an articulated question. It is conceptual and factual. Its goal is persuasion. As such, I want to emphasize, in all its forms, resolution based on the knowledge of entities and cosmic operators known to religion alone *is not faith* ... it is an *ersatz science* that functions on a motivation of individual calculation.

Religion, therefore, has become identified with beliefs, dogmatic concepts, doctrine, other worldly facts, "truths." Religion has been treated as an area of quasi-scientific rational interest, when perhaps it might have continued to answer experience with *experience* in the form of mythic narrative and participatory ritual as it did in its more primitive versions.

Religion, however, as we have it in its modern form, has become a series of reassuring propositions based on a knowledge of another world. Nevertheless, it is important to emphasize that the *vitality and passion* of our experience of *being-here* ... and our sense of helplessness before the evanescence of "being" ... is no more faithfully represented (much less resolved) by religious concepts or their rational logical extensions than it was by clan religion in its more primitive myths and rituals. **The ultimate goal of religion in all its forms, primitive or modern, ritual or intellectual is the same: the transformation of existential insecurity into existential reassurance through the agency of the local community.** It is the attempt to stabilize the individual and therefore provide coherence to the social group through the interpretation and elimination of *existential insecurity*. In all cases, Religion is ultimately a function of social stability.[29]

faith

Finally there's **faith**. ~~Faith~~ is the third and most non-conceptual feature of our religious landscape. ~~Faith~~ is not *knowledge*. It is *intersubjective relationship*. It is a personal disposition, an act of trust, a decision, an embrace, a surrender. ~~Faith~~ is not "beliefs," which is another way of saying that *faith is not traditional religion* with its alternative knowledge — "facts" dogmas and required behavior. Dogma, as knowledge, is contrary to the true notion of ~~faith~~. ~~Faith~~, which is a personal response (*not an "answer"*) to the anguished question about *existence*, is a self-surrender that overrides (*but does not erase*) conceptual darkness. *It is not knowledge.* It is a personal intentionality consciously embraced, not necessarily with any cognitive content, but with an active acceptance of the dynamism of *existence* as benevolent. I want to emphasize: *faith is not conventional knowledge*. It surrenders to its own identification with *existence* — its own **conatus** — and *thus* discovers this supposedly threatened existence to be, paradoxically, its very refuge against annihilation. *But it does not know what it is*, much less does it have or demand any control over it. *~~Faith~~ is the trusting surrender to existence chosen in the face of apparent existen-*

---

29 Joseph Campbell *Thou Art That,* New World, Novato, CA 2001, p.13, comments on this feature of religion and quotes Jung as saying that one of the principal functions of religion is to protect us from religious experience.

tial disaster and conceptual emptiness. It is a relationship with a somatic, bodily, component. *It embraces, it does not dispel, the darkness.* It is in this *act of ~~faith~~,* I contend, that the sense of the sacred is revealed to have a new, transcendent and *intersubjective* dimension.

Religion, taken as metaphor and symbol, may validly mediate *~~faith~~,* but religious beliefs taken as fact, pre-empt and preclude it. The resolution based on putative religious fact *does not work.*

~~faith~~ and *understanding*

The *understanding* (not knowledge) of *existence,* which is the goal of these reflections, is derived only *subsequent* to this experience of ~~faith~~. *Understanding,* then, is a somatically driven cognitive assessment of the nature or character of *existence* as appropriated in *~~faith~~.* It is an interpretation *that includes the salient features of the act of ~~faith~~ itself. **It is faith that informs understanding**. The understanding of existence* is the cognitive side of what is experienced exclusively in *a trusting relationship.*

There is a circularity here, made inevitable by the possession of *existence* by the subject of the act of ~~faith~~. The one who surrenders to *existence* is necessarily surrendering to what is, after all, him or herself. The "objective cognitive content" of that interpretation, such as we may be able to articulate it, was elaborated in the first chapter. But here I want to underline: its unique data-source is ~~faith~~. ~~Faith~~ is the **only authentic source** for *understanding* the intentionality of *existence.* The benevolent subjectivity of *matter's existential energy* is only apprehended in *relationship.*

What's been called religious experience is always a dialogic phenomenon: question and answer. Religious experience may couple with *~~faith~~,* though often it connects to *religion* as a rationalized reassurance. Religious experience is the realization of the *shocking vulnerability of* an *existence* that was presumed invulnerable. It is the very essence of paradox.

Traditional religion answers the question about existence with a knowledge of facts we call "beliefs," the central one of which in the West is the (Judaeo-Greek) concept of an other-worldly "God" projected as the trustworthy personal giver and guarantor of existence. For this same reason a belief in the providence of an anthropomorphic "God" is an invariable feature of this belief structure. It resembles the trust in the intentionality of *existence* by ~~faith~~, but *I want to state emphatically, **it is not.*** Religious belief by itself is not *~~faith~~* nor its resultant *understanding.*

The fact that both ~~faith~~ and *religion* run along parallel lines as the potential responses to existential anguish has contributed to the confusions surrounding the connection between the two. But I'm saying that it is precisely the ersatz *knowledge* proposed by the religious "answer" that skews the issue and turns religion into a *part of the problem* for Western man rather than the solution we would like it to be. **For there is no such "knowledge" of supernatural entities** and when that becomes clear, religion becomes a game of words willfully sustained and obsessively promoted by those who have become dependent on its illusions or who benefit from and therefore exploit them. Conversely, it is only the non-conceptual dimension, the unknowability, the "darkness," validly preserved, perhaps, in religious metaphor, but in any case *embraced in the act of trust,* that guarantees *understanding.* And it is only *understanding the void* that will not be subverted into the division and disdain, and often the mayhem and manslaughter carried out in the name of a non-existent "knowledge" that now riddle the religious life of a great part of humankind. We must recognize that the ethno-centrism expressed in religious hostility and hatred — justified if not caused by doctrinal disagreement, which may not even be conscious at this point in history — is not an insignificant element of the human problem. And it is exclusively due to the various religions' claim to "facts."

B. religion is "hardwired"

Sociobiology proposes to understand human social phenomena as a function of the evolutionary elaboration of the human genome. The biological basis for such a proposal is that environmental features installed or embraced by human society will eventually result in human genetic modifications. Over time, certain learned and repeated characteristics become "hard-wired" — fixed features of human life because they have been "selected." Selection in a human social context becomes increasingly exercised by society itself through the preferences of individuals in choosing mates. Partners select socially desirable characteristics in one another, and over time the character of the entire population changes accordingly. The desired qualities become genetically programmed, and to all extents and purposes, on the time-scale relevant to social decision-making, immutable. The social-religious dimension, I submit, is one of these. We evolved as socially religious beings. This evolution has been

etched in our flesh; it is cemented in our genome. It is potentially rever-
sible following the same process by which it developed, but that is not
relevant on our time-scale.

What this hypothesis says is that our religious interest is not a matter
of happenstance, or contingent historical occurrence. It has been socially
selected and therefore it is not eradicable. It is only modifiable within certain limits. It is a response anticipated by our very genes, encoded in elements of our DNA. They predispose us to act and react in certain ways
regardless of time, place, culture or history.

Religion is a socio-biological phenomenon.   Religion's foundational
narratives, conceptual structure and sacred rituals are community property
that originated in the ancient past. This fact has its *biological origins* in the
necessary role of the local community, the clan, in human survival. At the
most primitive level, the clan, which in *all* respects has been essential to
the survival of the individual since time immemorial, also has had to deal
with the problem of the *social disruption* caused by the human individual's
unavoidable existential insecurity caused by the anguished **conatus**.

The utter dependency of the individual on the immediate community of
survival — the clan — for virtually all its needs is a sheer fact of biological
anthropology. We evolved as social survivors; our existence as individuals is biologically tied to society. Our very bodies are the organic adaptations to social environments that human beings have chosen. At this point
we could not survive as individuals in the wild. Relative to the natural
environment, individual dependency on the local community was as true in
the Pleistocene epoch as it is today, permitting the human species to survive such adverse conditions as millennial glaciations. We are familiar
with the clan's provision of basic items like food, clothing, shelter and mates; but, I insist, it also included religion. Because of the intimate connection between the individual's general helplessness and the security necessarily provided by the community, *existential fear* also triggers a community response: *religion is that response.*

Religion, therefore, and the local community as its agent, draws on
the energies generated by the existential dread that arises from the human condition-toward-death and answers with local clan traditions that go
back beyond recorded history. This remains an invariable pattern. No
matter what the level of social complexity, religion responds to existential
vulnerability and therefore is created by the social group as the linear

extension of the clan-community's provision of support in all areas of life. In return, the local community is fed by the energies it has been effective in servicing. The clan is assimilated to the god or fetish that is its "savior." It is the co-guarantor of survival and shares in the divine power that saves. In creating *religion,* therefore, the clan simply extends the scope of its providence beyond food, clothing, shelter and family to cover the issue of *existential anguish* itself. This analysis asserts that religion comes from biologically based social mechanisms that emerged as a function of group survival. Society, in other words, is *an essential component* of the religious phenomenon, and its cohesion is in turn nourished by it. *There is no religion that exists apart from a social context, and there is no organic society that does not address existential fear, i.e., that does not provide religion in some form or another.*

This challenges the enlightenment theory that religion and society were fundamentally separable. They thought religion was a matter of individuals' beliefs, and once "reason" won out that religion would eventually disappear. They were wrong. Religion, to the chagrin of many, has not disappeared. And I claim, because it cannot. Religion is a communitarian phenomenon. The factors that generate religion are permanent features of the communitarian nature of the human organism which cannot disappear.

Reciprocally, then, the human genome has been formed in the context of the increasing importance of the community as a factor in individual survival. The biological individual, whose existential needs give shape and focus to human society, is in turn the *ultimate product* of human society. Specific individual developments, including intelligence, temperament, character, even physical features, have been and still are *selected by society* for their benefit to society. And if there is a gene responsible for the religious instinct, I believe it can be safely assumed that society has selected for it as well.[30]

Religion is created in this organic social setting. The group as "savior" of the helpless solitary individual offers a primary and indispensable reso-

---

[30] Cf *Scientific American*, 9/27/2004 review by Karl Zimmer of the book by Dean Hamer, *The God Gene, How Faith is Hardwired into our Genes*, Doubleday, NY 2004. Hamer's book is also discussed by another *Scientific American* columnist, Michael Schermer, in his book *The Believing Brain*, Times Books, NY 2011. Cf especially pp.165-174 where Schermer claims that belief in "God" is hardwired in the human brain. See pp 170-171 for his comments on Hamer's work.

lution to the feeling of existential fear. Therefore the "religious sentiment" is *always* found within a strongly bonded societal context. The sense of "reverence" that it generates — whatever focus on a god it may have — always *includes the group, the community*. The group bathes in the aura of the saving god whose power it conjures, brokers and co-authors. Separation from the group under these circumstances is nothing less than catastrophic, for it means separation from the clan's "god" and its saving power. Hence "exile" in theocratic Roman society, and "excommunication" in its later ecclesiastical counterpart, the Catholic Church, were considered punishments worse than death. Ethnic religious identities as in Northern Ireland, or the Balkans, with their religion-based violence may be understood as examples of this same phenomenon; they are rooted in the connection of the clan community with its particular protective "god." The intrinsic connection between the god and the community may be subconscious, or only subliminally perceived, but if there is an ethnocentric feeling, i claim it is necessarily associated with a religious vision.

civilizations

As society evolved from a local self-defense clan into the large civilized state, the religious dimension expanded along with it, and local religion became transposed into a universal key. The aggregation of small communities (clans) into large multi-ethnic agglomerates called "civilizations" — a process which began in all the centers of high social organization, Egypt, Mesopotamia, India, China, Mexico, Peru thousands of years ago — created the conditions for a religious homogeneity that transcended local clan and tribal identity.   As local religions were universalized in these great "empires" other important modifications accompanied the transition. The shift from narrative rituality (myth and its re-enactments) to dogmatic conceptualization and a codified, rationalized morality were elements that contributed to the universalization of the terms of the religious answer. Under the pressure of political consolidation, the natural tendency was to strip religion of its local clan associations and universalize it. The emergence of "academic" or philosophical religion is part of this phenomenon and it happened in all the great civilizations at roughly the same time.[31]

---

[31] Cf Karen Armstrong, *The Great Transformation*, Knopf, NY 2006, *passim*; the "axial age"

Universal religions have been with us for exactly the millennia that those totalizing civilizations have been with us. They are simply aspects of the same socio-cultural phenomenon. The claim of religion to relevance for the whole of humanity corresponds to the same expansion of the locus of group reverence — and collective salvation — from the local tribe to larger society, which, for these ancient all-embracing civilizations, comprised the then "known world," i.e., believed to be the entire human race. Therefore all the major religions evince a sense of *absolute universality* and by their association with some present or past epiphany of *centralized hieratic political authority* which was thought to cover the entire known world. *The universal religions are all the products of universal empires.*[32]

(From this analysis, a second hypothesis of future prediction arises: that any new universal empire will similarly project its own universal religion — an eclectic composite of earlier versions, or the syncretizing ascendency of one of them.[33])

church and state

Similarly, from this it's not difficult to understand the intimate, organic relationship between religion and the state. It is common knowledge that religion has shown itself to be particularly vulnerable to absorption by the state apparatus. Christianity, for example, achieved transcendent historical importance by being integrated into the Roman Imperial state machinery. And similarly, the inability of the state to resist succumbing to the agenda established by religion, is also historically undeniable. Christianity, to continue the example, after its canonization as the religion of the Empire, in short order turned the power of the Roman State to serve its own needs. Roman military force was routinely activated for the suppression of heresy and schism and the implementation of a Christian moral

---

[32] According to our hypothesis the reverse can also be assumed: universal religions may regressively become the "clan religion" in localities that have somehow become marginated or separated from the universal community. Thus the ethno-religious wars in Northern Ireland and the Balkans reflect an anachronism — an historical regression — pitting two or more "universal" religions, now functioning as local ethnic clan identifiers, against one another in complete contradiction of the universalist tenets of each.

[33] The allusion here is to my belief that the global "American Empire," if it has much of a history, will generate the next "universal" religious formulation of humankind, for better or worse.

and ritual program. No matter how large and powerful the State, religion remains identified with it and they tend to merge.

The apparent "separation" of Church and State promulgated in the national constitutions inspired by the enlightenment, masks two social realities that contradict the endeavor. The **first** is that these constitutions allow for the continued existence and right of expression of religions that have *absolutist premises and goals*. The modern constitution is theoretically open to the possibility that one or another of these absolutist religions may *convince the majority* to accept its beliefs, necessarily undermining the foundational principles of the state. In other words, the religion / State conjunction is always potentially revivable under these constitutions, and therefore remains ideologically unchallenged.

Separation of Church and State is a formality that is enforced only at the level of the apparatus of government; it does not penetrate the non-governmental levels of society which continue to be grounded, as always, on absolutist universal religions and the dictatorial exercise of authority. Thus we have the absolutely undemocratic authoritarianism that characterizes every sub-altern institution in our supposed "democratic" society — businesses, schools, religions, governmental agencies, etc. The only time democracy is exercised in an unmixed way is in a general election, or in activities legally obligated by statute to vote, like jury trials, legislative assemblies, etc.

The **second** reality is that the constitutions of the enlightenment era are themselves religious for they are explicitly based on "God" as the guarantor of their system. They presume the existence of a deity who grants rights and freedom to individual human beings. The "God" that guarantees individual rights purposely avoids interfering with the individuals' social preferences which are assumed to be *religious* for the achievement of "life-after-death" — their church. The state simply acts as a referee between competing religions. Churches are recognized, protected and even encouraged by the state. The state is presumed to work in tandem with institutional religions. There is no expressed support for a non-religious population, and no explicit guarantee for atheism. Whatever rights are recognized in these areas are indirectly derived from the principle of non-establishment. They are accidental. They are not based on secular principles.

Reason as a substitute for religious superstition was a belief of our founders. Thomas Jefferson was personally convinced that once people were given the opportunity to live by reason, traditional religion would eventually disappear.[34] It was an enlightenment myth that has long since been dispelled. Traditional religion in Jefferson's own United States, shows no sign of disappearing. His ideology did not recognize that existential insecurity — the void — is the proper object of society's ministrations. Religion and society are not separable.

State and Church. The two are one flesh. We have our evolutionary heritage to blame. It's in our genes. Society is the first locus of *survival* and therefore, no matter what the level of social complexity or unification achieved, is always most naturally the first responder to the cry for "salvation."

theocracy

Religion is constitutive of society, and so historically theocracy has been the political norm; the secular state has been a rare and short-lived interlude. Since religion has such a unifying effect, the state will tend to use religion in one form or another, if it can, to maintain social stability through the imposition of a standardized system of values. Beliefs, dogmas, religious "truths," party lines, ritual, behavior, moral codes, become the foundational infrastructure of society. A homogeneous doctrinal / moral system gives the authorities an enormous amount of control over individuals whose energies are driven by the existential dread born of the **conatus**. The separation of church and state, in contrast, has been a precarious experiment that, even on the rare occasions in the long history of the west when it was attempted, was violated in practice, and ultimately abandoned. It may be made to work temporarily, but *it is not natural.*

The state is treated with a reverence commensurate with its role as agent in the resolution of existential distress. It doesn't matter that a particular constitution claims to eschew such a role. The state is assimilated to the saving divinity and becomes itself an object of religious veneration and to that degree impervious to criticism and change. We are all familiar with this phenomenon.

---

[34] Cf His *Notes on the State of Virginia*, query 17, and his letters to Adams and others on the issue.

Even though not yet fully developed, we can see such an eventuality in the process of formation in our modern American society. Despite two centuries of enlightened politics, religion is stronger and more irrational than ever. Along with the ascendency of fundamentalist Christianity as a political force, many see the current US involvement in the mid-east as a "crusade" against Islam. Theocratic Christian statements made by US Church people and military leaders alike support this interpretation.[35]

Church-State separation in the US, supposedly a constitutional principle, often fails in practice. It is not easy to ignore the social basis of human religiosity and therefore the religious basis of human society. It not only reveals the foundational role of religion in the structure of human culture and society at all levels, it also explains the deflection of the resolution of anguish away from faith, which *does not claim "knowledge"* or seek control, and toward traditional religion, which does. This means the answer to that harrowing question about *existence* will almost certainly be given in terms of knowledge and social convention — religion and its beliefs identified with the political authorities.

I do not want to be misunderstood on this question. I am personally in favor of the separation of Church and state, but I recognize it as unnatural. I believe, pessimistically, that the efforts to maintain the separation are fighting an uphill battle even in the US, and may not succeed. The existence of a secular state, like the ancient Mediterranean democratic *poleis*, is a worthwhile endeavor, and provides benefits for all while it lasts; but the forces emanating from the **conatus** — resulting in our experience of the void — will overwhelm anything that denies their central role in human life. They cannot be ignored. The only hope, in my opinion, is to recognize their hegemony, harness them through the reform and naturalization of religion, and then use that energy to further a political and social agenda that works for the benefit of all. To deny the radical *existential* insecurity of our condition, and that religion is the tool we use to defeat it, is to live in a world of fantasy and illusion. Religion cannot be eliminated or ignored; but it can be humanized.

---

[35] Seymour Hersh accused the American military of thinking of their present work as a "crusade" against Islam. The Washington Post January 21, 2011

C. ~~faith~~ contacts the void "mouth to mouth"[36]

The deflective resolution of religious experience in *religion* rather than in *~~faith~~* is a pervasive fact of human history, universally true of cultures and eras that in other ways are insuperably diverse. *Religion is not ~~faith~~,* and the unique authenticity of ~~faith~~ as a response to existential insecurity — the void — means that religion will always be challenged by ~~faith~~. The "realizations" that characterize the authentic response of *~~faith~~* will continue to question religion's conceptual certainties and political alliances.

The dream of breaking the bond between religion and society (the State) to create a purely secular society has proven to be an elusive endeavor. The ancient marriage of state and religion, with its dogmas and politics, despite surface appearances in the modern constitutional democracies, continues to hold sway all over the world. If there is a sociobiological basis for this phenomenon, as I claim there is, then we can at least understand it. The connections are hard-wired; we are genetically predisposed to find refuge in a local religious community. Religion is a biologically grounded social phenomenon, and wherever there is human society, some form of religion will appear. It cannot be eliminated or suppressed, *but it can be made human.*

~~faith~~ and religious reform

Religious reform — making religion human — is dependent on visionaries who can see through and beyond the dogmatic overlay and political symbiosis that constitute the sacrosanct traditions of a given society. We can call such people *witnesses* for they announce a new *vision* which they have gleaned from their own *act of ~~faith~~*. They speak of a new *understanding* to which they invite others. The strong anthropological determinants that underlie the genetic predisposition to clan religion, however, insure that any serious reform of mainstream religion will be initially interpreted as a hostile challenge to the integrity and sacredness of the social fabric. It will be fiercely resisted. Hence, those "witnesses" proposing doctrinal or structural modifications will, at least at first if not always, be considered enemies of the "sacred community" which eventually is identified with the state. The authorities in every era and clime assume a re-

---

[36] The phrase is from John of the Cross, *The Ascent of Mount Carmel*, Bk II, ch XVI, para.9.

markably similar attitude toward these reformers and act in a remarkably similar way. We should remember the Greek word for witness is *martyr.*

I claim that religion is not the source of the sense of the sacred. The sense of the sacred is an extrapolation of the **conatus**. Its correlate is not religion but ~~faith~~ which, without knowledge, re-affirms the natural thrust of the **conatus** to exist. Religion is subordinate to ~~faith~~ and can encourage it *by providing metaphors that confirm the reliability of the **conatus**.* In principle there is nothing to prevent religion from anticipating the "right moment," the *kairos,* the time of existential helplessness when the *act of* ~~*faith*~~ may be called forth. In this way, for those who realize the limitations of religion, it can be helpful *so long as it defines itself as ancillary to* ~~*faith.*~~ But, to the extent that religion considers its practices the only authentic response to the "existential problem," it tries to substitute for ~~faith~~ and so becomes an obstacle to it. Religion without ~~faith~~ can only be the insistence on non-existent knowledge — religious "facts" — and the claim to control them. It is an attempt to deny the void. In that form it is intrinsically alienating.

John of the Cross and Martin Luther

I would like to present from western Christian religious history what I think is an illuminating example of the phenomena we are examining in this section: ~~faith~~ and the reform of religion.

The sixteenth century Spanish mystic, John of the Cross, while claiming to function entirely within the orthodox parameters of the Catholic religion of his day, taught that an *act of faith* similar to what I have been describing was the universal call and destiny of every Christian and the unique source of contemplative development.

This is salient for our discussion on two counts: John of the Cross called for a "faith" that was conceptually blind, a notion that from the point of view of Roman Catholicism represented a radical departure from conventional doctrine. John gave a perfunctory nod to the official religiosity operating in the sacraments and the other Church instruments of salvation, but the real program he proposed for contacting "God" effectively was something else entirely. "Faith" was the word he used. It represented a significant re-ordering of priorities. It was clearly reminiscent of the descriptions of Marguerite Porete and Johannes Eckhart. I am suggesting, in other words, that the program of John of the Cross was, by the standards we are uncovering here, a true reform of religion based on the experience of ~~faith~~ camouflaged as an esoteric asceticism confined to contemplative monasteries.

It is especially remarkable the way Catholic *doctrine* is treated in John's vision. Dogma, as we know, has historically been the keystone of Catholic claims to be the "only true religion." Dogma was included in the word "faith" as used in the late mediaeval tradition; "faith" had a dense, detailed conceptual dimension. Faith signified beliefs, truths, *facts,* supposedly revealed by God, like the Trinity, the Incarnation, original sin, sacramental function, infallibly defined by the Church and therefore *clearly known* (though not fully understood), and requiring assent from every Christian. Faith meant dogma. One had "faith" by believing what the Church taught. It didn't matter if the motivation were just peer pressure or even fear. *A trusting relationship to the source of existence was not necessary.* The Church took the place of "God" and offered "knowledge" not available by any other means.

a different "faith"

Despite these ecclesiastical claims, John declared that, quite to the contrary, *God was completely unknowable,* and that it was the very unknowability of "God," encountered, acknowledged and embraced, that was the key factor for the *ascesis* of authentic contact and therefore by implication, holiness and salvation. *Authentic contact with "God" was achieved, said John, not by knowing but by* **unknowing,**[37] *not by faith as knowledge, but by faith as blind trust.* In the context of his time and ecclesiastical doctrine, it was called "mysticism," but it is not. It is simply religion as it ought to be.

John always admitted the need for *verbal assent* to the dogmas as demanded by the Church authorities, but he astutely turned this required acquiescence to the service of his message by saying the dogmas were **mysteries that could not be understood** and therefore were themselves a *constitutive part of the conceptual darkness* — the void — which was the necessary context for faith as he meant it.[38] Acknowledgement of the "truth" of the dogmas in such a context, from the point of view of conceptual "knowledge," amounted to an empty formality. It was not the ~~faith~~ that, according to John, led to contact with God.

---

[37] John of the Cross, *Ascent of Mount Carmel,* tr Peers, Image, NY 1958, Bk II Ch.4, #4, p.89
[38] ibid, Bk II Ch 6, #2, p.99

Martin Luther

As part of the changes in Christian theology initiated by the Reformation of 1517, John's insistence on the primacy of *faith-as-blind-trust* mirrored contemporary developments that were to dominate European Christianity for the next 400 years. In practice, if not in theory, John's teaching parallels the reforms of his near-contemporary, Martin Luther, who for his own part had no qualms about declaring "faith" to be the only authentic Christian program — for all, not just monks — in open challenge to the Catholic emphasis on obedience to orthodox dogma and code of morals, the power of ecclesiastical ritual and the (remunerated) intercession of the Church. It reveals the radical nature of these 16th century religious innovations, even though today the two contending denominations, Catholic and Lutheran, are eager to downplay their original clash. This is a concession on the part of the Lutherans, in my opinion, allowing Catholics to save face. For there is no way to deny that in the historical context of late-mediaeval magical mechanisms of salvation, upheld as standard doctrine and practice by the official Catholic Church, John and Martin were talking about an altogether new kind of "faith." It was a response that would bypass religious practice as it then existed and invite *the individual* to *an act of personal trust*. Faith for them was not knowledge or dogma, or mechanical practice, or paid intercession. *Faith was a relationship of reliance*. Catholics like John of the Cross muted the subversive implications of their reforms by presenting them as a subset of mainstream orthodox Christian doctrine designed for a monastic elite. For John of the Cross, this may not have been the intentional subterfuge my interpretation intimates, but in any case the alternative would have meant censure, excommunication and possibly the stake; the Inquisition had become a fact of Spanish life in the aftermath of the *re-conquista* of 1492 and the expulsion of the Jews. In 1517 in Germany, however, the Church had already lost control of the "secular arm." Martin's prince, for reasons of his own, supported the Lutheran reform. With little to fear from Rome, Luther did not need to disguise the separatist implications of his doctrine nor its universal relevance for pastoral practice.

John and Martin weren't the only ones speaking newly of "faith." The term "faith," at that time was going through a larger historical transition. For in place of its use in the "business" of salvation, "faith" was being given a guiding role as a theological source. Since the days of Duns Scotus and William of Ockham in the early 1300's, thinkers increasingly had recourse to a theological "faith" to ground the philosophical "truths" and "beliefs" that once were "scientifically certain" but now held suspect. By the 1500's, the era of the reformers, that new perspective counted on a large following. As western thought moved decisively away from its metaphysical roots in Platonism, the tendency more and more was to use "God" as a theological *deus ex machina*, speaking through scripture and the Church, to guarantee a "knowledge" of the invisible world that philosophy could no longer provide. This "faith" revised theology and broke the age-old union between reason and faith. If there is a divide between science and religion today, it began in that era.

But the 16th century Reformers, like John of the Cross and Martin Luther, went a step further. The faith that John described as "unknowing," and Martin claimed "saved" us, had to be different even from the faith that provided "knowledge" for the orthodox theologians. *For these reformers faith was not knowledge of any kind,* and therefore, not dogma. It necessarily presupposed a different relationship to reality. There is no way to avoid the implications of such a requirement. This kind of faith established *a relationship* where conceptual clarity was not important. *Unknowing,* unless it's a game of words, must refer to what *we do not know.*

~~faith~~ as unknowing: *apophatic monotheism*

"Unknowing" is a strange word. Most people are not familiar with it, and yet it is one of the oldest and continuously stable notions in western religious thought. Its unfamiliarity is easily explained: it is used only by the mystics, and we have been discouraged from reading the mystics. It was coined by Pseudo-Dionysius in the 6th century. But the roots of the concept go back even further — to the very foundations of Mosaic monotheism. That's when we were first introduced to a "God" who was "unknowable."

As recorded in Exodus, Moses had a vision of a god who spoke to him from a burning bush. He asked what he might call this god and the response was a *NAME* so sacred to the Jews that it was never to be uttered. It turned out to be something of a redundancy because the *NAME* itself, *Yahweh,* meant "unknowable." Translated into Vulgate Latin in the 5th century of our era, it came into Western Christianity as *ego sum qui sum*, in English, *"I am Who am."* This is not quite accurate, according to

Philo of Alexandria, the first century ce Jewish philosopher. The Hebrew words, he says, translate to ***"I am who I am"*** which was a not-so-subtle refusal to give any name at all. In the context of the ancient near eastern polytheistic culture which believed that having the names of gods gave humans power over them, the "no-name" response was a loud and clear declaration of divine independence. The ineffable *NAME* then became the very symbol of transcendent monotheism for the Jews. It was not the philosophical "being" the Greco-Roman world has projected, but along with the Judaic prohibition against any depiction of "God," the unutterable *NAME* evoked a presence that *transcended human knowing*. For the ancient Hebrews the closest they would come to representing "God" was an empty tent — the symbol of a nomadic "God" wandering with "his" nomadic people after their escape from slavery in Egypt. The symbol of the empty tent said that any imagery would be a distortion, a false god whose worship would be *idolatry.*

Moses' anger at his people when he came down from the mountain was not because they were worshipping a different god. They were still worshipping *Yahweh,* Moses' new "God" who had saved them from the Egyptians. No, his anger was directed, rather, at the fact that *they had created an idol,* and dared to represent the unknowable "God" in knowable form.

Tradition says the exodus is supposed to have taken place in the 13th century bce. It has been suggested that the source of Moses' vision came from a 14th century bce Egyptian religious revolution centered on the recognition of a single divine principle, *Aten,* and the absorption of the traditional national gods — *Horus, Anubis, Thoth*, etc. — as mere aspects of that one divinity. That brief interlude is referred to as the Armana period in Egyptian history because it involved the relocation of the cultic capital to that city. It indicated the intended seriousness of the conversion. It was a radical reform launched by the Pharaoh himself, *Akhenaten.* It upended traditional patterns and ran counter to the millennial habits of the Egyptian population kept obedient to their traditional gods through fear of punishment after death. The "new" unknowable "One God" precipitated a strong reaction from the established Egyptian hierarchs and supposedly accounts for the subsequent deliberate obliteration of representations of Akhenaten and his wife Nefertiti along with the rapid dismantling of the changes they made during their 17 year reign.

If the conjectured Egyptian influence is correct, it means that an *apophatic* — "unknowing" — religious vision, expressed as an *imageless monotheism* was not a unique revelation made by a supernatural "God" who chose to give this knowledge only to a "chosen people." It was rather a fragile and politically threatening discovery of the second millennium before the common era, picked up by enslaved people like the Hebrews who used this insight to defend their identity against subjugation by the Egyptian theocracy. Such a vision has always been marginated if not persecuted by officialdom. From its very inception it revealed the importance of belief in an unknowable god and the liberation of people from the hieratic mystifications used for the control and exploitation of diverse populations. *Apophatic monotheism was born and barely survived amid the empires of the ancient world.* Akhenaten's reforms were perceived by the Egyptian establishment as subversive of the state, and the Hebrew embrace of that vision a slave revolt. It was a declaration of independence — an event of political liberation. Liberation from "the gods" was an essential element of the Buddha's teaching as well. Why is this?

unknowing and liberation

The traditional religious interpretation is that "God" is a God of human liberation. But that ascribes an anthropomorphic intentionality to "God" that can only be taken as metaphor. I offer a simpler theory: *liberation from the gods means we are free from their illusory mystifications.* For the Hebrews, relationship to the unknowable god that Moses met in the desert freed them from the all too well known Egyptian gods who ruled over their captivity and exploited their labor.

And in our contemporary context, that is exactly what the "unknowability" of "God" still accomplishes. Admitting that *we do not know what "God" is like,* means we cannot claim to know *what "God" wants.* Hence, what makes "God" completely unknowable also puts us beyond any imagined obligation to obey. We are free. But notice, even for an anthropomorphic theism it works the other way around as well. Not-knowing "God" means there is no obedience or ritual act of ours that could control "God." Since we cannot "please" God, we should be disabused of any thought that we have a claim on "him." Not knowing "God" not only frees us from "God," *it frees "God" from us.* In the most orthodox of terms, it preserves the transcendence of "God" and refutes the arrogant attempt on the part of any human "authority" to exact obedience from human beings in "God's" name.

I submit for your consideration: the entire spectrum of religion-based violence, so much in evidence in our times, despite its apparent variety of forms and motives, is ultimately reducible to the *claim of knowing what "God" really wants*, and therefore of being in a position to secure his favor and avoid calamity. Violence born of that illusion is the primary thing decried so passionately by the "new atheists." The violence is multi-faceted. It includes the intergroup violence of war, exploitation and genocide ... the interpersonal violence of gender, family abuse and economic exploitation ... self-inflicted violence, ... and violence toward other species and the environment. Once that false constant — *"God's will"* — is eliminated from the equation, the lie that disguises the violence we perpetrate on one another is exposed. That does not mean violence will automatically disappear, but it eliminates one major reason why we don't see what we are doing even when it is staring us in the face. "God" issues no commands; the evil we do is ours; we cannot justify it in the name of "God," (nor as we shall see later, as the work of the devil).

unknowing vs. "knowledge"

"Knowledge" is a critical category for human beings. We use our knowledge of antecedent and consequent events to defend ourselves in an impersonal universe. The introduction of rational order into the welter of incoming data is critical to human psychological stability; it represents our control of an uncontrolled environment. The animals have their instincts and their extraordinary bodies built for speed, strength and the mastery of an environmental niche. We don't. We have only our minds and the representative imagery we generate about the world around us. It has allowed us to transcend the limited habitats of the animals, but it has also meant that we are individually weaponless against the world except for our ability to imagine "what's coming next" and adjust our collective labors accordingly. Traditional religion claims to have "knowledge" about existence itself, its divine source and its apparent loss in death — "what's coming next" — and how to deal with it, so we can continue to "survive." Traditional religion seems to make sense because it responds to the questions of the **conatus**; it is the linear extension of the very same strategy we use everyday to stay alive and prepare for tomorrow. Religion claims it "knows" and that *that* "knowledge" is salvation for the individual.

A different kind of religion — one that claims that *it does not know* — necessarily runs counter to the traditional resolutions of human anguish provided by mainstream religion. We call such alternative religions *"apophatic,"* speechless, meaning that they say nothing about "God." They eschew "knowledge." Apophatic religions function on "unknowing" rather than knowing ... on the *understanding* derived from *relationship* rather than "knowledge" ... and on autonomous self-actuation (compassion, justice and love — being "human") rather than obedience to law, because they do not presume to know the "will of God" and therefore they cannot codify "his" commands.

Mystics like John of the Cross are fully immersed in the apophatic tradition. Reading what they wrote helps us understand how this phenomenon impacts our social psychology. The mystics, when confronted with the impasse of "not knowing" what it is all about, either did not take the "knowing" road offered by religion, or quickly abandoned it. They left religion and its dogmatic knowledge and chose the path of unknowing, plunging headlong into their clear-headed ignorance — *the void,* which they fully trusted — convinced that at some point it would yield what they were looking for: the truth about existence, life and death. *The mystics, even the most institutionally loyal of them, universally rejected religious imagery (knowledge) as inadequate to their quest for contact with existence.* They counseled their disciples to embrace emptiness — the void — the mistrust of all clarity of ideas or images in the search for "God." For John of the Cross, the Spanish word for the void was *nada, "nothing."* They were convinced that the "answer" to life is rooted in the very unknowability of God ... and therefore what initially seemed the unsolvable question turned out to be the very answer they were looking for ... it was the key. If you want contact, they said, it was made by *unknowing, not* by *knowing.*

"In order to arrive at what you do not know," said T.S.Eliot, "you must go by a way which is the way of ignorance."[39]

It seems that at some point an "enlightenment" occurred for the mystics that did not turn ignorance into knowledge but rather into an *understanding or realization* of the ultimate "goodness" of things just the way they are. The mystics realized they were in a *relationship.* That meant they were absolutely where they were supposed to be, doing exactly what

---

[39] *Four Quartets,* East Coker.

they were supposed to be doing; **there was nowhere else they needed to go, and nothing else they needed to do.** Their quest ended not because they had found a new entity or had arrived at a new place or obeyed a different code, but because they realized *they had been there all along.* They discovered that they were already in the "heaven" that they were taught that they should "go to" in another world, *for the relationship was already alive and well in their own personal existence.* Eriugena, following Gregory of Nyssa, taught that heaven was not a place, but *a state of mind*.[40] The world such as it is, was dripping with the very love and benevolence they had roamed so far and wide to find. They called this enlightenment "unknowing;" for while it provided *understanding* there was no new knowledge. The Buddha said it was as if we had a "third eye" and it suddenly opened.

I claim that what these people encountered was nothing but **themselves** immersed in that "in which all things live and move and have their being" ... what some of them call "God."

unknowing or ignorance?

But why were the mystics so enamored of the word *unknowing*?

Unknowing is not the same as *ignorance.* *Ignorance* is passive; *unknowing is active.* Ignorance refers to the simple absence of knowledge. We are all automatically ignorant of everything we do not know. The ignorant have no necessary relationship to what they are ignorant of. Most likely they are not aware of all the things they do not know, and wouldn't care if they were. This absence of human engagement may help explain why the word "ignorant" is often used as an insult. Brute animals are also ignorant.

But notice that you never find the word "*unknowledge*" in the mystical literature either. I think it is true for the same reason. Such a word would suggest a bare lack of knowledge. But the term *unknowing* does not refer to a static condition. It is an *action word*; it refers to a living relationship in which *the darkness and emptiness are embraced and **understood**. To understand*, as I use the word throughout the *Mystery of Matter*, conforms to Wittgenstein's concept of "showing" or "pointing to" when referring to things that do not fall under the normal categories of logic-controlled third-

---

[40] John Scotus Eriúgena, *Treatise on Divine Predestination, (c. 850 c.e.),* tr Brennan, U.of Notre Dame Pr., 1998, p.125ff.

party observable knowledge. You do not "know" a tautology, like *"I think, therefore I am,"* but you *understand* it implicitly and you can "point to" it.

Unknowing implies an active, even passionate engagement in what we do not know. More than a search for an allegedly absent knowledge, it goes further and suggests some sort of grasp with a cognitive dimension that bears enough of a resemblance to "knowing" that it validly uses that notion as a base. What can this possibly mean?

Chapter One in this book tried to elaborate the notion of ~~faith~~ as the active appropriation of our common possession of *material energy.* That discussion turned on the fact that in the case of *existence,* the subject and object of knowledge is one and the same thing. It meant that it was impossible for the enquiring subject to "objectify" *material energy (existence)* and study it as if it were "something out there" to which s/he could relate as to what is *other. Understanding existence* does not correspond to the ordinary meaning of knowledge. The searching subject, *as active,* is itself always within the circle of the question that it is searching to *understand*; it can never become "object." We are in the realm of *tautology* here. It was one of the central conclusions of *The Mystery of Matter.* It meant that our relationship to matter, and therefore *what it is and what I am,* was not the object of "knowledge," but of *understanding.*

> *Author's Note: This is the fundamental reason why **physical reductionism,** which may be of value as a scientific strategy used by certain limited disciplines, **does not work as an ultimate philosophical position**, because the "condition" of the matter studied by physics or chemistry in isolation does not take into account the other "conditions" that very same matter assumes later ... in life ... in the higher animals ... and in us. Physics is a limited discipline. It cannot be the sole judge of matter. If you are trying to determine the "nature" of quarks and gluons (the most basic components of ordinary matter known to date), the quark in my heart or brain, functioning as an integral component of conscious, compassionate and committed human ethical behavior, is no less a quark nor are its true abilities any the less **immediately** on display in my human activity than in the CERN particle collider. To talk validly about the nature of "quarks" therefore, you have to look at the way they behave everywhere they are found. Obviously they are capable of existing and functioning in more than one "condition."*
>
> *A trans-disciplinary science like cosmo-ontology, using methodological tools designed for the purpose, is indicated. To accept physics as the ultimate arbiter of the "nature" of matter, is an <u>arbitrary</u> projection. It is not warranted. It is assuming that reality is structured from the bottom up, and not from the top down. **Logically speaking** there is nothing to prevent the organizing dynamism to work from an informational high ground (like the DNA of higher organisms) gathering and assembling the substructures it needs to exist and function. The direction of the sequential*

*elaborations of evolution, which are definitely "bottom up," do not necessarily deter- mine the direction of the organizational dynamism of biological construction. And un- less you are going to claim that "informational DNA" is something **other than** material energy, to insist that matter is **only** as studied by physics is pointless.*

What this means is that there is no way for us to know matter without "knowing" *ourselves,* for we are matter. Since we are driven by a **conatus** that is passionately committed to continuing to exist — derived from the very energy of matter itself — to fail to appropriate its dynamism is to fail to *understand* matter *as it is;* and that means we fail to *understand* our- selves *as we are.* The uncomplicated recognition that *that* dynamism is also us ... and *constitutive of us **as it is*** ... is the basic "cognitive content" of the act of ~~faith~~. *~~Faith~~,* then, as I define it, is the active embrace of *exist- ence, matter's existential energy,* for what it is, as we experience it in all its manifestations, which primarily includes our driven selves.

*Matter is what it is. And what it is, is what you see it doing right before your eyes **everywhere that it is doing it,*** including your body-person. Any arbitrary "reduction" in the scope and range, depth and intensity of its actual, real, observable functioning is an unwarranted limitation, an *a priori* assumption.

The use of the cross-out for ~~faith~~ is a reminder that ~~faith~~ is a *complete- ly natural* human act. There is no supernatural agency or substance or entity of any kind required or implied. Unfortunately, the word has been wed to religion's supernatural illusions for so long that it is easy to forget that it is an everyday human phenomenon. But it is precisely in that way that the word is intended here. *~~Faith~~* trusts *existence, matter's energy,* as it would its mother or father, or even ***itself.*** Why? Because the subject of the act of ~~faith~~ is *nothing but **itself**, matter's energy.*

Unknowing, therefore, is just another word for *~~faith~~.* And it is exactly the kind of ~~faith~~ that John of the Cross said put us in contact **boca a boca,** "mouth to mouth," with the source of existence. That source for him was "God," for others, like the Buddhists, a dynamism some of them choose to call *súnyata,* "emptiness." Others refuse to give it any name at all. But that is not so strange. Even at the birth of our own Judaic tradition, nam- ing it as we saw, was forbidden. **Faith is the act of surrender to the dynamic benevolence of existence, such as it is, unknown by us but fully understood in the intimate depths of our own being-here.** It is an **act,** not an item of knowledge or a bit of information. It is an **act** that accepts everything that *material energy* can be validly said to be by science, including its constitutive presence *as my organic self.*

That this **act of faith** may resemble the dynamic which is observable in some acts of religious faith is not surprising. Trust in the solidity of *existence* is a natural instinct of the **conatus.** That *that* trust had been directed to "God" as the metaphor for the *creative self-donation of existence,* would follow naturally from having identified a humanoid "God" as the source of *existence.* In fact, for those who are aware of the metaphoric nature of this attribution, nothing is lost or distorted if the word "God" continues to be used to name the source, the "other pole" in the relationship. But that means, of course, that "God" now includes my own *existence* and the *existence* of everything in the universe, shared and sharing itself. For such a metaphoric application to work, "God" can never be conceived as a separate humanoid entity ever again.

So we see that it is not the use of the word, but the absence of any conceptual specificity presuming to identify **a discrete divine entity that thinks and acts in history as a "person" existing separately from all things** that distinguishes ~~faith~~ from faith. ~~Faith~~ trusts in *existence;* traditional religious faith trusted in a separate humanoid "God." Depending on your way of conceiving "God" and what you trust "God" will do for you, they may or may not be the same thing. But if you understand, as I do, that there is no other world, then you also understand there is nothing supernatural. You realize that "God" is not "other than" the natural order which includes you. In that case it doesn't matter if you call the object of your trust "God" or *material energy.* It is the same thing. The word is unimportant. What is important ... the only thing that is important ... is the relationship, *the trust. Existence,* this *material energy* that "fathered" us, can be trusted.

It is good to *be-here.*

peroration: we need religion

Religion must be reformed ... for two reasons. First, it's not going away, and if we allow it to continue to exist in the forms we have inherited, it will continue to produce the individual and social damage with which we are all too familiar. We can destroy ourselves and our planet home, and the religions we have now will help us do it. That is not acceptable. It is everyone's concern that the madness stop. In that regard the "new atheists" are right on target. And we can't trust religions' authorities and many of their theologians to do it, as we have seen over and over again. Their important positions in society have them too wrapped up in keeping things the way they are.

But we can't walk away from it for another and more important reason: *we need religion.* We cannot afford to live without a tool that supports our sense of familial belonging to this universe of matter. We need something that helps us relate to life as a precious gift ... that encourages the sense of the sacred that grounds benevolence toward other people and respect for other species and the planet without which life becomes a hell. It is sheer madness to dismiss our needs for collective celebrations and community mournings ... the myths and metaphors, poetry, art, ritual, symbols and songs that elicit awe, respect, gratitude, compassion, forgiveness, pathos, empathy ... and service. Poetry is our thing. It's what we do. It's our virtual song to our virtual "creator" *whatever it may be.* We can't *be-here as human beings* in this universe without it. *Religion is our public poetry.*

It's time we acknowledged that religion is our common concern. It is our way of identifying who we are in this universe — what we have been given, and what we owe in return. We humans have been treated with great deference and privilege. We live and see and love and feel as no other organism on the face of the earth and possibly in the vast expanses of spacetime. Besides our own life which is a source of endless joy to us, we see the marvels of the existence around us with eyes no other species has. No organism has been given as much intimacy with the inside story of this astounding universe as the human being. *How does that affect who we think we are?* That is the question we ask our religion to answer.

And, God help us, *we have to make sure it answers correctly.*

PART TWO

toward a restructuring of Christian doctrine

Part One was about religion in general. In this part I will begin to address some of the specifics of Christian doctrine. These pieces are meant as examples only. There is no attempt to be exhaustive.

Christianity is the foundational religion for our western culture. Other religions in our corner of the world have been so affected by Christian predominance that their programs and even their doctrines have come to resemble it. But even when that was not true, the culture absorbed Christian perspectives and values, and after so long a period of tutelage, reproduces them routinely without even being aware of their origins. We have already alluded to some of them; they all have positive and negative sides: ... *an individualism that can overwhelm the communitarian nature of reality ... a disciplined control over bodily urges sometimes to the point of repression ... a self-questioning mistrust that can lead to an immobilizing non-specific guilt ... a focus on rationality sometimes to the detriment of bodily wholeness ... a pride in origins that can result in ethnocentrism and xenophobia ... and a technical prowess and daring that produces unimaginable marvels even while it brings about the extinction of other species and the possible destruction of the planet's life-sustaining capabilities.*

In this Part, Chapters IV and V, are on original sin. This doctrine was singled out for a more in-depth look because it is so central both to the western Christian view of the world and the predominant characteristics of the western personality. A culture establishes the values both as ends and means that construct the individual selves. "Western man," as a traditional personality type, with its positives and negatives, I contend, has been forged in large part by the Christian doctrine of original sin.

The entire western Christian view-of-the-world, thanks to Augustine's iron-clad logic and self-deprecating presumptions, rides on this one doctrine as on no other. His particular vision — which does not necessarily represent the only ideological configuration that Christianity is able to live with — collapses without original sin. Those who want to restructure Christian doctrine, in my opinion, must start here.

Chapter VI, titled "To Whom Shall We Go?" was written in the late '90's, and is reproduced here as something of an overview of the prospects for the reform of Christian doctrine. It represents what was a first effort on my part to reinterpret Christian doctrine as metaphor. Many of the perspectives assumed in that chapter have been revisited in later essays and in some cases transcended. I offer it here revised but essentially as it was written. I repudiate nothing and make no apologies. It was an attempt to point out for Catholics the direction in which a new, more universal spirituality might move. Others may find it helpful. A spirituality, utilizing the older Christian imagery **as metaphor,** is the first step in the development of a new view-of-the-world, for I am convinced that *theology follows spirituality and does not lead it.* That chapter is the fruit of what has been forged in the crucible of the anguished transitions lived by many of my generation during our time under the sun.

The ultimate theological or doctrinal "reform," however, is beyond our ken. There is no pretension here of pre-empting the work of future generations who will, hopefully, recast religion in entirely new terms, perhaps terms we would not today recognize as Christian. My efforts here are the first halting steps in that transformation. Religion, especially in the United States, has been shanghaied and pressed into service to reactionary views that contradict the very core of what I consider the fundamental religious project ... *a sense of the sacredness of existence.*

Chapter IV

original sin (1)
the doctrine and its consequences

I. THE ORIGINS OF THE DOCTRINE

One of the more remarkable things about Christianity is that it is not simply a "religion" in the expected sense of a moral and ritual program. From very early on, it presented itself as a full-blown *metaphysical, cosmological system,* grounded in *literal facts* of a scientific nature which claimed to describe universal reality and fill in gaps in physics and history. Even today, there are some facts about the universe for which science not only can find no evidence, but actively disputes, that traditional Christianity in the past and the Roman Catholic Church today affirms as infallible truth.

Among those items is an event of transcendent historic importance that Christians say entailed vast cosmic repercussions. It is **original sin**: the act of disobedience of the first humans to a command of "God," preceded by the "fall" of invisible beings, angels, which made them "devils." According to Christian belief, this is not just some ancient fairy tale like the stories of the gods of Olympus or Valhalla, despite appearances. The Church claims that these were **actual historical events** — a physical and metaphysical catastrophe that changed the very nature of the universe, and its eternal destiny. The Catholic Catechism, published by the Vatican in 1992, reaffirmed these beliefs and insisted on their factuality.

The claim that by Adam's disobedience human beings lost a supposed original immortality is a relatively familiar part this belief. It is also well known that the human organism is said to have suffered a "darkness of mind and weakness of will" that accompanied "disordered" *bodily desires* that "inclined" humans to sin. But not many are aware of the more fundamental claim that *the entire material universe* lost its "spirituality" when Adam sinned, and that it was *that* general cosmological debasement that has brought such suffering to humankind.

That claim goes well beyond the effects on human beings. Death for animals and plants, natural disasters like earthquakes, *tsunamis,* hurricanes, plagues, etc., are all events that *would never have occurred* if Adam had not disobeyed. St Augustine could point to passages in Paul's epistle to the Romans where it was said that "all of creation groans under this burden" and "has been made subject to corruption" produced by the sin of Adam.[41] In this scenario the "redemption" effectuated by Christ on the cross was in fact a necessary **cosmic rescue** of the entire material universe from a physical dysfunctionality caused by the "fall."

Needless to say, science in general and evolutionary biology in particular belie all of this. Cosmic development, as far as science can tell, has been a seamless uninterrupted process whereby *material energy* has found ways to survive by aggregating and integrating its constituent elements in a self-elaboration that has produced every structure and organism in the universe. This self-construction was driven and accompanied at all times by the threat of extinction and the competitive struggle for resources. Death, in the view of science, far from being *unnatural,* is a natural part of the cycle of life for all living organisms; and the threat of death is itself a driving force in organic evolution. Furthermore, the universe has not "become worse" over time, but in fact, almost all observers would say "better," meaning more complex, more intellectually agile and sensitive, more empathetic and compassionate — more "spiritual" and communitarian — as it has evolved ever more sophisticated organisms through the eons.

Even were the case of humankind to be isolated from the rest of the developing biota, there is no evidence of an abrupt change from an idyllic state where human suffering and struggle did not exist to one where it did. Besides, immortality for humans alone would have been a most conspicuous exception in a world where all other complex organisms, whose bodies resemble ours to a remarkable degree, die.

The "Christian doctrine of original sin," so glaringly contrary to this picture, seems to suffer from the shortsightedness characteristic of all prescientific "theories" of reality which come down to us in the form of myth. We know the ancients did the best they could with what they knew. That the ancient peoples of Western Europe believed the biblical stories to be

---

[41] Letter to the Romans, 8:22

fact, is completely understandable. But this incredible phenomenon — that highly educated Catholic authorities at the turn of the 21st century should continue to insist on it despite the knowledge gained by the sciences — is so irrational as to border on insanity. Fundamentalist Christianities, which include Roman Catholicism as it seems to be evolving in our times, cling to this insistence. Given the pre-formed commitments of these churches, I submit, there is good reason for it. For the fundamentalists' doctrinal complex and their Christian self-definition collapse without it. This is not insignificant. Allow me to explain.

the linchpin

"Original sin" is the linchpin of the western Christian religious view of the world. The traditional theory of redemption by Christ hangs by this one single thread. For if there were no original sin and its associated fall, it would mean there never was any of its alleged effects or consequences: ... humankind never lost the friendship of God ... the cosmos and all of material reality including the human body never lost immortality or was made "subject to corruption" ... death is not an unnatural condition whose existence is entirely due to Adam's sin ... hard labor, the pain of childbirth, suffering, disease, human violence and natural disasters are, however unwelcome, simply part of the natural order of things. Without original sin *the entire traditional western Christian interpretation of reality, as we have inherited it, collapses. There was no need for a cosmic redemption requiring that "God" become man ... because there was no cosmic catastrophe to begin with.*

This is not a minor issue. After a deconstruction of this magnitude, the main claims of traditional Western Christianity lose their *rationale*. The entire doctrinal chain that has evolved consistent with cosmic salvation — like Christ's death as a sacrifice to placate an infuriated "God" or to "buy us back from Satan" ... Christ's "divinity" co-equal to the Father, necessary to accomplish "redemption" ... the establishment of the Church and its sacraments as the unique vehicle for salvation for the whole of humankind ... the powers exclusive to holy orders ... the infallibility of the Church's magisterium (and the Pope), ... not to mention heaven and hell and the hierarchy's power to control who goes where — these "doctrines" *all become groundless.* Their only *raison d'être* is **original sin.**

Christians have traditionally claimed that Jesus is a divine cosmic redeemer and not just a moral "Teacher of Righteousness." But, if the traditional interpretation becomes meaningless and absurd, "Teacher of Righteousness" is what remains. Jesus, then, would be exactly what his words, sifted out by consensus scholarship from the larger narrative of the gospels, reveal him to be: a Jewish teacher of wisdom ... a human being of great spiritual depth, intensity, simplicity and compassion ... but not a "divine cosmic redeemer." Many would see this adjustment as a most welcome assist to a moribund Christianity. For without all that Greco-Roman baggage, the "real Jesus" can stand up and be what he always was, *a faithful Jew, a human being, a Mensch,*[42] and perhaps his words and spirit can get done — finally — what he originally set out to do: *teach others how to be fully human* through a new understanding of the loving fatherliness of the traditional Jewish "God," *Yahweh.*

the catholic doctrine of original sin

The traditional western Christian version of the doctrine as elaborated by Augustine in the 5th century is preserved in the formulation found in recent documents like the *Catechism of the Catholic Church,* promulgated by the Vatican in 1992. It interprets the Genesis account as a literal cosmological event which caused a *metaphysical metamorphosis* that re-configured the very inner structure of reality itself. This new articulation of it is laid out in the Catechism, ## 388 – 412.[43] I reproduce the most salient passages **in bold** here, along with my comments *in italics*:

389. **The Church ... knows very well that we cannot tamper with the revelation of original sin without undermining the mystery of Christ.** *The point is relevant. For without original sin the entire tapestry of the western Christian worldview unravels.*

---

[42] I do not address the issue of whether "Jesus" is a real historical person or a mythic composite. The controversy that claims he is an *avatar* of the "Teacher of Righteousness" mentioned in the Dead Sea Scrolls *is irrelevant* to the coherent personality presented in the gospels. It is the message of that "personality," mythic or not, that was used to launch a new religion. The controversy is even less relevant to the later doctrinal complex which I am calling "greco-roman Christianity" that now undergirds western culture and its major institutuions. For even if there were no historical "Jesus of Nazareth" these powerful "memes" remain. Human virtual reality is *real*, whatever its origins, and however *virtual* it may be.

[43] *Catechism of the Catholic Church,* Libreria Editrice Vaticana, pp. 98-104. The Catechism was promulgated by John Paul II in the Apostolic Constitution *Fidei Depositum*, October 1992.

390. **The account of the fall in Genesis 3 uses figurative language but affirms a primeval event, a deed that took place *at the beginning of the history of man.* Revelation gives us the certainty of faith that the whole of human history is marked by the original fault freely committed by our first parents.** *(emphasis in the original.) There is no doubt that original sin is being affirmed as an historical fact; the language, the Catechism says, may be figurative but the event is real.*[44]

(391 to 394) *Here the Catechism recounts the "fall of the angels" as the event in which "Satan" and other "devils" were supposedly spawned. This angelic "rebellion" is said to precede the fall of man and is declared to be an irrevocable rejection of "God." None of it is present in Genesis. There are only the vaguest of allusions to it in the rest of scripture.*

395. *The Catechism speaks of Satan's action in the world and says even though it ...* **may cause grave injuries — of a spiritual nature and even, indirectly, of a physical nature — to each man and to society, the action is permitted by divine providence ... . It is a great mystery that providence should permit diabolical activity** *... A mystery indeed! In this conception, the "providence" that gives permission to the activity of the "devils" turns the business of living a good moral life into a dangerous game ... with the principal dangers provided by "God" himself for no apparent reason. Unleashing the devil initially on Adam and Eve, it must be noted, was totally undeserved. It was not part of the "consequences of original sin" because the serpent, taken to be "Satan" in the Christian view, was given access to them before the "fall."*

Also, please notice the mention of "injuries of a physical nature." This is a diluted residue of what was a traditional Christian belief: namely, that natural disasters were caused by the devil, given permission by divine providence, as punishments for "sin." It was the Christian version of the beliefs of most pre-scientific people that natural disasters were caused by supernatural forces — punishments willed by the gods, or "Nature" itself for violations of correct behavior.

---

[44] Some theologians, in their obsession to reconcile this interpretation with the discoveries of paleontology, actually suggest the event must have taken place among *homo habilis* or *homo erectus* — early sub-species of homo that preceded *homo sapiens*. Cf. Raymund Schwager, *Banished from Eden*, Gracewing Publishing 2006 p.76

400. [After Adam and Eve's disobedience] ... **The harmony in which they had found themselves ... is now destroyed: the control of the soul's spiritual faculties over the body is shattered; the union of man and woman becomes subject to tensions, their relations henceforth marked by lust and domination. Harmony with creation is broken: visible creation has become alien and hostile to man. Because of man, creation is now subject "to its bondage to decay." ...** *Death makes its entrance into human history.* *(emphasis in the original).*

401. After that first sin, the world is virtually inundated by sin. There is ... the universal corruption which follows in the wake of sin. *The language of 400 and 401 speaks of a universal condition which in fact does not exist. "Shattered control ... lust and domination" as universal conditions were fantasies that emerged from Augustine's repugnance for his own lack of sexual discipline. Sexual license, justified and excused as "natural," was a cultural permission enjoyed by the Roman upper classes to which Augustine developed a lifelong aversion. These attitudes are consistent with Paul's personal problems with the "Law" in Romans 5 which was expressed in similar terms, and some suggest may also have been of a sexual nature.*

404. By this "unity of the human race" all men are implicated in Adam's sin ... . Still the transmission of original sin is a mystery that we cannot fully understand. ... It is a sin that will be transmitted by propagation to all mankind, that is, by the transmission of human nature ... it is a sin "contracted" and not "committed" — a state and not an act. *Such an organismic transmission, explicitly defined as "by propagation" not "by imitation" (Council of Trent, Session V, June 1546, #3),[45] directly contradicts the Prophetic pronouncement in Ezekiel 18 (which re-states Exodus 34) that each person's sin is their own individual responsibility. There is hardly to be found in the entire Bible a command more explicit than Ez 18 verse 3, referring to the proverb about children suffering for the sins of their fathers: "As I live, says the Lord God, this proverb shall no more be used by you in Israel." It is summed up in verse 20: "The son shall not suffer for the iniquity of the father." Sin is not passed down from parents to children.*

---

[45] The word "imitation," used by Trent, was the term Pelagius used to explain how Adam's sin affected his descendants.

405. [human nature] **has been wounded in the natural powers proper to it; subject to ignorance, suffering and the dominion of death, and inclined to sin — an inclination to evil that is called "concupiscence." Baptism ... erases original sin ... but the consequences for nature, weakened and inclined to evil, persist ..."** *One of the main arguments of the mediaeval Jewish theologians in their disputes with Christians was that if the Christian claim that Jesus' death conquered the "effects of original sin" — death, labor, the pain of childbirth — were true, why have they not disappeared.*[46]

407. *By original sin* **the devil has acquired a certain dominion over man ... a "captivity."** *This "belief" accounts for the application of the word "redemption" which literally means "buying back" and in the Christian era was used to refer to ransom paid to captors for the return of a hostage. The thought that "Satan" could actually come to "own" humankind so that it needed to be "bought back" ... and that Satan was satisfied by the death of Christ on the cross can only be a metaphor, a kind of "as if" catechetical device. It cannot possibly be meant literally. And yet here the Catechism is asserting it as factual and with emphasis.*

409. **"... the whole world is in the power of the evil one."** *This can only be a figurative statement and a gross exaggeration. Claims that Christ's death was some sort of payback to the devil are as literally impossible as claims that an enraged tyrant "God" would be placated by the death of his own son. These are, at best, metaphorical "as if's" that might work as motivational devices in those cultures where such notions are meaningful. Apparently the "enraged, insulted emperor" was a meaningful image for Augustine and Anselm of Canterbury who between them provided justification for the "restitution" theory of redemption. But it does not work for us, and at any rate it runs directly counter to the image of a loving father evoked by the entire OT from Exodus through the prophets and emphatically reprised in Jesus' teachings.*

It is relevant that the Roman liturgy, created in this era, transformed the eucharistic meal into the "sacrifice of the mass" and its dinner-table into an "altar," where a "priest" offered "sacrifice" to "God" amid clouds of incense, customarily used in pagan rituals to cover the stench of slaughtered ani-

---

[46] Cf *The Vikuah of Nahmanides,* the report of the sole Jewish protagonist of the disputation at Barcelona, 1263, reprinted in Hyam Maccoby tr., *Judaism on Trial,* Fairleigh Dickenson U. Press, 1982, p.118.

mals. None of this was characteristic of the original eucharistic meal as re-counted in the NT — the central symbol of Christian community, familial love, and the equality among Jesus' followers.

412. But why did God not prevent the first man from sinning? *the Catechism asks ... and it answers, citing three separate sources, that "sin" led to even greater supernatural gifts through Christ.*

We can see from this very recent official statement promulgated by the Pope himself, that The Roman Church continues to preach the doctrine of original sin fundamentally unchanged from what was elaborated by Augustine early in the in the 5th century of the common era.

According to Augustine's theory, all our troubles, physical and moral, are due to sin, not because of cultural transmission or familial inheritance, but because "Adam's sin infuriated "God." "God" punished us *all* for Adam's sin by physically taking away our immortality, and then burdening us with hard labor, the pain of childbirth, and worst of all *abandoning us to our "concupiscence"* which accounts for all the pain we heap upon one another out of selfishness. All this is punishment from "God."

This is a collective sentence. It was directed at all of us because Adam was the first of our species and contained within himself the "seed" of every human being who would ever be born. But, the collective aspect is quickly transferred to the individual. Each newborn human being, before becoming pleasing to "God" in baptism, is destined for eternal punishment. Even after baptism, we are still on our own as individuals. Salvation can be lost and eternal punishment awaits each one separately.

The Christian doctrine of original sin generated the image of an omnipotent "God" who is obsessively focused on his own slighted dignity. It blamed all the suffering of life on "God" punishing each member of the species for the sin of the one individual who actually insulted him. Each one of us is personally saddled with this entire collective guilt; no one can avoid it, not even in the absolute innocence of infancy. It is the individual who must be baptized, the individual who must make use of the sacraments and avoid sin, and it is the individual who will be judged at death for her / his behavior.

But it must be acknowledged, for Augustine it was an intellectual *tour de force.* With his theory of original sin, Augustine was able to accomplish the intellectual integration of a multiplicity of disparate factors that otherwise would have remained unconnected. In one fell swoop, he "explained" (1) the Genesis account in detail, item for item, (2) the need for the redemptive death of Jesus (Anselm would expand it later using the same reasoning), (3) all the suffering of life including death, (4) immoral human behavior, (5) the salient passages in Paul's epistle to the Romans, (6) the remarkable similarity with Plato's theory of a "fall," (7) the Church practice of infant baptism, (8) the absolute indispensability of the Church and its sacramental ministrations. And last but *by far* not least, (9) it provided a *rationale* for the already published belief that *outside the Church there is no salvation* which was used by the Roman Empire and later "Christian" States to justify ideological homogeneity, theocracy and imperialism.

This last point cannot be emphasized too strongly: it served to confirm Christian states in their power projections for the conquest and domination of others. It was particularly useful for providing justification for the Crusades against Muslims and heretics, the suppression of the Jews and the *conquista* of foreign lands like the Americas in later centuries which involved the enslavement and forced conversion of untold numbers of "heathen."

the roots of the doctrine

To understand the Christian theory of original sin we need to look at the influences that combined to construct it. It has two ancient roots: (1) Hellenistic culture, especially as represented by Platonism; and (2) the narrative in chapters two and three of the Jewish Book of Genesis which recounted the temptation and disobedience of Adam and Eve in the Garden of Eden and their banishment.[47]

Greek philosophical theories, principally those of Plato and the Stoics, were key to the development of the doctrine. I will expand on this shortly. These philosophies were known by the authors of NT material, most likely absorbed by them through diaspora Jewish teachers like **Philo of Alexandria** and his school of thought that formed a bridge between the Jewish and Greek visions of reality. The disconnect between the core of Jesus' message (as derived from the *logia,* or "sayings of Jesus) and the earliest

---

[47] In this regard it is interesting that *no direct antecedant* has been found for the story of the temptation in the garden. The mesopotamian Gilgamesh epic, its nearest analogue, contains many of the same themes, but the narrative is entirely different. Cf Joel Rosenberg "Biblical Narrative" in *Back to the Sources*, Barry Holtz, ed., Simon & Shuster, 1984, p.53.

depictions of the Christian world-view created by the architects of Hellen-ized Christianity, is most significant for our study. Those "missionaries" were responsible for transforming Jesus from a moral and spiritual re-former of Judaism into a divine agent of cosmic proportions that "saved" the entire universe and all of humankind from destruction. The theory of original sin was later developed to justify that transformation. It resulted in Christianity as we know it — something that Jesus, clearly, never had in mind.

Besides these foundational sources, 400 years later the contemporary influences acting on **Augustine of Hippo,** the final architect of the doc-trine, are relevant. Among these there is, first, Augustine's status as a member of **Roman social elite**, which in his case included training as a rhetorician ("lawyer") in the classic manner. It would have insured his familiarity with and loyalty to traditional Roman *mores* and values. There were also those unwritten "permissions" of the Roman upper classes to the sexual exploitation of lower class women that figured so prominently in Augustine's sense of his own moral depravity. Connected with that, there was Manichaeism, a radical flesh-hating sect that had a large following among Romans. Augustine had joined that sect as a young man and its condemnation of all sexuality *including marriage* reverberated throughout his theology. Against the background of his own self-perceived degener-acy, Manichaeism helps explain his strange insistence on moral power-lessness and the need for divine grace just to lead a decent human life — the keynotes of his theology of original sin. Finally there were the **Chris-tian influences**: the New Testament itself, 350 years of Church Fathers, but most importantly, *Constantinian Imperial Christianity* — almost 100 years old by the time of Augustine — that had already "defined" the Trinity and the divinity of Christ at Nicaea and Chalcedon and dominated Roman political life. Christianity had evolved doctrines and attitudes that were vigorously promoted by people like his mentor, Ambrose of Milan who was a political advisor and confidant of the Emperor Gratian and assigned to the episcopacy by him which required that he be quickly baptized and ordained. Roman political needs and the detailed collaboration of the authorities were, unfortunately, an important factor in the development of Christian doctrine, and especially original sin.

the greeks

Platonism may not seem the proper place to begin a short survey of the background to the Christian doctrine of original sin. Plato, after all, lived 350 years before the time of Jesus and in a land far away. But I want to start there because I believe more than any other influence, despite the antiquity of the Jewish story of the Garden of Eden and Jesus' own strictly Jewish perspective, it was Platonism that gave the essential character to Christianity and its doctrine of original sin. Platonism not only reworked every detail of what was inherited from the Hebrew scriptures, it suffused every statement and action of Jesus, effectively re-interpreting his message in the light of Platonism's own fundamental assumptions. The essential meaning of the Christian doctrine of "original sin" did not come from the Jews or from Jesus of Nazareth. It was the product of Platonism and Hellenic culture.[48]

The first point is that Platonism, as philosophy, was believed to be the rational correction of the outlandish stories of the gods of Mediterranean mythology. Platonism, in other words, considered itself not a religion, but more like **science**; it was a reform of religion initiated by rational enquiry and logic. Christianity eventually identified with Platonism, and picked up this "scientific" pretension, at least from the late second century. By the time Athenagoras wrote his *"Plea for the Christians"* to the Emperor Marcus Aurelius around 175 ce, it was on full display.[49] Christianity was *truth*, said Athenagoras, in the scientific sense of literal, factual and historical truth; the stories of the gods were "mere" myths. Christianity never lost that self-projection. The apparently factual accounts of Jesus' life in the gospels, and the frank narrative of failure in his execution by the Romans, corroborated the feeling that with Christianity the days of legends and myths were over and the age of truth had dawned.

But while Plato claimed to correct the false ideas that Greek mythology propagated, he did not challenge its basic premises, and in fact reinforced them. The only thing he disputed were the fantastical stories told about the gods and the *absurd infantile character* of the divinity they portrayed.

---

[48] The primary agent of this penentration was Philo of Alexandria, a first century diaspora Jew whose books were widely known. Diaspora Greek-speaking Jews like Saul (later Paul) of Tarsus would doubtless have been familiar with his work.

[49] *Early Christian Fathers*, Cyril Richardson tr and ed., Macmillan, NY 1970, pp.290ff.

But for Plato, there was indeed another world where the gods, whom he imagined were pure spirit, dwelt and acted.[50]

Plato imagined the gods were minds, "spirits" with ideas, that inhabited another world different from this world made of "matter." But then, he asked, how was it that in this earthly world of matter there were *minds, spirits,* that use *ideas* to survive, grow food, build their families and their empires? These "spirits" didn't really belong in a material world. How did they get here? The original human being, he conjectured, must have been all spirit, and must have done something in that other world, by mistake or by malice, and as a result "fell" into matter. Human nature as we know it, in other words, is not as nature intended; it is the result of a tragic misstep. *Humanity is the product of a catastrophe that joined two substances that were never meant to be together.* Spirit was exiled into matter as into a dungeon, and its true nature drives it to escape its place of torture and return to the world of ideas and minds from which it came. All of human work, struggle and the social, political strife that seems to accompany us wherever we go, is explained as the effort *to get back home* to that other world — *the* world that the myths of the "gods" had so grossly mis-represented. Plato's philosophy set out to rectify the false impressions of that other world created by mythology, and to set the correct course for "getting back home."[51]

Plato was different in this respect from other contemporary Greek philosophers like Zeno of Citium, the Stoic, who did not believe in the existence of any other world.[52] **Stoicism** vied with Platonism for popularity and while it had a non-dualist materialistic physics and cosmology, its views on these fundamentals are often glossed over in favor of its spiritual program. Historians tend to focus on Stoicism's highly disciplined moral agenda which Jews and Christians have always admired. Its ethical views, however, cannot really be understood outside of the context of its cosmology.

> ... the Stoics, make God material. ... the Stoic God is immanent throughout the whole of creation and directs its development down to the smallest detail. ... It is important to realize that the Stoic God does not craft its world in accordance with its plan *from the outside*, as the demiurge in Plato's *Timaeus* is described as doing. Ra-

---

[50] This is clearly sketched out in Plato's *Phaedrus*

[51] The imagery of the "fall" and the "return" is found in Plato's *Phaedrus.*

[52] Zeno of Citium (334-262 bce) founder of Stoicism is not to be confused with Zeno of Elea (490-430 bce) pre-Socratic from Southern Italy who was part of Parmenides' school of philosophy.

ther, the history of the universe is determined by God's activity internal to it, shaping it with its differentiated characteristics. The biological conception of God as a kind of living heat or seed from which things grow seems to be fully intended.[53]

Please note: **the Stoics did not believe in the existence of two-worlds**, nor any alleged "fall." There was no thought of another life after death. Their practical moral program had to do with how to live in this world *such as it is*, not how to insure "salvation" in some other. Hence their "stoical" attitudes toward suffering. What is most relevant for our study, however, is that there was a deep affinity between Stoicism's ethical goals and the message of Jesus of Nazareth, and both differed significantly from Platonism's emphasis on returning to the "other world" and Christianity's "life after death." For the Stoics, and as we shall see for Jesus, the moral act was its own reward ... a good human life for the individual and for the community.

The word "stoic" originally referred to the porch (*stoa*) from which Zeno delivered his lectures. But the term has come to be used in all European languages to mean endurance in the face of suffering, and a cold, bloodless acceptance of the meaninglessness of life. With such a negative assessment, it is no surprise that its metaphysics has been ignored by western historians, the majority of whom have been Christians. Stoicism believed reality had a spiritual dimension, but it was not, like Platonism, metaphysically *dualist.* There were not two distinct realities; the spiritual, for Zeno, was an aspect of material reality.

The belief that spirit was *different from matter* and belonged to another world was Plato's novel idea. Platonism reified the notion of spirit, and with it established a scientific basis for the existence of another world, a spirit-God who resided there, and the human hope of returning there after death. Thus the primitive Greek fascination with the life of the gods and their immortal divine-human offspring was made suddenly and ecstatically accessible to ordinary mortals through the possibility of "return to the other world" offered by Platonism. Plato persuaded many that we belonged to the world of the gods, and their divine immortality was ours *if only we could discover the formula for how to get back home*.

---

[53] Dirk Baltzly, "Stoicism", *The Stanford Encyclopedia of Philosophy (Winter 2010 Edition)*, Edward N. Zalta (ed.), URL = http://plato.stanford.edu/archives/win2010/entries/stoicism/.

My commentary on Plato uses the categories developed by Baruch Spinoza in the 17th century. Plato's promise of immortality tapped into the infinite wells of energy stored in humankind's **conatus,** the drive to survive. The **conatus**, our blind physical thirst for existence, a force as irrational as it is insuppressible, resident in every cell and oozing from every pore of our bodies, was fatally seduced. Western civilization as we know it was the fruit of that seduction. Platonism out-competed Stoicism because the "denial of death"[54] — a derivative of the **conatus** — was served by the belief in a separable spirit and Christianity, as we know it, embraced Platonism.

Christianity as it has come down to us was a subset of that generalized Hellenistic enthusiasm — the quest for immortality — given wings by Plato. It rejected the simple stoic wisdom of Jesus' one-world Jewish message, made it subordinate to life in another world and put Jesus in that world by making him divine. The Christian phenomenon represented the same preference for the fantasy of life after death as Platonism. They were really both part of the same cultural event. Rome's "Catholic" version of Christianity is Platonism in ritual and juridical form.

the jews and genesis

The Hebrew *Book of Genesis*, which scholars say was redacted at the earliest in the 8th century bce,[55] provided a vivid account of the "first sin" that the Greeks saw as a confirmation of Plato's vision.

In the days of the Alexandrian conquests around 325 bce, barely a generation after Plato, the Greeks "discovered" that the Jews had an ancient "Book" (gr. *biblos*) that contained the story of an "original sin" committed by the first man and woman that accounted for death, suffering and the violence among humankind. The correlation with Plato's theory of a "fall" was striking — so much so that some Jews were convinced that the Greeks had somehow gotten hold of the scriptures and transposed them

---

[54] Cf Ernest Becker's *The Denial of Death*, 1974, and its sequel, *Escape from Evil*, 1975. It was a great mystery to Becker that this "denial of death" — which he saw as responsible for a great part of humankind's self-destructiveness — functioned so invariably and uncontrollably across cultures and time. Becker's exclusively psychological approach to the etiology of this phenomenon may explain his bewilderment at its persistence.

[55] *The Jerome Biblical Commentary* ed Brown et al, Prentice Hall, 1968; ch 67, ¶22, (Vol II, p. 519)

into a philosophic key.[56,57] In a similar manner, Christians would later claim the resemblances between the story of Jesus' resurrection from the dead and those of Dionysus and other gods of the mystery religions, were due to "demons," who knowing of the future redemption by Jesus', created the mystery myths with a death-and-resurrection scenario in order to confuse and deflect faith in Christ.[58]

The Bible is a Jewish Book. It was written by Jews, for Jews, as a family record of the origins and history of the Jewish relationship with "God." By default, one would think its interpretation belongs to the Jews. The book of Genesis opens the Bible with the story of humankind's first *contract* with "God" (as a foreshadowing of the Mosaic covenant) in the garden of Eden. It was a story designed to help Jews stay faithful to their contract as it evolved through time.

What is the Jewish interpretation? Very simply stated, the Jews say the basic intention of the original author(s) of the story of the Garden of Eden is "etiological." That means it was an *account of origins* ... beginnings.[59] Genesis was designed to explain how things came to be the way they are: why there is an earth, seas and a sky, the sun, moon and stars,

---

[56] Eusebius, *Preparation for the Gospel* (transl. Gifford), XIII, 12 quotes Numenius: "Plato derived his idea of God from the Pentateuch. Plato is Moses translated into the language of the Athenians."

[57] For Philo, Greek philosophy was a natural development of the revelatory teachings of Moses. He was no innovator in this matter because already before him Jewish scholars attempted the same. Artapanus in the second century B.C.E identified Moses with Musaeus and with Orpheus. According to Aristobulus of Paneas (first half of the second century B.C.E.), Homer and Hesiod drew from the books of Moses which were translated into Greek long before the Septuagint. http://www.iep.utm.edu/philo/ n.

[58] Cf Justin Martyr: (c. 100-165): Christian Apologist. (*Dialog with Trypho*, ch. lxix.): "Be well assured, then, Trypho, that I am established in the knowledge of and faith in the Scriptures by those counterfeits which he who is called the Devil is said to have performed among the Greeks; just as some were wrought by the Magi in Egypt, and others by the false prophets in Elijah's days. For when they tell that Bacchus, son of Jupiter, was begotten by [Jupiter's] intercourse with Semele, and that he was the discoverer of the vine; and when they relate, that being torn in pieces, and having died, he rose again, and ascended to heaven; and when they introduce wine into his mysteries, do I not perceive that [the devil] has imitated the prophecy announced by the patriarch Jacob, and recorded by Moses? ... And when he [the devil] brings forward Aesculapius as the raiser of the dead and healer of all diseases, may I not say in this matter likewise he has imitated the prophecies about Christ? ... And when I hear that Perseus was begotten of a virgin, I understand that the deceiving serpent counterfeited this also."

[59] Joel Rosenberg "Biblical Narrative" in *Back to the Sources*, Barry Holtz, ed., Simon & Shuster, 1984, p.46, 55, 59 and Gerhard von Rad *Genesis*, Westminster Pr 1961, p.83, 89.

why there are animals and plants, men and women, why work is hard and childbearing painful ... and why we die. It tries to imagine the origins of this sexuality of ours that creates children and families and villages and nations, ... it tries to account for why men and women have unequal roles when God made them equals[60] ... and why women seem to carry an undue share of the burdens of life.[61]

Jewish scholar Joel Rosenberg sees the garden story as:

> ... *paradigmatic,* typically repeated in every lifetime ... . The story of the expulsion from a paradisic "Garden" is thus a kind of metaphor, a parable of human maturation. The episode of the woman's temptation by the serpent is a kind of parable-within-a-parable: it translates the loss of innocence theme into a moral context; it makes the event the fruit of a "transgression." This grafting together of anthropological with moral lore is perhaps the story's main point.[62]

And he sums up his overall interpretation:

> ... it is a fable about the human life cycle (all of its stages have been represented: birth, adolescence, leaving of the "parental" household, marriage, sexual awakening, procreation, labor, and death); about the differences between beast, man and divinity; about the origin of human society, its economy, culture and technology (recounting in the process the origin of clothes, agriculture, breadmaking, toolmaking, subordination of woman and beast to man); and about disobedience to God and its consequences. While the temptation scene is homogeneous and self-contained, it takes its place in a complex collage of cultural themes.[63]

One of the principal goals of the Genesis story of creation was to make it unambiguously clear that the world was made by "God" alone. Unlike

---

[60] Rosenberg, *op cit,* (Jewish), and von Rad, *op cit,* (Lutheran), both eminent scholars of the Hebrew Old Testament, comment on Genesis 2: 21-23 that before the fall, the human couple are called *Ish and Isha* in Hebrew, which both von Rad (p.82) and Rosenberg (p.56f) say denotes **equality** ... after the fall their names are changed to *Adam and Havvah* (Eve) which emphasize their unequal roles and status.

[61] Gerhard Von Rad, *Genesis,* Westminster Press, Phila., 1961, commenting on 3:16, p.90. "[After the fall] ... severe afflictions and terrible contradictions now break upon the woman's life. ... Whence these sorrows, these contradictions, this degradation of the woman's life? It is not a small matter that our narrative absolves God's creation of this."

[62] Rosenberg, *op cit,* p.57f.

[63] *Ibid.,* p.59

the creation myths of the peoples around them, the Jewish version insisted there was no other deity involved, and the world "God" made was *entirely good*, with no admixture of evil. If it weren't for sin, they said, this
world is a "paradise." The story of Adam and Eve was clearly intended to
eliminate any doubt: if evil has entered "God's" creation, it came from
humankind, and from nowhere else.[64] Biblical scholars insist that the
myth of the Garden was created precisely to say that evil does not antedate humankind.[65] The serpent is not "Satan," but a symbol of rational
calculation and the "selfish intent" is nothing but the natural bent of the
unchecked **conatus**.[66]

For the Jews, the story of the Garden was a fable, an allegory, intended to teach a moral lesson and spur its readers to lead a moral life. Even
Jewish literalists who see the narrative as a record of actual events, are
careful to confine the guilt and any liability to punishment to Adam and
Eve. They also take pains to emphasize that their "God" is the compassionate, forgiving "God" of Exodus who saves his people from oppression
and showers them with great gifts — land and freedom. He "does not visit
the sins of the fathers upon their children."

The Roman rhetorician, Aurelius Augustinus, however, claimed to discern the *real reality* behind the story of the garden of Eden. He never
consulted Jews about how to interpret the story of Adam' sin. He was not
only a literalist, he expanded the story into the theory we saw laid out in
the Catholic Catechism as "original sin." What is most astonishing is that
this doctrine is *at such variance* with what Jews say the story means. It
actually reverses the Genesis authors' intention. Working from exactly the
same text, he said the story explains how the *whole universe* became
irreparably corrupt by the sin of Adam, and fell from perfect order toward a
primeval chaos and into the possession of Satan *by the will and acquiescence of "God"* who, for all his almighty power seemed powerless before
"sin." It was a change so profound as to virtually make *evil into an original
organic condition* for everyone who came afterward ... and it turned "God"
into an ego-driven psychopath. For the loss of paradise and immortality
were not sufficient punishment; the guilt for the insult to "God" passed to

---

[64] Von Rad, *op.cit.*, p.85, 87
[65] Rosenberg, *op.cit.*, p.59
[66] Von Rad, *op.cit.*, p.85

each human being in equal measure meriting *eternal torment*. The catastrophe was so complete that "God" himself would have to perform a **cosmic rescue** — virtually a *new creation* — to reverse those effects. Jesus of Nazareth, he declared, was God-in-person made man who came to earth in order to accomplish that task.

jesus and christianity

Just who was this Jesus that the Roman Emperor and the Roman Catholic hierarchy of the 4th century claimed was God Almighty? Information from the gospels, corroborated by non-Christian sources, says he was a Jew who lived in Palestine under Roman occupation in the first century of the common era. He was an itinerant preacher who explicitly characterized his message as *Jewish, directed exclusively to Jews for the reform of Judaism.*

Similar to the disconnect between Christians and Jews about the events in Genesis, it is quite remarkable that what Christians say about Jesus is also *at great variance* with what Jesus said about himself as recorded in the gospels. Jesus clearly denied being "God."[67] He never suggested that the cosmic effects of the sin of Adam were the essence of the "human problem" requiring divine intervention ... much less that he himself had come to rectify that problem and that it was the sole reason for his being here. He seems to have had no disagreements with the traditional Jewish understanding of Genesis. In fact, by all available evidence he had no intention of transcending Judaism in any way whatsoever. His mission, as he himself made clear, was to restore "Israel" to a filial relationship with a loving Father.[68]

Finding out exactly what he said, however, is not an easy task. Jesus has been poorly served by his followers. Unlike the Buddha, whose disciples preserved their teacher's original sayings, and kept them separate from their own with the result that we have a fairly good idea of what he actually said and thought,[69] that didn't happen with Jesus. Within a generation of his death, Christians had set his words in constructed narratives

---

[67] Mark 10:18, Matt 19:17

[68] Mt 10:6; 15:24: *"I have been sent only to the lost sheep of the House of Israel."*

[69] "The Authenticity of the Pali Suttas", by Thanissaro Bhikkhu. *Access to Insight*, 30 January 2011, http://www.accesstoinsight.org /lib/authors/ thanissaro/authenticity.html).

that gave them meanings that he never intended. What happened? Why did they feel they could take such liberties with their rabbi?

The excuse we often hear from Christian sources is that the ancients were poor historians. That is complete nonsense. In fact, the astonishing capacity for memorization among ancient and non-literate people is a well known phenomenon that belies any such excuse. You can be sure Jesus' words were memorized when they were uttered and at some point most certainly written down. But they have been lost. If the gospel authors failed to transmit *exactly* what Jesus said and did, it was not for lack of documentation. There is only one reason: *they did not feel it was necessary or important.*

The fact is that what Jesus said and did, and what he claimed to be, was Jewish. Jesus' followers who wrote the gospels, on the other hand, were not Jews, they were Greeks. For the Greeks to accept Jesus' message as he gave it would have meant becoming Jewish. They were not about to do that ... they were interested in a religion that would replace the myths of their capricious gods recently "deconstructed" by the philosophers. They adapted the man, message and mission of Jesus to suit their religious and philosophical projections. This process had already begun when the gospels were composed in the latter half of the first century more than a generation after the events. It is not insignificant that *there are no Hebrew or Aramaic versions of the gospels*, and all conjectured sources like the "Q" document or other collections of *logia* ("sayings"), which certainly existed, have been lost. All the gospels are in Greek, and according to the scholars, *show no signs of having been translated.*[70]

The Christians who wrote the gospels were Greeks convinced that *"the real truth"* had simultaneously been discovered by Greek philosophy — especially Plato. The Jewish Philosopher Philo of Alexandria encouraged that conviction. Philo lived in Egypt in Jesus' time and spent his life comparing the Jewish writings with Greek philosophy. It was he who insisted that Judaism and Platonic philosophy were **one and the same thing.** The Jewish "Book" (the Bible), he taught, was simply Greek philosophy repackaged in the form of legends and stories for uneducated, non-philoso-

---

[70] This true even of "Matthew" which Papias claimed was based on Aramaic logia. But, whatever his sources, Matthew's Greek "reveals none of the telltale marks of a translation." Geoffrey W Bromiley, *The International Standard Bible Encyclopedia*, 1959, Eerdmans, Grand Rapids, p. 281

phical people. Both Moses and Plato agreed there was only one God, and so according to this school of thought, there could be only one truth. That truth was expressed *literally, factually, scientifically* by Greek philosophy and allegorically, metaphorically, symbolically by the Jewish stories in the Bible. It was philosophy alone that *had the literal truth and expressed it in scientific words.* And the Greek Christianity created by Paul and "John" caught that football and ran with it. So for example, they took the word "Messiah" and they translated it to mean Philo's *Logos,* the firstborn of all creation, the very "Wisdom" by which "God" created all things. These were Greek philosophical categories syncretized with Judaism; they were not originally Jewish and they were certainly not Jesus'.

Those who wrote the gospels reported *what they chose to remember* of what Jesus said, and put it in terms that *they believed and understood it to mean.* Through their "vision of faith" they were convinced they knew the real truth, and the results are the mixed narratives we call the gospels. They actually generated a re-interpretation of the Jewish Scriptures designed to justify Christians' perception that Jesus was the Messiah, the chosen messenger of God, along with adumbrations of his divinity. These were claims that Jesus himself never made. That fact is clearly present in the gospels and available for verification by any careful reader.

What they did to Jesus, they also did to Genesis ... and to any other part of the Bible they looked at. They disregarded what the Jews thought, just as they disregarded what Jesus said and meant, and imposed their own interpretation. But it should not be a big surprise: *Jesus was Jewish ... and his Jewish message was ignored and his mission transcended just as the Jewish Bible was ignored and its meaning transcended.* The Greeks were not interested in Judaism; they had the "truth" in Platonic philosophy, and integrated everything they found into its worldview including Jesus and his message.

This process was inchoate in the first generation after his death; but it was just the beginning. As for all virtual "memes" trying to survive within their virtual environment, the subsequent three centuries saw a remarkable evolution of Christian doctrine and practice molded by the pressures of Greco-Roman society.

Greco-Romans took Jesus' words as they had received them, already adapted by the Hellenic gospel accounts, and wrapped them in ever more culturally appropriate doctrinal packaging and ritual practice. It was nothing less than the total reinvention of Christianity assimilated to the class stratification, authority requirements, religious prejudices, ritual customs and philosophical assumptions of the Greco-Roman world. In 350 years, from the founding of the first communities as recorded in Acts to Christianity's emergence as the chosen religion of the Roman Empire, an egalitarian spiritual and moral movement of the lower classes morphed into an organization providing a magical "saving" ritual rigidly controlled by the bishops and priests of an upper-class hierarchy. No documentation has been found that traces the details of exactly how that happened. All we have are the results.

That transformation eventuated in Christianity becoming "Catholicism" — the official religion of the Roman empire at the beginning of the 4th century. *That* was the event that put an abrupt end to its spontaneous evolution. From that point forward Christianity became subject to the standardization and codification imposed by its new imperial managers. It guaranteed there would never be a return to its roots in Jesus' Judaism. The changes that had already taken place were the very things that made a once threatening anti-imperialist Christianity attractive to the emperors, and any changes allowed from then on would be carefully monitored by the Roman authorities to make sure they continued to fit into the Imperial agenda. What suited their purposes they set in stone; what didn't, they made sure were anathematized, and their proponents exiled. The empire would not tolerate division or uncontrolled change in *its state religion.*

This helps explain why the now-Christian Romans had to violently suppress Judaism — something they had never done before. The Jews had proprietary rights to the Scriptures and their interpretation. If the Christian revision of a thousand years of Jewish fidelity, reflection and scholarship was not to be exposed for the usurpation that it was, Jewish claims had to be eliminated. The empire would not permit a challenge of that scale to the very wellspring of its "divine power."

This is the "Christianity" we have inherited, and the version preserved in the Roman Church is its most representative and least reformed repository. It bears little resemblance to the mission and original intent of Jesus, whose words, if not totally lost, were buried in the "inspired" text of early commentaries called "gospels" — which themselves became buried later under centuries and centuries of "infallible" *magisterium, dogmas* and pontifications. Unearthing Jesus' original message at this point is as daunting an enterprise as an archaeological dig.

The fact remains, **Jesus was a Jew.** The doctrine of original sin is one of the extreme examples of Christianity's arrogant disregard for Jewish tradition as well as the worst possible reversal of the Jewish religious values which were the source of Jesus' teaching. It turned the Jews' liberating compassionate *Yahweh* — Jesus' "loving Father" — into a tyrannical Roman psychopath. It displays all the typical penchants of Greek philosophical thought: they interpreted everything as the allegorical expression of their cosmological and metaphysical convictions. It is a standing contradiction of the traditional Jewish interpretation of Genesis as legends of origin and the goodness of God.

II. THE HUMAN SIGNIFICANCE OF THE DOCTRINE

We have examined the questionable sources of the Christian doctrine of original sin and from every angle there seems to be very little to support it as a valid representation of reality. It is contrary to science and to the Jewish Scriptures. It was never mentioned by Jesus and was not fully formulated for 350 years after the founding of the first Christian communities. It was limited to the Western Church. Eastern Christians reject the Augustinian interpretation as non-apostolic.[71]

Based on the gospel principle that *"by their fruits you will know them,"* it remains to examine the doctrine from the most important angle: how it has worked out in practice. What are the *consequences* for western Christians and their culture after 1600 years of living with the "doctrine of original sin." I have selected seven areas where the accumulated evidence over time has proved the doctrine to work against the spirit of Jesus' message and what is good for people.

---

[71] In *Ancestral Sin*, John S. Romanides ... asserts that original sin (as inherited sin) is not a doctrine of the church nor cohesive with the Eastern Orthodox faith, but an invention of later church fathers such as Augustine. http://en.wikipedia.org/wiki/Eastern_Orthodox_Christian_theology

(1) one-world vs. two-worlds

Plato's theory of the "fall" was the model for Augustine's interpretation of "original sin." By Augustine's time, Christianity came to be completely dominated by the Platonic paradigm, and Augustine with his theory of cosmic sin and cosmic redemption reinforced it. The fundamental view of Platonism and the Neo-Platonism that followed it was that there were two worlds — a world of spirit and a world of flesh, and "salvation" meant leaving the one and going to the other. I contend that this was not the focus of Judaism, nor was it Jesus' who was a Jew. Quite the contrary, theirs was a "one-world" vision. That means that the Christianity we have inherited is different from the message of Jesus. What I want to do in this section is to show how momentously significant that difference is, in the context of what we have learned about the doctrine of original sin.

In Augustine's Christianity the fall split the world in two. There was the cosmos before the fall — the world as "God" intended — and the cosmos after the fall — reality as we know it. There was no way of recovering our true humanity or that original world in this life, except in seed ... a seed of Christian holiness that would not blossom until after death in another world, the world of spirit. Entrance into that other world is not guaranteed. It must be won.

This "two-world" vision sets up an inexorable dynamic. Once you assert the existence of another world and the human destiny to return there, you necessarily create an *ethos* that is directed by and to that other world. This entails some unavoidable consequences:

Revelation. There has to be some way of finding out what you need to get there. By definition, these worlds are separate and diametrically opposed; so the requirements for entrance will not be readily available in *this world.* At best, Plato thought, since the *real* realities exist in that other world. they can only be adumbrated, i.e., *inferred from the shadows they cast* in this one. The nature of the situation requires that if we are to know for sure what we must do to get to that other world, there has to be some kind of "revelation" from that world to this. This helps explain the endless western enterprise that we are all familiar with: of ascertaining exactly what "God said," and what "God wants." We should remind ourselves of the centuries of conflict and rivers of blood spilt on the question of *the "will"* of God. It was inevitable. Once you have convinced yourself that in order to be "saved" you *need to know exactly* what "God" wants, not only do you become obsessed with getting it right, but your tolerance for other views evaporates. "Knowing the will of God" not only destined the divergent factions of European Christians to endless wars, but it also served as justification for the colonial plunder, enslavement and genocide of people in Africa, Asia and the Americas who, because they were not Christian, obviously did not know the "will of God."

Individual self-interest is the core motivation of the two-world program; it cannot be avoided. Hence *ulterior motivation* will always be suspected. Jesus' moral program, however, was not driven by self-interest. It was not based on reward and punishment of any kind, nor any form of selfishness no matter how "spiritual" or refined. Jesus did not offer heaven as a motivation, nor hell as a deterrent. Much of what is paradoxical in Christianity — like the conflict between compassion, forgiveness and the implacable punishments for moral or ritual lapses — can be attributed to the difference between the dynamics that rule these two contrary worlds. Once the influence of the "other world" is allowed to disappear, these anomalies tend to disappear as well.

In a two-world system the kind of compassion and forgiveness that would characterize a this-worldly ethic like the one Jesus promoted, is always secondary to salvation in the "other world" and to loyalty to its master. Compassion tends to be treated as an unnecessary indulgence attributable to an excess of sentiment; it becomes religiously significant only when "performed" as a disciplined obedience to a command from "God." Forgiveness does not "gain grace" unless it is performed as a hard-nosed self-interested compliance-for-salvation.

In this two-world system Jesus' program of forgiveness was in fact claimed to be an other-worldly law. It said Jesus came to give us a "new law" which "commands" us to forgive as God forgives. The incongruence here is revealing. Such a "command" could only have been meant *metaphorically*. For If it is taken literally, it eviscerates the very meaning of compassion; it undermines the spontaneity of love and trust in God, and it is damaging to human autonomy. Just how free and generous are you if you are ultimately always "taking care of yourself," gaining grace and building your nest in the "other" world? "Obeying law" is contrary to the ultimate point of Jesus' ethos, which is the development of a new type of personality, a "new human being" with a *new psychological identity* that functions on a new set of interests, emotions and motivations.

The real focus of Jesus' Jewish message was that **to live humanly in this world is to be like Yahweh.** To be fully and deeply human one had to imitate "God" who gives ... and forgives, gratuitously, spontaneously, unreservedly, generously, without expectation of recompense ... like a "loving Father." His message was very simple, much too simple, in fact, to leave any room for the self-interested coercions western culture insists *must* drive all human interaction. The complex theological labyrinths produced throughout the millennia of "Christian thought" can be understood as just so many elaborate fabrications needed to contain and neutralize that simplicity ... and, on the opposing side, the titanic efforts required to deconstruct those fabrications.

As far as **moral content** is concerned, a program of "living wisely on earth" — characteristic of *one-world visions* — will almost never work for "two-worlders" for the simple reason that the earth and *living on it* is not the object of their respect; its only value is as conduit to another world. Attention is necessarily directed there, and since it is a world of *immaterial* spirit, the concern will be for one's own "spiritual" acquisitions ... *not the human body of my brother and sister struggling to survive ... much less the eco-systems that support us and all the other species with which we share the earth*. In a "two-world" system, the moral agent cannot really care all that much about life on earth because matter is the place of banishment and frustration, soon to be left behind. In fact historically, the two-world view has caused people to *despise* earthly life and the human body.

jesus' jewish reform movement

A very strong case can be made for saying that the very object of Jesus' message was *precisely to* overcome the obstacles created by the "reward and punishment" mentality of a Judaism that, according to Christian claims in the NT, had come to be dominated by an excessive legalism. While Judaism did not subscribe to the existence of two-worlds, the Jewish belief that "God" *rewarded or punished in this world,* set up the same *quid pro quo* dynamic. The *old contract* — the "covenant" — between Israel and Yahweh had precisely to do with *national prosperity in return for obeying the Torah.* It is not at all irrelevant that some Jewish theologians recognize this as a phase in the evolution of mature Judaism as reinterpreted by the prophets, who saw the *contract* as well as the law in more moral and mystical terms.[72]

Jesus was part of the prophetic movement toward a universalist Judaism built on love for humanity. For him it meant *imitating our "loving Father" who loved without measure.* His message emphasized not obedience to law, but *compassionate behavior in this world*, in a way that was not unlike the Greek Stoics. John Dominic Crossan, a Catholic New Testament scholar, highlights the similarity of Jesus' message to a philosophical system he identifies as a lived version of Stoicism popular in Jesus' time. He categorized the moral program and *intentional simplicity of life* of this movement as one of the diverse ways in which people "*respond to the world when salvation from evil is no longer the issue.*"[73]

Given this background, it is not surprising that Jesus did not point to the commands of "the Book" for the content of his vision.[74] *He elicited it from the hearts and minds of his listeners.* It was embedded in his teaching method: **he taught in parables.** It meant people had to look *inside themselves* to discover what was right and wrong. Clearly he thought his listeners were up to the task. Correct conduct was theirs to discover and decide. How many times did his parables end with a question ... "which of these was truly a neighbor ... a faithful servant ... a true son"? He called forth the "law" written in their hearts, not on tablets of stone. He encouraged attitudes of empathy, forgiveness, sincerity, humility, compassion, loyalty that may have been mentioned in the Jewish Torah and were certainly the spirit behind it,[75] but were not the direct object of a written "command." Jesus was so far from making morality an act of legal obliga-

---

[72] Abraham Heschel, *The Prophets*, Harper Torchbooks, 1969, *passim*; cf Edward Greenstein, chapter "Biblical Law" in *Back to the Sources*, Barry Holtz, ed. Simon & Shuster, 1984 pp. 83-103. *passim.*

[73] John Dominic Crossan *The Historical Jesus* 1991, Harper Collins, p.72. Cf the entire *chapter 4, "Poverty and Freedom,"*pp.72-88. Crossan explores the striking similarity between the text and attitudes found in Matthew chapters 5 and 10 and the moral program of the "movement" of Stoic-Cynics in Greco-Roman times. Crossan had hinted earlier that the proximity of Nazareth to the ancient Roman city of Sephoris, only 4 miles away, would suggest that Jesus was more aware of these non-Jewish Greek movements than we realize. His respect for them may or may not have induced him to include them in his preaching, but at any rate he seemed to share their values.

[74] The only "command" he cited was the paraphrase of the "Sh'ma Ishrael" – Love God with your whole heart ... and your neighbor as yourself. Hardly a "law."

[75] Edward Greenstein, op cit. says colloquially, "God is a *mensch.*" P.89

tion that he even encouraged his people to *judge their religious authorities by the standards they found in their own hearts.* "By their fruits," he told them boldly, "*you* will know them."

Do not misunderstand. I am not claiming that Jesus himself or the Judaism of his time actively rejected life after death. But we know that to them it was a disputed possibility, not "dogma"[76] and therefore not the basis of a two-world morality. At any rate *Jesus ignored it* and concentrated conspicuously *on this world alone.* I say "conspicuously" because it stands in such sharp contrast with the other worldly perspective that dominated the later Christianity erected in his name. *Jesus was not a Christian, he was a Jew.* I contend that the program offered by Jesus functions perfectly in a universe where there are not two-worlds ... but not without a "loving Father."

In a two-world system we must always be ready to make whatever sacrifices are necessary in order to "obey the will of God." Barbara Newman underlines the hardhearted attitude that such a belief inspires; she quotes Bernard of Clairvaux as saying: *"It is the height of piety to be cruel for Christ's sake."*[77] With such a mentality we are *not* encouraged to listen to our hearts, and respond to our neighbor with empathy, as Jesus asked of us. We are warned only to "obey God," and, of course, those who claim to speak in "his" name.

While the doctrine of "original sin" was not solely and directly responsible for all this, it became the ultimate justification for the worldview that was. Catholic authorities of Augustine's time found it consistent with the Roman Christian agenda.

two world politics and original sin

There is a political dimension implied in all this that I want to make explicit. The belief in two-worlds discourages commitment to justice in this world and excuses collaboration with exploitive economic and political systems. Please take note: justice is a communitarian virtue. The Platonic two world view based on the doctrine of original sin, is necessarily individ-

---

[76] Cf Jesus debate with the Saducees on exactly this question: Mark 12:18-27, Matthew 22:23-33, Luke 20:27–40. This was not a settled question in Jesus' day.

[77] Barbara Newman, *From Virile Woman to Woman Christ,* Phila., U of PA Pr, 1995, p.81, cf Chapter 3 "Crueel Corage" pp. 76-107 *passim.*

ualistic. Individualism is a transcendent feature of Western civilization. It's important to see how this works in Augustine's system which dominated Western Christian life in thought and practice from the 5th century right up to today and continues to function in the culture whether westerners are Christian or not.

In the Christian scheme of things, no one's destiny is tied to anyone else's. If you are living for your individual reward in another world, what happens to others in this world is secondary. Even when it does not explicitly encourage escapism, the attitude permits those who have no interest in redressing injustice (perhaps because they are profiting from it) to rationalize their inaction or complicity.

I believe it was the two-world system that helps explain how the *non-violent resistance* to Rome's self-idolatry manifested by the early martyrs, could have been followed less than a decade after the last persecution[78] by the Christian acceptance of cooperation with the Empire. What the martyrs opposed was *idolatry*, and they faced death fearlessly because they believed they were going immediately to the other world. Refusing to throw incense on the fire may have included their opposition to the Empire's dehumanizing exploitation, but there's no evidence for it. They were "two-worlders." Personal reward after death motivated their courage, they were explicit about that. Please notice: that exclusively "religious" motivation meant that once Rome declared it would worship the "true God," Christian resistance to the empire evaporated. Belief in the "other world" permitted if not encouraged support for the Empire without requiring that it cease its exploitive *modus operandi*. Justice — a communitarian imperative — did not have a sharp focus among Christians *because a two-world system intensifies individualism*. The result has been the hieratic maintenance of two millennia of imperial machinery and the justification, *in Christ's name,* of the exploitation of defenseless isolated individuals by a class of elite predators as a characteristic of western political structures.

There is a spontaneous human outrage at injustice that parallels the spontaneous empathy that stirs our compassion. Both these are communitarian "this worldly" instincts that can be vitiated by the refined selfishness encouraged in a two-world belief system. And a non-violence driven

---

[78] The persecution of Diocletian ended in 303. Constantine endorsed Christianity in 312.

by unconcern for this world can actually work in the service of this selfishness.

In our time some have erected "Christian non-violence" into a new moral imperative. But there is no guarantee that just being non-violent in the face of injustice always promotes the common good, and may not itself simply be an excuse for indifference or even selfishness. Don't get me wrong, there is even less guarantee that violence in and of itself will secure justice. The point I am making here is that non-violence is not an end in itself. It is a tool of action and receives its value from the ends it is used to pursue. It must be directed against injustice.

(2) western individualism

In a version of "individualism" that we are familiar with today, our *culture* teaches that happiness is an individual achievement and possession, and that society's role is to protect the individual's ability and opportunity to achieve happiness. In more extreme versions it is considered perfectly acceptable that the competition that allows the "winners" to achieve, entails the actual physical extinction or economic destitution of the "losers." Such attitudes assure the continued existence of a menial underclass, marginaled and miserable, a phenomenon that has characterized our societies for so long that it has come to be considered "natural." An off-hand remark by Jesus, "the poor you will always have with you," by which he meant to turn his disciples attention to his own impending death, has been taken out of context and used to confirm that view of things.

How did this come about? I believe that such a conviction is the ultimate product of a cluster of ancient beliefs that were centered on the existence of an individual "spirit-God," who judges, rewards and punishes each individual "spirit-person" separately in a "spirit-world" after death. It is a corollary of a "two-world" view of reality, and it is supported by the doctrine of original sin. In such a universe there is no group survival or "salvation." Everyone is on their own. An intense concern for oneself has been introjected deep into the western psyche. It has endured long after the Christian religion which promoted it stopped being the official state-sponsored object of belief.

"Original sin" is the foundational Christian doctrine making **individual selfishness** the very definition of adult behaviour. It is significant that this teaching was elaborated in its most toxic form by the Roman philosopher Augustine less than a century after Constantine's "conversion." But, early as this was in Christian history, it was still a full 350 years after the birth of Christianity, and could hardly lay claim to original authenticity.[79]

"Original sin" advanced individualism on three levels simultaneously. (1) It declared that each was born with "original sin" and thus punished **individually** for Adam's affront to "God." (Even newborn babies, if they died without baptism, would be damned for all eternity.) (2) It entailed a proclivity to sin, which meant the individual was **innately selfish** — constitutionally predisposed *not* to consider anyone but him or herself. And (3) it meant **individual damnation**, unless sin were forgiven and remedied — individual by individual — with the ritual ablutions administered *exclusively* by the Empire's Church. Augustine's Roman imperial theology proclaimed that *"outside the church there is no salvation."* It gave the empire all the justification it needed for external conquest and internal control.[80]

In tandem with belief in the *individual immortal soul,* "original sin" was perfect for Roman imperial purposes. Your fallen humanity guaranteed that your selfish body would always predispose you to sin, and you would always have to go to the authorities of the Empire's Church for forgiveness. Terrified of dying and going to hell, you knew that there was no one **except them** who could help you avoid eternal damnation. Christian doctrine rendered irrelevant family and village — the primary human survival communities — and put the Empire's Church, offering individual survival in another world, in its place. To effect that transition, you had to be convinced that you were a spirit from another world, that you really belonged to that other world not to this one ... *and the Church controlled the keys!* Family, clan, village and language group were absorbed into the community of the theocratic State, once declared dead by the martyrs and

---

[79] The early source cited for "original sin" is the NT Epistle to the Romans. But what Paul expressed there did not in any way justify where Augustine went with it. Augustine's version is thoroughly hellenic, individualistic, a reprise of the Platonic theory of the fall of spirit into flesh, denigrating matter and permanently grounding individual guilt. Paul's was hebraic, communitarian, symbolic, using the story of Adam's sin to evoke the re-creation of humankind accomplished by Christ alone — establishing a new communitarian relationship to "God" **for all people,** *without law, guilt or sin.* Similar to what he did to the book of Genesis, Augustine *completely reversed* the meaning of Paul's imagery.

[80] 16th century Christian colonization of primitive peoples in the Americas entailing their exploitation and enslavement was universally justified as "Christianization." Imperial Christian doctrine has always motivated and justfied conquest while rendering the conquered submissive — a lethal combination.

now brought back to life by the kiss of the Imperial-consort. And all of it was based on the central dogma of the spiritual individual, the existence of the "other world," and the corrupt nature of everything in this one *because of "original sin."*

"Original sin" established the premise that unregenerate, non-Christian human nature is inherently corrupt and selfish. It would follow, then, that any attempt at forming "human community" outside of the salvific community of the Empire's Church must be the product of some kind of *selfish materialist dynamism* ... if it claimed to be altruism, it must be the work of Satan, for outside the true Church all is corrupt, *all is the work of the devil.*

Doctrinaire capitalism, as the ultimate violent self-projection of the individual who arrogates to himself as "owner" what belongs to all, is inevitable in such a world. Since fallen humanity is *intrinsically selfish* and insatiably greedy, it is a condition that *cannot be changed.* Thomas Hobbes in 1651 *said*: "man is a wolf to man .... In the state of nature profit is the measure of right." Note: Hobbes was Christian. The "state of nature" is life in this world without the effects of "grace" mediated exclusively by the sacraments of the Church. To be selfless in Hobbes' terms *is supernatural — that means it is not human.* The best that could be done for unregenerate humanity is to harness and direct its demonic energy.[81]

Besides, those who are convinced that they are utterly despicable before God, develop a need for a compensatory mechanism that will allow them to function psychologically. The accumulation of wealth as a sign of divine favor was a solution that came to be institutionalized by the Calvinist version of Christianity in the 16th century. We still speak of the well-off as being "**blessed by God**." This morphed into the popular belief that the wealthy were *morally superior — elected by God to teach and to rule.* The plutocracy that today rules the world and that we all accept came from there.

The insuperable individualism that we have been brought up to believe is the norm, therefore, is the result of a very long, intense and continent-wide cultural programming in the lands we know as "Europe." For more than 1500 years, Europeans were subjected to this Christian indoctrination telling them who they should think they are and what they should think

---

[81] Thomas Hobbes, *Leviathan*, 1651

of this world we live in. The result was to breed a continent of isolated individuals, vulnerable, defenseless, terrified of "God," distrustful of themselves, their neighbors and this material world which produced their own material bodies.

The doctrines of the Empire's Church formed the soul of Europe and its political structures. Western colonial conquest over the past four centuries, energized by this vision, has exported that mindset and insured its globalization. European capitalism and its associated pseudo-democratic plutocracy is the product of an ancient imperialist ideology; and in our times they have come to dominate the planet.

(3) a schizoid deity

The doctrine of original sin concocted by Augustine of Hippo projected a schizoid personality of the "God" that presided over it. For despite having been rendered *merciful* toward humankind because of the sacrifice of the cross, he was required to simultaneously stay *furious* at original sin.

Why did Augustine say that "God" remained angry? Because the cross *obviously* had not reversed the dreadful punishments allegedly imposed on humankind at the time of the "fall." Sickness, hard labor, subjugation of women, pain of childbirth, violence between brothers, concupiscence of the flesh, "darkness of the mind and weakness of the will" and, most bitter of all, death itself ... none of these "punishments" were eliminated despite redemption. It's interesting that at the disputations between Jewish and Christian theologians at Barcelona in 1263, this was one of rabbi Nahmanides' principal arguments against Christian belief in a "redemption" already achieved.[82] Augustine claimed that the suffering borne by humankind is so overwhelming that it could only be a sign that "God" was *still enraged* with humankind for original sin — despite Christ's sacrifice. The attempt to reconcile the co-existence of these two opposing characteristics — God's anger and his forgiveness — has occupied not a small amount of theologians' time and hard labor through the subsequent centuries. Rather than concede that the contradiction proved the premises

---

[82] *The Vikuah of Nahmanides*, the report of the sole Jewish protagonist of the disputation at Barcelona, 1263, reprinted in Maccoby tr., *Judaism on Trial*, Fairleigh Dickenson U. Press, 1982, p.118.

flawed, theologians devised contorted "solutions" that led to ever deeper contradictions.

Martin Luther was one of those who came up with a complicated formula designed to explain the paradox. He said that "God" decided *gratuitously* (i.e., not forced by the *logic* of justice) to accept the death of his son as compensation for the insult to the divine majesty. But please notice what Luther meant: it was an *extrinsic imputation*; it really did *not* get to the root of, or delete the injustice of Adam's sin which was eternally there, in a real sense indelible, and therefore fundamentally **unforgiveable.** The baptized Christian was simultaneously reprobate and reprieved, guilty though forgiven — as Luther put it, **simul justus et peccator,** "both righteous and a sinner"[83] — and thus did a schizoid "God" generate a western European Christian population with a schizoid identity, unsure of its own integrity, questioning its own worth and goodness, made so in this "God's" own image and likeness. You and I are part of that inheritance.

What complex of concepts could possibly be functioning here to require that "God" be of two minds? Why isn't "God" either angry or forgiving? The popular understanding that "God" is angry or forgiving **by turns** — meaning that his moods and choices change in response to events — is unacceptably anthropomorphic. Theologians have always rejected any such solution because in classic theology "God's" mind cannot change. They had to come up with a formula whereby "God" could be "eternally" of two minds. (If it seems to you that we are in a surreal world here, you are not alone.)

Luther, following Augustine, seems to suggest that "God" had to "find a way" ... i.e., had to use some kind of "*stratagem*" to get around his "obligation" to be angry. Are you following me here? The traditional Christian view of redemption, in other words, implies a *state of reality over which "God" has no control* ... and "God," if "he" is to forgive humankind, like any conniving Greco-Roman godling, is reduced to finding ways around that reality. This is utterly preposterous. But there are ideological and institutional reasons why this constellation of incoherent ideas has existed in

---

[83] Martin Luther, *Lectures on Romans*, 260 cited in Tatha Wiley, *Original Sin*, Paulist Press, 2002, p.89. Luther's memorable image for the extrinsic imputation of forgiveness for the baptized Christian was "a dunghill covered with snow."

Western theological thinking for 1500 years and I want to spend a few paragraphs reflecting on them.

These reasons are cultural and exist at two levels: the philosophical ... and underneath that, the earlier, pre-philosophical. Let me explain ... and please be patient ... we are trying to understand a language we no longer speak, but which formed our view of the world.

(a) First, *philosophical-theology.* The Greeks, remember, were stone idealists. That means they believed that at the root of everything is "God's" self-contemplation — *ideas.* Now ideas, for the Greeks, were rational. That means they followed the rules of logic *necessarily;* it is of their very nature. Therefore the ultimate structure of reality *has to be rational.* Even "God" must obey it, for "idea" is of his very essence; *idea is what "he" is.* It is not a question of power — who's boss. It is beyond "will" altogether, whether divine or human, *ideas must obey the "laws" of logic.* This is the Greek mind.

As a Platonist, Augustine subscribed to this view of the world. In the case we are considering, his "God" was bound by the inescapable "logic of justice" that lay behind the juridical principle of *restitution* in conjunction with an ancient category of tort called *laesa majestas* (in English-speaking jurisprudence, *lese majesty*). It stated that if you insult (*laesa*) a person, you have committed an *objective* violation of the order of justice; and the grievousness of that violation is determined by the "objective" importance or dignity (*majestas*) of the person insulted. All such injustices rob the insulted person of a dignity they have a right to.

In an aristocratic society this dignity varied according to status. It determined one's standing in the eyes of others. It is what gave you your place in society. This "dignity" is a possession. So, robbing someone of their dignity is "stealing," a crime that demands more than retribution, *it demands a restitution of the dignity lost.*

Now, in the case of "God," insulted by Adam's disobedience, the theft *cannot* be paid back because the "person" offended is *infinite,* the dignity lost is infinite, and the restitution owed is infinite. No amount of mercy or forgiveness can erase that fact. If the objective "order of justice" is to be restored, therefore, it requires that "God" be paid back his dignity by humankind, and *"being forgiven"* does not do away with the requirement of *restitution,* much as a thief still owes restitution even after serving his time in jail. Hence the redemption of Christ.

In that aristocratic system, restitution of "dignity," was accomplished by a public display of remorse and obeisance that restored the offended "person" to his proper place in the eyes of others. Jesus' death on the cross was considered the public recognition of the supreme dignity of "God" paid back by "God" himself. Romans would have understood such a connection because they were accustomed to the Emperor demanding outrageous compensation — suicide, for example — as punishment for an affront to his Imperial person. In the case of Christ, it was an "obedience" that outmatched the "disobedience" of Adam. It was a display of submission that was itself appropriately *infinite* because it was performed by "God" himself (under his aspect as the "second" person of the Trinity). A very tidy package, indeed, for the Greco-Roman mind, and a brilliant bit of mental gymnastics by a Platonist Christian, Aurelius Augustinus ... our beloved "Saint" Augustine.

(b) But we are not finished. There is another level down — where philosophy is formed and fed by the often-hidden springs of the earlier *culture* from which philosophy arose. I believe what we are looking at here is the unconscious preservation of the ancient **pre-philosophical Greco-Roman belief in "fate"** as an objective mindless, inhuman "force of nature" which ruled the universe, imposing punishments for the violation of prescribed patterns *whether the perpetrators were aware of them or not.* Fate was the infrastructural bedrock of all reality ... an unwritten inner essence of things to which everything, *including the gods*, must conform.

So from this quick review we can see what went into creating and sustaining the western Christian doctrine of "redemption." It required a literal cosmological original sin and an imagined humanoid "emperor-God" personally insulted and enraged by it, and powerless to dismiss a restitution to his dignity demanded by the "order of nature." This fate-driven "God" was placated only by the death of his son; hence each human individual, unless "bathed" by that death in baptism, remained the object of "God's" eternal wrath. *It is all absurd to us.* It was a rationalization justified by obsolete juridical principles and class assumptions that perhaps at one time made sense in a different virtual world ... but not in ours.

(4) the jews and natural disasters

There are traditional features of the doctrine of original sin that have been conspicuously omitted or muted by the Vatican Catechism's reprise, that actually had great impact on the lives and behavior of

Christians in past centuries. One is the belief that **natural disasters** stem from the "corruption of nature" caused by original sin, and God's fury at "Adam's humanity." Catastrophes naturally occur throughout corrupted nature, but if they occur in Christian lands, it may be assumed that it is because of *the presence of the unbaptized* in the region where calamity strikes ... because "God's" wrath is uncontrollably directed to those who have not been forgiven through baptism. These were the direct implications of Augustine's formulation. Mediaeval Christians took them as fact and applied them unfailingly. It was believed that Satanic forces are free to do their worst where the "power of the cross" is not present. The vampire legends reflect that belief.

The conviction that God is eternally insulted by Adam's sin was sufficient cause through most of western history to precipitate *genocidal pogroms of Jews* every time a major catastrophe struck. Jews were not baptized, and because they were also "Christ-murderers" they had to be the principal object of divine wrath. Paranoid persecutions which aimed at the *physical extermination of heretics* and witches followed this same logic. The recent claim by fundamentalists that the natural disasters in New Orleans in 2005 and Haiti in 2010 were the products of divine punishment unleashing satanic fury on those displeasing to "God," is evidence that these beliefs are not some quaint myth of the ancient past but travel with us still. This is all the inheritance of the "doctrine of original sin."[84]

I believe it was the cultural residue of these convictions that provided the obsession for the holocaust under the Nazis. To say that the irrational hatred of Jews does not have a religious etiology, however lost in the mists of the past, is to be blind. Hitler's attempt to camouflage his loathing with the then recently constructed theory of "Aryan" racial superiority hides the real truth from no one. Even were they as convinced of their own superiority as they claimed, the Nazis had no plans to exterminate everyone but blond Germans. Why heap such opprobrium on the Jews alone? James Carroll's condemnation of Catholic complicity with Hitler, detailed in his 2001 book, *Constantine's Sword,* points to the answer:

---

[84] Cf Alan Jacobs, *original sin, a cultural history,* Harper One, 2008, who quotes Augustine in his tract against Julian of Eclanum, exclaiming "You slanderously boast that my words contradict one another ... *as though it could not be true that one and the same evil is inflicted on sinners both by the devil's iniquity and God's justice.*" p.61

Because of the *"dark symbiosis"*[85] *of ancient Christian Jew hatred and modern racism*, Hitler's anti-Jewish program even at its extreme was not that offensive to the broad population of Catholics. ... The Vatican's silence ... was only a version of the choice countless Europeans made to pursue their own welfare without regard for those outside the circle of their concern — the Jews.

   That choice had been nearly two thousand years in the making. It is the last consequence of the long story this book has told ... . This story is itself the source of the Pope's silence and the meaning of it. *This is the moral failure of Catholicism, and of the civilization of which it is so centrally a part.*[86]

The Holocaust, I believe, was the ultimate Christian *pogrom*, the "final solution." It was the attempt to realize the inveterate dream of Christian Europe that it could once and for all rid itself of the perennial source of misfortune by exterminating the unbaptized in its lands. God's blessings had to follow. Was this atheist Hitler's conscious intention? Certainly not. But the unconscious archetype ingrained over thousands of years of Christian "belief" made Jewish extermination desirable, even without knowing why.

   I am convinced the ultimate cause of the holocaust was the Augustinian doctrine of original sin.

(5) racism and the third world

But the "dark symbiosis" Flannery spoke of is with racism. The doctrine of original sin served as a logical support for the disdain and genocidal plunder that Christians *universally* visited upon the more primitive dark-skinned people they "discovered" in Africa, Asia and the Americas beginning in the 16th century. This is the root of Western racism. The thinking here was exactly the same. These people, clearly identifiable by the color of their skin, never even heard of Christ. They were "heathen." *They had to be in the possession of Satan.* The forced conversion and subsequent *lifetime of slave-labor* under the tutelage of a "Christian" master allegedly for the purpose of "Christianizing" these "heathen" was institutionalized in the *encomienda system* of the Spaniards officially approved by Rome. It functioned in the Latin American colonies until the 18th century, despite its exposé and condemnation by Bartolomé de las Casas. The Portuguese slave trade, the principal source of supply

---

85 Edward Flannery, *The Anguish of the Jews*, NY, Paulist Press,1985, p.225

86 James Carroll, *Constantine's Sword*, Mriner Books, 2001, p.534-5 *(emphasis mine)*

for American plantation slavery, crucial to the build-up of American economic power, was an extension of the same attitudes and policies. To this day racists are still wont to call blacks "heathen" and yet they have no idea where their hatred and disdain for dark skinned people originated.

I contend it came from the "doctrine of original sin."

(6) The damnation of unbaptized infants

Probably the most outrageous application of the theory of God's enmity with those still unbaptized is the ancient Christian belief created by Augustine's insistence that all *unbaptized babies* went to eternal damnation. "Augustine," says Alan Jacobs, "did more than anyone else in the Christian Church to convince the world that unbaptized infants, because of the sin of Adam, would burn in eternal conscious torment."[87]

Not everyone agreed with Augustine, but none could compete with his ideological dominance. Julian of Eclanum was a contemporary bishop whose diocese was in southern Italy. He launched a sustained attack on Augustine's doctrine of original sin for its outrageous claim that "God" damned unbaptized babies. Jacobs recreates a vivid exchange between Augustine and Julian:

> Augustine [said] that these infants surely descend into "everlasting fire" with all the other sinners. To this Julian howled with outrage: "Tell me then, tell me, who is this person who inflicts punishments on innocent creatures ... You answer: God. God, you say! God!" Julian cites scripture after scripture telling of God's love for us; he reminds Augustine that God loved us so much that he sent his son to die on our behalf. Yet "he it is who sends tiny babies to eternal flames"? ... [Augustine answers] chillingly, "This is the Catholic view; a view that can show a just God in so many pains and agonies of tiny babies".[88]

It is hardly necessary to challenge the Augustinian position; its utter absurdity condemns itself. What might be of more value for our purposes is how to account for it. That the "loving Father" whom Jesus trusted even unto death could seriously be accused of tormenting innocent babies for eternity just for being human beings, is a clear manifestation of the rationalist and *authoritarian priorities* of the Greco-Roman mindset. For the theory was not only an idiosyncratic fantasy of one sick old man suffering

---

[87] Jacobs, *op.cit. p.64*
[88] *Ibid, p.62f*

from a sadistic inversion of his sexuality, but it was *embraced by the entire western Church.* Based on Augustine's accusation, Julian was condemned for heresy — Pelagianism — and banished from his see. He died in exile 25 years after Augustine. His 12 books of invective against Augustine have all been (predictably) "lost." Original sin became an integral part of mainstream Christianity in the West for the next 1500 years. Why did the whole western church accept this insanity?

To my mind there is only one answer. As we saw in the first section of this chapter, original sin as Augustine conceived it was *the linchpin of the indispensability of the Church* and its sacraments. Inclusion in the Church was established only by baptism. According to Augustine's theory, without baptism the necessary salvation of Christ is not applied, and you are still locked into the sin of Adam. If this theory was not to be toothless, *it had to have no exceptions*; without baptism, *everyone* goes to hell, *everyone!* or people would consider baptism optional. Hence unbaptized babies *had to go to hell.* Augustine's logic was unassailable. What was flawed were his facts and his premises. There was no original sin, as a matter of fact, and therefore there was no "necessary redemption" by Christ, nor any "necessary" Church with its indispensable sacraments to apply it. And besides, *the premises that there was a "God" who was powerless before his own injured ego, and a human nature incapable of being human, were also false.* What was truly inhuman in all of this was Augustine's diseased mind and the bloated Imperial attitudes that had infected him.

Catholicism was the Official Religion of the Roman Empire. Romans *had to be* Christians. Church and State were two in one flesh. Augustine's rigid interpretation provided the sufficient and necessary grounds for the total control and obedience the Roman Empire had come to expect as "God's" agent chosen "to execute wrath on the wrongdoer," a sacred role assigned to the Empire by Paul himself.[89] The Christian accommodation to the Empire was signed and sealed by Augustine. It was never seriously questioned until the protestant reforms of 1517, and then, many would argue, *not really.*

---

[89] *Romans*, 13:4

(7) the debasement of women

The Genesis account has traditionally been cited as "proof" of the moral inferiority of women and to justify their being demeaned. It "blames" Adam's fall on the instigation of Eve.

It's easy to see how this would appear to be the intention of the narrative as written by the original Jewish authors. It cannot be ascribed to an Augustinian misinterpretation as were other aspects of the traditional doctrine of original sin. The story specifically cites the pain of childbirth and women's' submission to their husbands as direct punishments for the act and conspiracy of disobedience initiated by Eve.

But if as Joel Rosenberg says, the Jewish authors' intention was allegory — a poetic attempt to include, by means of entertaining narrative, the *current condition* among near-eastern people at that time — there is no fixed "law of nature" being established here. The fact that others later took the story that way, was attributable to a literalist *scientistic* reading not to the intention of the authors. Traditional Christian literalism was due to the penchant of Greco-Roman *philosopher-scientists* to "ontologize" or "reify" everything. What was intended as a fable was turned into literal history and the justification for women's' debasement was the result. The obvious corrective for this is to return the Genesis account to the metaphor it was meant to be by the Jewish authors. In this case, the theological task is to assess the purposes to which the doctrine has been put, recommend the proper interpretation ... *and insist that it be disseminated*.

> ... the systemic bias of sexism accompanied the idea of original sin in the writings of early church theologians. The doctrine legitimated male privilege and the exclusion of women from full participation in the richness of religious and cultural life.[90]

Fundamentally, in doctrinal terms, this can only mean the traditional Christian version of "original sin" must be repudiated. And it's hard to see how that can effectively be done without a public declaration and an acknowledgement of the damage to women through the millennia.

---

[90] Tatha Wiley, *Original Sin*, Paulist Press, 2002, p.208

(8) original sin among the eastern orthodox

The Eastern Orthodox position on original sin holds literally that with the disobedience of Adam and Eve, humankind lost the "perfect" idyllic existence in which it had been created by God. Because the first humans sinned, death entered the human condition, work became laborious and difficult, childbirth became painful, women were made subordinate to men, violence erupted between brothers, etc., etc. Those beliefs were the same as Augustine's. But the Greek Church disagrees on a key issue: *it does not believe that each of us is born with the guilt of Adam's sin, and merits damnation.* That is the major difference, *and it is huge.* It follows that for the Orthodox — whose claim to an unbroken tradition going back to apostolic times is at least as good as the Roman Church — it is completely absurd that God would send infants to hell.

> This [the Eastern Orthodox] view differs from the Roman Catholic (Augustinian) doctrine of original sin in that man is *not* seen as inherently guilty of the sin of Adam. *According to the Orthodox, humanity inherited the consequences of that sin, not the guilt.* The Orthodox Church does not teach that all are born deserving to go to hell, and Protestant doctrines such as Predestination that derive from the Augustinian understanding of original sin are not a part of Orthodox belief.
>
> In the book, *Ancestral Sin,* [theologian] John S. Romanides ... asserts that original sin (as inherited sin) is not a doctrine of the church nor cohesive with the Eastern Orthodox faith, but an invention of later church fathers such as Augustine.[91]

Joroslav Pelikan contrasts Eastern and Western views citing the 6th century theologian Maximus the Confessor:

> ... Maximus spoke of sin and the fall in an apparently Augustinian fashion. But Maximus' doctrine, while referring of course to the sin of Adam, did not have in it the idea of the transmission of sin through physical conception and birth.[92]

In the light of this contrast, the iron consistency of Augustine's position reveals the transparently authoritarian cattle-prod that lay hidden behind it. In order to make the Church *indispensable* for salvation, Augustine disregarded common sense and displayed an insane willingness to project the kind of sadistic motivations onto "God" that one would hardly believe of a hardened criminal. He showed that his "image" of "God" was formed by psychopaths like Caligula and Nero, who bear no resemblance to the

---

[91] http://en.wikipedia.org/wiki/Eastern_Orthodox_Christian_theology *(emphasis mine).*
[92] Joroslav Pelikan, *The Christian Tradition,* vol 2, *The Spirit of Eastern Christendom,* U.of Chicago pr., 1974, p.182.

compassionate "loving Father" that Jesus tried to paint for us. Augustine's image of "God" — the image embraced by the Roman Catholic Church to this day — was the Emperor of Rome.

The Western Legacy

I believe we must squarely face the transcendent psycho-social effects of this legacy. Two thousand years of Western Europeans were formed in this mentality. It is the cornerstone of what Herbert Marcuse would accuse as being "instinctual repression" in the service of exploitive domination by an elite class,[93] and Paolo Freire would identify as the "internalization of the oppressor."[94] Original sin prepared the European people for a life of guilt and self-loathing that could only be assuaged by the submission of an over scrupulous conscience in blind obedience to an exploitative authority. What westerners have always pointed to as qualities in which they take great pride: their efficiency, their dedication to work, attention to minute details, punctuality, self-discipline, ability to obey orders, self-restraint, self-repression, come dangerously close to resembling an unhealthy personality configuration produced by the Augustinian nightmare of original sin. I would feel less assured about my negative opinion of "Western Man" if westerners did not at the same time despise third world peoples for their "lack of discipline," their "laziness," their relaxed attitude about time, their lack of a technological sense, their willingness to work menial jobs, to be content with their poverty, their sentimentality, their emotional volatility and absence of sexual shame. The self-denigration and emotional repression required by the doctrine of original sin builds a world of fear, rigidity, ethnocentric xenophobia and narcissistic self-absorption ... not of joyous self-acceptance, appreciation of human diversity, inclusive generosity, compassion, forgiveness and the willingness to accept our mortal destiny as human beings. *"By their fruits you will know them."*

The comparison between the two cultures may be lost on many of us ... as the jazz song goes, *"compared to what"?* ... we may never have known anything else.

---

[93] Herbet Marcuse, *Eros and Civilization*, Vintage, NY 1962, p.15ff, p.79f.
[94] Paolo Freire, *The Pedagogy of the Oppressed*, Penguin, 1993, *passim.*

Chapter V

original sin (2)
evil and redemption

I: SIN AND "EVIL"

Underneath it all, the ultimate underpinning for the doctrine of original sin is the assumed notion of sin itself, and more fundamentally, *evil.* We assume we all know and agree with what sin and evil mean. But do we? What exactly are we talking about when we use these terms, and does it make sense?

S*in* has a more specific meaning than "evil." It is generally used to refer exclusively to disobedience to "God." And therefore it requires an anthropomorphic concept of "God" as a person.

Disobedience is the dominant notion. It assumes there is a *relationship* between "God" and humankind where *the terms are* behavioral compliance on our part to a command of "God's." That means there are "laws" regarding prohibited or required behavior which come from "God" himself. It's different when we talk about breaking human laws. That disobedience we call a "crime," or a "tort;" we don't use the word "sin." It is only sin in the case of "God."

Disobedience to "God" is considered an act of ultimate disrespect to "him" **as a person.** It is assumed we will be punished for this disobedience-disrespect. The *personal element* here is paramount. It is precisely what constitutes "sin" as opposed to some other form of moral violation.

Based on everything we have said about the impossibility of an anthropomorphic "God," I claim this is all patently absurd. There is no such reality as "sin" because "God" is not a person like we are. "God" issues no commands. The "sense of sin" is simply a feeling in the mind of the "sinner," operating on very bad information about "God." The concept of "God" assumed by the disobedience theory, is **humanoid,** and quite impossible, even by traditional scholastic standards. All manifestations of sequential moods, attitudes or commands on the part of "God" are necessarily metaphorical projections.

Furthermore, *there is no "other world"* where disobedience will be punished. There are no spirits, nor any other metaphysically separate plane of existence. This material world is all that exists and the behavior we have labeled "spirituality" is its intrinsic potential.

We are not self-originating; there is a "God," by which I mean the source and genetic origin of our existence. But "God" is not a separate immaterial person-entity who gives commands. "God" for us is the *existential material energy* of the things that exist. What we have been traditionally calling "God" is a projection, a metaphor that springs from our **conatus,** the drive to survive, the force of all evolution and desire for continued life and existence. We all share in this energy and our lives come from there. "God" is our source and sustainer, the matrix in which we live and move and have our being.

there is no "sin"

Even the scholastic concept of "Infinite Spirit" cannot co-exist with the finite *humanoid* qualities implied by the word "person" derived from a naïve literalist interpretation of Biblical stories. By "person" the scholastics were referring to abstractions. "God" is not a finite "person." "God" has no "will" as we humans understand the term, has issued no commands, is neither threatened nor insulted by disobedience, and rewards and punishes no one (you may have noticed!).

If there is no such thing as "sin," *a fortiori* there is no original sin ... there was no insult to "God" ... no fall from friendship ... no need for a second "deity" to placate the feelings of an offended "God." Whatever has been handed down on this matter is, at best, allegory and metaphor, and at worst, pure rubbish. Since Judaism's concept of a "personal" God — an ancient pre-scientific myth — is not true, the "personal" element necessary to make human behavior a "sin" is not there either. There can be no "sin" because "God" does not relate to us interpersonally. All laws are promulgated by human society and the claim of divine authorship is a common fiction designed to elicit a willing compliance. These stories are quaint and endearing; we may appreciate their intent and their poetic imagery, but they are fairy tales.

evil

E*vil,* on the other hand, is a term that evokes a broader concept than sin; it does not immediately imply disobedience to a lawgiver-person who has a will and issues commands. "Evil" refers to something contrary to "nature" that portends disastrous consequences beyond human control. It has often been identified with "God's will" in a non-personal sense, i.e., not as articulated in a specific set of commandments but as the very intrinsic structure of reality. What could possibly be the origin of such a concept?

I offer a conjecture. As it became clear to hominids evolving into humans that they could no longer rely on the instincts of organic nature as a guide to behavior, people realized they had to determine *their our own way.* But evolution was slow and incremental and that awareness did not come all at once. I think this emerging realization must have been a source of an anxious insecurity for our primitive ancestors and elicited a confused nostalgia for the time as animals when *behavior was determined by instinct.* Their bodies told them what was "right and wrong."

It is not implausible that humans would tend to cling to the assumption that there was some "natural" way of doing things that for some reason they did not know about, or perhaps forgot, which would bring disaster if violated. That violation, because of the consequences, would be "evil."

Evil, then, in this conception, is a projection that translates to "unnatural." It would assume that there is some objective reality to which human behavior must conform as to an inescapable *standard — even if humans were not aware of it.* It is more like a physical or biological "law" of nature than morality. In a second step it is easy to imagine that just as a parent warns a child not to put her hand in the fire, and if she violates their command she gets burned, so too the natural "punishments" for breaking natural laws can be imagined as contravening a command from a parent-deity. Natural disasters of all kinds, sickness, plagues, earthquakes, even death itself, would then be conceived as the natural outcomes of having violated some "law of nature."

Evil would equate in a broad sense to "natural law" and the projection of a command from a personal parent-deity would generate the notion of "sin" as a derivative. Traditionally it has been claimed that the ten commandments were natural law imperatives re-promulgated by "God's" direct command. So by that theory, "sin" is more fundamentally "evil" compounded by its re-iteration in the "personal" command of the divine law-giver. But in any case, evil is something natural that *I do not know but need to find out,* or things will go bad for me. "God's" commandments, under these circumstances, might actually be considered a boon. They may be thought of as giving us necessary information about hidden realities that otherwise we would not have.

Under this category of "evil," would fall the concept of "fate," mentioned in the previous chapter, in the sense of an impersonal "Way" — the expression of the force of destiny to which everything, gods and men, must bow. "Evil" is whatever fate, "the Way," commands. It is as rigidly predetermined as any other natural requirement, once again in roughly the same category as physical, or biological "laws" whose violation entails disaster ... and moral choice or intent has nothing to do with it. I believe that with the introduction of rational analysis, Greek philosophy *replaced the ancient pre-philosophical notion of "fate" with logic,* and began to separate morality from "nature." Logic, rationality, morality, exercised the background role once performed by "fate;" logic was a natural force to which even "God" was obligated to conform, as we saw above. Thus the rationalization of nature was begun well before Christianity and certainly before the modern era.

The Greek concept of **hamartía** was a corollary of this phenomenon. It is often translated "sin" but the Greeks used it to refer to human behavior that is *an objective distortion of the nature of things* that the perpetrator may not even be aware of. It was a violation of "destiny" understood as "natural law." It referred not to an immoral choice, but rather to a kind of "unnatural act" stemming from some personal inevitability — the source of tragedy — an act which, the perpetrator's innocence notwithstanding, shattered the delicate harmony of nature. Such shattering, depending on the magnitude of the transgression and the "importance" of the people involved, could cause the earth, heavens and seas to be loosed from their moorings and fall back into chaos. Hence it was "evil" that caused and explained natural disasters.

oedipus

The tragedy of Oedipus dramatized by Sophocles in the 5th century before the common era is the most familiar example of this pre-philosophical belief in the role of fate. Killing his father and marrying his mother — despite his total ignorance — was considered a heinous violation of the natural order. A plague of livestock infertility and crop failure was unleashed on Thebes in punishment, *and Oedipus had to go in search of the reasons why.* He discovered his "sin" (*hamartía*) only in that search. But his "sin" was not an immoral choice as we understand the term. It was a kind of triggering of a curse or spell. Behavior conformed or did not conform to "nature" as the ultimate force in the world. "Destiny" did not respond to calls for forgiveness *for it was not human.* Thebes was not punished by the will of the gods. The gods may have carried it out, but they were the mere agents of fate. The gods themselves had to obey fate; they were powerless before it.

This, I submit, was the background mentality that Roman Augustine had internalized from his culture and to which he subordinated the loving "Father" whom Jesus, following the Torah, tried to paint for us. Augustine's Romanized "God," so vividly functional a thousand years later for a terrified Martin Luther, was as determined by the eternal decrees of "destiny" (logic) as Chronos or Zeus. In this scheme of things, *even "God" was bound by the "laws of nature."* That's why Augustine could claim that "God" had to send babies to hell while at the same time "scheming" to devise a redemptive "plan" that would out-smart fate and bring salvation to sinful humankind. The schizoid nature of the divine personality in this conception is clearly manifest. It is thoroughly Greek. This Christian "God" is simply an expanded version of the godlings of the Mediterranean pantheon, prone and impotent before "fate." It is really "fate" that rules the universe; and in its new guise as *logic,* rules "God" as well.

The Judaic "God" of the "Book," very different from the Greco-Roman version, on the other hand, may have been an anthropomorphic fiction, but at least the buck stopped with him. There was no other. There was no "fate" which ruled *Yahweh* ... no Tao or Nature to compete with him, much less to tell him what to do. Hence Job's complaint was completely trumped. Job had no basis for redress, for there was no objective justice to which *Yahweh* had to bow.

The ancient Greeks could not imagine such a "God;" they conceived their mythological deities as "persons" like themselves, subordinate and obedient to fate. When called upon later to characterize the one Judeo-Christian "God" with its Trinity of persons, what they came up with was simply a composite mega-version of the gods of their pantheon. This anthropomorphic deity was also the obedient agent of an objective justice which harnessed his power and ruled his behavior ... only now it was rationality and its *logic,* not fate.

What we are looking at here, I believe, is that very juncture in the foundational infrastructure of Western Civilization where the Greco-Roman Mediterranean mindset expropriated and adapted Judaism to salvage its dying empire and decadent culture. That adaptation is Roman Catholic Christianity. What it salvaged and passed on to us as our legacy is nothing less than *the Roman Empire itself* embedded in "Christian doctrine" — the institutionalized expression of ancient Mediterranean cultural beliefs and values. The Roman Catholic doctrines are the hidden DNA, the genetic code for reproducing the last and most successful of a chain of empires that dominated the western world from the Atlantic Ocean to the Ural Mountains for a thousand years.

So ... here we are: If (1) there is no "sin," because there is no personal "God" who is offended that "his" commandments are disobeyed, and (2) there is no "evil," because there is no implacable, punitive "fate" or "natural law" to which all must conform, it becomes a major problem for our traditional view of the world. For without these criteria, not only do the reasons traditionally given for the importance of Jesus' death evaporate, but it seems to leave us with a much more fundamental question: *how do we decide what is right and wrong?*

pragmatic morality.

I propose we drop the word "evil" altogether along with "sin," and consign them to our verbal museums; they are myths from the past. We construct our morality on a different basis; we don't need fairy tales to tell us how we should live.

Despite all claims that "right and wrong" are derived from moral absolutes deducible from human nature, I believe "right and wrong" are, in fact, and always have been, determined *pragmatically* through the assessment of the *consequences* of human behavior. "Right and wrong" is what works for human beings. What "works" is what enhances human survival and well being over time. There is no other criterion because, like evolution itself, I believe both individual and social morality can be judged only at or toward the end of a series of events that "prove" whether certain behavior is "good" or "bad" for us. What is morally good is what benefits people, what is morally bad is what damages people. None of that can be determined without the accumulation of experience, thoughtful analysis, quiet reflection, thorough discussion and the consensus of the community. A moral code is the end result of a long-term communitarian process. It is a pragmatic morality.

The moral significance of an entire chain of activity only becomes clear over time ... it is emergent. It is something that could not have been known at the beginning of the sequence because it requires seeing how the whole complex works out in practice. Traditional morality is the result of an age old pragmatic test of truth. "Evil," if we must use the term, is what tradition finally decided "does not work." The rest, to my mind, is pure idle speculation. There is no absolute intrinsic evil; and there is no "will of 'God.'" Unlike the animals, we make our own laws, but we are not arbitrary about it. Our laws are all about "what works" for us and the world we care for.

Without the pragmatic test of value, I contend, evil is simply in the mind. The French proverb, *mal y soit qui mal y pense* ("evil is where you think it is") sums it up. It says evil is a subjective perception, mediated by the culture. Virtually any human activity could be considered either evil or good (or neutral) depending on the cultural preferences of the people involved, and therefore such preferences are worthless *as objective determinants*. I deny there are any "absolute" values that can be established *a priori,* in advance, by deduction from absolute and objectively true premises or from a definable "human nature," ... and I *absolutely* deny there are any "commands" issued by a "person-God."

Now, that having been said, I want to be clear that I am not suggesting that cultural factors, however "subjective," should not be taken into account in determining a moral course of action *in practice*. You may consider walking into a Church with your shoes on, for example, to be a perfectly moral and harmless action. But to Muslims not taking off your shoes when you enter a Mosque is sacrilege, and it would be an act of such disrespect *as perceived by those offended* that it enters the moral sphere almost as an "objective" factor. The "pragmatic test of value" in this case necessarily includes taking "subjective" or "relative" cultural values into account. At what point circumstances demand that these taboos ought to be violated is not an easy call. But when they are, it is because we have subjected traditional "morality" to the *pragmatic test* and what benefits people is determined to take priority even over hallowed traditions.

The collective wisdom of the community over time has come to conclusions about what is good for people that must be taken into account. Such inherited determinations, of course, must be reviewed and monitored in the light of the pragmatic test of value. Respect for the ancient solutions embedded in traditional morality forces us to look at value as it emerges in the long run, and not jump to short-term conveniences whose claimed benefits turn out to be ephemeral. To establish morality by a "pragmatic test of value" therefore does not necessarily imply anything myopic, superficial, lax or reckless.

In fact, it may be more demanding than many will be unwilling to entertain. If the test were applied, for example, to our technological innovations and industrial patterns, it seems to me, a great deal of what constitutes modern economic activity might be considered *immoral.* But that is emerging only now, after 200 years of technological and industrial revolution, because it is only now that we see the environmental and societal damage that some of these activities have produced. There was no way we could have known it earlier.

The same may be applied to the military institutions of all the world's nations. By the pragmatic test of value, a case could be made for saying that *the very existence of an organized force trained to kill people, is immoral.* The claim that what has arbitrarily been called a "nation" has the right to create and maintain such a force, is simply a conventional agreement that does not necessarily pass the *pragmatic test.* Many agree and, were conditions conducive, would be willing to call for a morally imposed prohibition against the formation of national armies.

Here's another example: If we look at the question of the *habitual use of tobacco,* smoking for many years was not considered immoral because what it does to the human body was not known. Now, in my opinion, it has become a moral issue, not because of some arcane principle, but solely because of its failure to pass the pragmatic test. Why, therefore, is it not *immoral* to smoke at the levels known to cause serious disease? If "behavior damaging to life and health" for oneself and others is not a criterion for immorality, then I ask, seriously, *what is?*

What the *pragmatic test* does is to substitute a practical criterion for determining right and wrong that is not based on rationalist abstractions, or cultural traditions. Those who complain that it opens the door to a "relative" morality, fail to realize that the *pragmatic test* is also quite capable of establishing absolutes of its own, just as imperious and inflexible as the rationalist model. So in this regard, relativity is not the issue, superstition is. "Figuring out" the morality of a line of behavior based on its value for life is exactly what real people do everyday in the real world, because most situations do not conform to codified laws. Refusing to consider the present moment — act, intention and circumstances — by falling back on some *a priori* rationalized "principle," is an abrogation of responsibility, whether the principle comes from *pragmatism* or philosophy or from religious tradition. And in the practical order this evaluation is essential to a "human" morality. What is truly *in*human, in this view, is the refusal to bring moral care to each *situation* — to respect the uniqueness of the people involved, the responsibilities they are trying to carry and the circumstances in which they find themselves.

In all cases, moral choices should be made based on the analysis of what is best, not on pre-determined rules. For, indeed, I ask, without the clear commands of a personal "God," or "God's" infallible representative, or "God's" inspired word, or the deductions from someone's *a priori* philosophical system, whatever would those rules be based on?

guilt

Guilt, in this view, is simply the disconnect between what you think is right (dependent upon the opinion of the community of your peers) and what you see yourself doing. You can erase your guilt in either of two ways: (1) by changing the behavior that is causing the guilt, thus earning the approval of society ... *or* (2) changing what you think society thinks (or should think) is right. Fundamentally the second option means that right and wrong are not in any way pre-set by nature ... or even the culture, and certainly not by the "will of God." Consistent with the pragmatic view, good and evil are determined in the here-and-now by our perception of the evolution of events and the dynamic assessment of human action-intention-circumstances *always in a social context*. There is no "state of guilt." Genetic, inherited or metaphysical "guilt" is just as much a childhood fantasy as primeval "innocence," and both are derivatives of the obsolete archaic belief in a personal commanding "God" and a "human nature" whose demands are set in stone.

The *perception of yourself as evil,* a phenomenon which has figured so prominently in the religious history of the West, and most recently the source of an endless need for "therapy," is a *non-specific guilt*. It corresponds to what Christians have traditionally called the "state of sin" derived from original sin. In my opinion, it is the equivalent of the nightmare of a child who has mis-interpreted his parents' scolding as *ontologically penetrating*, and self-defining. Unfortunately it has been confirmed and nourished by the doctrine of original sin; it has been given "reality" by the Church, and can no longer be dismissed for the bad dream that it really is. Moral maturity consists precisely in transcending the false identity created by parental disapproval (and the disapproval of parental surrogates). Maturity means the adult assumption of responsibility. *Responsibility* involves determining morality by exercising a running moral assessment — *the pragmatic test* — that evaluates behavior. It constitutes moral goodness and represents an *instantaneous return to "innocence."* But even putting it that way concedes a reality to guilt that it has no right to. *For the mature person is neither guilty nor innocent, but morally responsible and therefore free.* The categories of guilt and innocence disappear along with the infantile mentality that spawned them. Mature persons are "good" not because of their "genetic make-up," their past behavior, the opinions of others or the "forgiveness of 'God,'" but precisely *and only* because they are personally committed, at all times, to discover and do what they perceive is "good."

The doctrine of original sin has functioned to prevent this maturity from occurring. The doctrine actually promotes belief in human moral impotence. It insists on surrender to non-specific guilt created by nothing other than our natural urges and instincts falsely identified as the residue of "Adam's sin." It discourages the assumption of responsibility and generates emotional pathology. It does not pass the pragmatic test. It is of no benefit to people *at all.* It should be publicly denounced and repudiated.

"resident evil"

I have used the word *dualism* to refer to a metaphysical theory that claims there are *two* kinds of distinct "substances" in existence: *spirit and matter.* Each is said to have properties that are diametrically opposed to the other. All phenomena of whatever kind in this universe can be explained by one or the other. I have consistently maintained that this dualism is erroneous, and in the west, because of its undisputed sway over the popular imagination due to religion, distorts the human project.

But there is another kind of dualism also fostered by religion that is much more dangerous. It is a *moral-cosmic theory* that imagines the world ruled by two contending supernatural powers, *good and evil*. I will call it *"cosmic dualism."* This theory entered the Mediterranean by way of Persia before the beginning of the common era and ultimately meshed with Plato's dualist division of "spirit and matter." Matter became associated with the evil power, personified in "Satan," and spirit with the good championed by "God." Since we are made of matter, in this view the evil, and therefore the demonic, *resides within us ... in our very flesh*. It is the origin of the image of "resident evil."

The Genesis account of the fall has been re-interpreted by Christians in these cosmic terms; Christians identified the serpent as "Satan." But the original Jewish authors had no such thing in mind. Commenting on the biblical account Van Rad says:

> The serpent ...in the narrator's mind is scarcely the embodiment of a "demonic" power and certainly not of Satan. ... The mention of the snake here is almost secondary; ... the narrator is obviously anxious to shift the problem as little as possible from man. It is a question of man and *his* guilt; and therefore the narrator has carefully guarded against veiling evil in any way, and therefore as little as possible has he objectified or even personified it as a power coming from without.[95]

But exploring the significance of cosmic dualism is not just an academic exercise of theological or biblical criticism, it has an all-important practical side. For cosmic dualism has produced catastrophic effects among us. It seems there are no limits to the violence that people will employ to protect themselves from what they are convinced is an alien annihilating force against which they have no defense. *Jihads* and holy wars are spawned and justified by the fear of "Satan" and the immanent evil of which he is the source and energy.

A fanciful term I use for this imagined force is "resident evil." It comes from the horror movies and games. The "resident evil" storyline imagines a parasitic "t-virus" capable of turning humans into man-eating zombies. Once infected, humans become agents of the evil force. It evokes fear of an *implacable inhuman enemy embedded in our own flesh.*

Belief in "resident evil" and its Satanic source has not only been used to excuse *unthinkable* behavior like pogroms and genocide, but it also unleashes an unparalleled ferocity — demonic hatred, visceral repugnance, and blind rage. The entire phenomenon represents a self-inflicted

---

95 Von Rad, *op.cit.* p.85

human torment that far exceeds what any other species suffers from the predation, natural disasters, diseases and death that are common to all living things. Self-destructive suicidal and genocidal behavior is absolutely unique to humankind. That fact alone should tell us that the explanation lies in what makes us different from the animals — *our heads.* "Resident evil" is one of our virtual realities. It is a product of the human imagination.

our heads

But it has been traditional to ignore that clue, and to ascribe such behavior to the coercions of an *alien force.* The argument claims that self-destructive behavior itself is sufficient proof of that. After all, who attacks themselves? There must be an enemy out there somewhere that makes us do such things*! But there is no "enemy."* It is exactly this *reification and externalization of "evil"* — the claim that "evil" is an objective reality independent of human imagination and choice — that is one of the principal justifications for human violence. This deflection is functioning even if we attribute "evil" to an innate corruption — a "flaw" — of the human organism stemming from Adam's sin, because such a flaw is *considered an alien reality.* Introduced by the devil, it is not **we** who do evil ... it is the "flaw" — "original sin" — dwelling in us. We are all familiar with that phrase and those sentiments; I am referring to Paul's lament in his letter to the Romans, 7: 15-20. Every version of "resident evil" no matter how simple or how sophisticated, identifies *something foreign, inhuman,* outside and made to reside inside us as the source of all evil.

The Christian doctrine of original sin is, of course, the prime example. Look at what it tells us: the traditional version says that, *at the instigation of the "devil," matter* became corrupt after the fall and no longer obeys the commands of the spirit. *Evil, now, resides in our very flesh.* Our "carnal" lusts and desires, grotesquely deformed from the way "God" created them, refuse to follow the dictates of "spiritual" reason. The body doesn't belong here the way it is. It is *alien* and follows the promptings of "the evil one." That means first of all, it has to be *exposed* for the imposter that it is ... for it comes disguised as ourselves. It has to be treated as hostile ... and subdued, *or it will destroy our "souls."*

Some very committed and knowledgeable Christians took this quite seriously. The great theologian Origen of Alexandria, who died a martyr in 253, actually castrated himself in an attempt to control what he was convinced was "concupiscent evil" resident in his human flesh.

This theory became the accepted wisdom of the western world. If those who believed such things hated the "Resident Evil" in themselves, they necessarily hated it in others. Hence, being "Christian" did not correlate to an appreciative wonder at human diversity around the globe ... rather it meant learning how to mistrust people, especially those of other traditions *who were not aware of the contagion they bore in their flesh.* Thus was human nature demonized by Christian theory, and it opened the door to the denigration, plunder and enslavement of primitive peoples everywhere, identified as "heathen" by their lack of shame about the functions of their bodies and, coincidentally, *by the color of their skin.* Western racism comes from there, and *from nowhere else.*

freud

Then there is a more sophisticated version of "Resident Evil" proposed by Sigmund Freud. He said there was a "death wish" embedded in organic matter which explains human self-destructive suicidal behavior. Freud's hypothesis (outlined in *Beyond the Pleasure Principle*)[96] was that the forces of equilibrium, which might be identified with *entropy* in physics, exert a pull on living organic matter to return to the inanimate state — the pool of inert particles from which all life emerged. Called *thanatos* by Freud, the "death wish" counterbalances *eros* — the "pleasure principle," the drive to live, to reproduce, to preserve the vital integrity of the organism (what Spinoza called **conatus**).

While Freud's theory may be said to correlate, in a general sense, with science, it is not science. It is pure conjecture. But it preserves the core dynamic we found operating in the theory of original sin. *Thanatos* is an *embedded* organic drive, totally subliminal, beyond any human consciousness or control, *responsible for self-destructive behavior.* Self-destructiveness is *entirely* attributable to something *alien* to human free choice. It is an example of the archetype of "Resident Evil."

I find Freud's theory difficult to accept for two reasons. First, if, as he claims, it is the insuppressible "pull" of all living matter to return to the inanimate state, *then every form of life would manifest self-destructive suicidal and genocidal behavior.* And yet none does, only humankind. That is our clue to understanding things correctly. For what does human-

---

[96] Sigmund Freud, *Beyond the Pleasure Principle*, tr Strachey, Bantam Books, NY, 1959 (1919).

kind have that no other living organism possesses? We have *the power to imagine and reference those images with words* to create the virtual worlds that we live in. If there is an explanation for our unique self-mutilating inclinations, it must be *in what we think and choose to do,* not in the quarks and gluons of pre-integrated *material energy.* The problem is not with matter, it is with mind.

The second is that Freud ignores the fact that he discovers *thanatos* in the culturally conditioned environment of early 20ᵗʰ century Europe. There is no attempt on his part to adjust for the influence of the very long history that has molded Western man with Christian doctrine. To fail to take into account such an intense, long-term and universal belief system disregards the influence of social conditioning. What Freud was studying and trying to explain, I am convinced, was the effect on the European psyche of two thousand years of Christian "spiritual" formation based on the doctrine of original sin. If he thought he was looking at the human psyche in some raw pristine state, he was mistaken. In my opinion, he was looking at a vision of things that resulted from Augustine's personal pathologies.

satan

But the most incredible, untenable, and damaging belief is the personification of evil in "Satan," imagined to be the god-like ruler of an evil empire. Not only has the existence and function of Satan, the "Devil," never been repudiated by the Church, it was actually officially reaffirmed in 1992 with the Vatican Catechism.[97] In **##391 to 395** the Catechism speaks about the "fall of the angels" as an event in which Satan and other devils were supposedly spawned. Here are the words of the Catechism:

> 391 Behind the disobedient choice of our first parents lurks a seductive voice, opposed to God, which makes them fall into death out of envy. Scripture and the Church's Tradition see in this being a fallen angel, called "Satan" or the "devil". The Church teaches that Satan was at first a good angel, made by God: "The devil and the other demons were indeed created naturally good by God, but they became evil by their own doing."(IV Lateran Council, 1215)

> 392 Scripture speaks of a sin of these angels. This "fall" consists in the free choice of these created spirits, who radically and irrevocably rejected God and his reign. ...

---

[97] It might not be just coincidental that in the early '90's Cardinal O'Connor of NY performed exorcisms and publicized it.. He adduced fear of the Devil as a "help to maintaining belief in God."

393 It is the irrevocable character of their choice, and not a defect in the infinite divine mercy, that makes the angels' sin unforgivable. ...

394 ... "The reason the Son of God appeared was to destroy the works of the devil." In its consequences the gravest of these works was the mendacious seduction that led man to disobey God.

395 The power of Satan is, nonetheless, not infinite. He is only a creature, powerful from the fact that he is pure spirit, but still a creature. He cannot prevent the building up of God's reign. Although Satan may act in the world out of hatred for God and his kingdom in Christ Jesus, and although his action may cause grave injuries - of a spiritual nature and, indirectly, even of a physical nature - to each man and to society, the action is permitted by divine providence ... . It is a great mystery that providence should permit diabolical activity.[98]

Satan, the "Devil," is claimed to be a "person" of god-like abilities, hell bent on destroying "God's" masterpiece, the human species. He is attended by hordes of minor spirits — devils — who do his bidding. They are all "pure spirit," and therefore invisible, able to change locations with the speed of thought. They were traditionally believed to be responsible for natural disasters and human birth defects[99] as well as human temptations in the form of visions and fantasies that assault the brain.

But even in the Vatican's traditional categories these claims are totally incoherent. Given the supposed resistance of the human body to control by its own "spirit" after the fall, how these "evil spirits" are able to exercise such total control over matter which is not even their own is not explained. Are we to believe that "God" miraculously erased the restraints of nature and even "the effects of original sin" in order to give the devils this transcendent power over nature? The devil and his minions would then become the direct agents of "God," *created for the very purpose of producing evil*. That would obviously make "God" the real author of evil. Absolutely absurd*!* Is no one held accountable for propagating such garbage?

Besides, if these "devils" were damned to hell, how is it they are out and about and able to cause so much mayhem? It could only be with *special divine permission*, making "God," once again, complicit in what they do. Also there is no explanation of how Satan controls these follow-

---

[98] *Vatican Catechism*, Librería Editrice Vaticana, pp. 98-99

[99] In *Contra Julianum*, one of Augustine's "proofs" for Satan's "ownership" of the unbaptized infant were the occurrence of birth defects (which naturally preceded baptism). He never explains, however, why since they are all the possession of Satan all children are not born defective.

ers of his, i.e., what coercion he applies to prevent each of them from going their own way. They are, after all, by definition, "little devils."

The "angelic rebellion" which spawned the Devil and his minions is declared to be an irrevocable rejection of "God." This "irrevocability" is itself a part of this whole inane fantasy. It is traditionally grounded in the metaphysics of a branch of mediaeval theology called "angelology," which claims that each angel's essential being is ratified in a single self-actuating choice. It is outside of time — naturally, because there is no "matter" involved. How these "once-and-for-all" essential spirits can then begin to react to the sequence of temporal events on earth in order to corrupt and seduce humankind is not explained. What we are looking at here is pure hogwash. This Church, simply because of its millennial prestige, can get away with saying anything it wants, no matter how absurd just because it is "traditional." If there is any proof that there is no *providential "God"* to protect us against such imbecilic rubbish, this is it.

The Catechism says, "It is a great mystery that *providence* should permit diabolical activity." Thus, to my mind, does the Roman Church in its official doctrine *blaspheme* by painting "God" as a malevolent trickster who uses "evil" as a plaything to trip people up. If this stupidity were true, it would mean that *any decent human being is morally superior to "God."* It is pure drivel*!* The Church that would *insist* that all this actually occurred, makes a mockery of itself. But that such things are, moreover, declared to be *infallibly true,* in my opinion, borders on the psychotic.[100]

In all these cases "evil" cannot be conquered without divine help. "Original sin" is imagined as an insuperable flaw, dwelling like a parasite in the human organism, a "resident evil," passed on from parents to children *"by propagation, not by imitation"*[101] that cannot be extirpated. With Satan, we have an insidious intelligence, a god-like power, hordes of obedient servants and a fiendish passion that *we cannot defend* against. Only the miraculous power of "God" can save us from these sources of depravity and destruction. So it is no great surprise that the self-serving Roman Church promotes the factual reality of both these theories of "evil." In such a world, evil can come at us at any moment from anywhere, outside

---

[100] There is a traditional warning that says that to deny the existence of Satan is a clear sign of diabolical influence. Definitely a fail-safe mechanism that still rules peoples' lives.

[101] Council of Trent, Session V, June 1546, #3

or inside, and it can "devour" us because we have no ability to withstand its supernatural power. We are utterly dependent on "divine" help against Satan and our own innate degeneracy. The combination — a true one-two punch — is devastating. The only thing we can do without divine help is to try to *eliminate* the source of the evil by exterminating it. *Does this sound like something that might inspire genocide?*

"natural" evil

Whereas the fact is, there is nothing "supernatural," independently personal, or inescapable about evil. Evil does not exist outside of human perception, choice and behavior. Evil is not a "thing" or a person or an open suppurating wound. Evil is a *virtual reality. It is what we do* when we allow our **conatus** — the urge and instinct for self-preservation and self-enhancement — to be improperly directed at things that have nothing to do with our self-preservation. The *terror* that "resident evil" evokes in us is the fear of annihilation ... and the full force of the **conatus** rises to destroy it. *Evil is what we do when we don't know what we're doing.* It has no independent existence whatsoever in any form or fashion. There is no "corrupt matter," there is no Satan, *there is no "resident evil,"* and most certainly there is no "God" who "gives permission" to Satan to torment, punish and test humankind. It is all fairy-tale and ghost stories. Evil is simply human error set in motion by a misinterpretation of what is really threatening to our well being, or conversely, what is really of benefit to us. *What is evil is what does not work* ... it's what we do when we haven't yet figured out what does.[102]

A brief aside. Forty years ago I was in "group therapy." Two of the people in the group were a young married couple, and the young woman was slowly emerging from a severe catatonic breakdown. (Catatonia is a psychosomatic disorder where *the body,* entirely or in part, "shuts down." The victims can actually lose the ability to see, to hear, to speak.) The cause of it, in her case, was "shunning." She belonged to a religious com-

---

[102] There is no intention to deny the immobilizing effect of emotional disorder. Emotional equilibrium is a pschosomatic balance that can be severely disrupted. The intense anxiety that may attend these conditions may yield to the kinds of religious imprecations that have been directed in the past against "resident evil," because that's the symbolism they take on. I am not denying human vulnerability to emotional disturbance or to any number of other "mental" disorders. I am simply saying that none of it has a metaphysical ground. It is all in our heads, and we use our heads to neutralize its power over us as best we can. Prayer may be effective for that purpose.

munity that was so strict about marriage with outsiders that when she married the "wrong kind" of person, the community, including her family, shut her out completely. The effect of this isolation on her fragile psyche was devastating. When I met them, she was doing better, and working hard to understand what had happened to her. It was a revealing experience that I never forgot.

There is no way to explain this phenomenon except by recourse to an imagined *binary* belief system, a form of cosmic dualism. There has to be a "world of light" separate from and opposed to a "world of darkness." The "sinner" falls into "darkness" and the rest of the community must "shun" her to keep the darkness from spreading to them all. It is the psychic equivalent of *annihilation*, and the young woman's psyche "got the message" and reacted accordingly.

the dilemma

If evil exists *independently* of human perception and choice, then there are only two possibilities: there has to be *EITHER* an independent, absolute "*principle* of evil," i.e., a separate Satanic "god" as powerful and original as the "good God" to explain it, *OR* the "evil" world would have to exist *dependent on* "God" himself. Now, the latter scenario is exactly what our tradition has always maintained, because it insists that "God" controls everything. But please notice: *this makes "God" complicit in evil.* Think about it: God has total control ... Satan and his buddies can do nothing without divine permission. *It is totally absurd.*

But if the only "evil" there is, as I claim, comes from a false application of the energies of the **conatus,** then all these absurdities disappear. "Evil," like every other thing we do wrong is a **mistake**, whether inadvertently or maliciously chosen, and reflects a failure to include all the relevant effects of our choices before we choose. As the Jews have always said, the purpose of the Genesis narrative was to say that "evil" is a purely human product. It was not part of "God's" creation before *or after* Adam's sin.

If there is *no* world of damnation into which we descend, then all immoral activity, even the most heinous and tragic, is simply an erroneous choice. It is radically reformable,[103] and the agent of that error does not have to be annihilated or exterminated.

It is interesting that Paul Ricoeur's acclaimed book on evil confines itself to the **symbolism of evil**, it does not tackle the issue of its independent reality.[104] And his pamphlet-sized follow-up volume, is revealingly entitled "*Evil: A problem for philosophy and theology.*" Of course it's a "problem" for people like Ricoeur who are committed to a religious vision. They hide behind their "phenomenology" to avoid directly challenging the cosmic dualist claims that there exists a Satanic Kingdom of Evil, which remains a fundamental belief of all the religions of the book. They address the "psychology of evil," but say nothing about the real existence of cosmic metaphysical personified evil despite its damaging effects. But I have no such loyalties. *There is no "evil," cosmic or resident.* Evil, I say, is in the mind and choices of man; nowhere else. This concurs with the Jewish interpretation of Genesis which we examined in the last chapter. If evil has any abiding presence in the human organism it is through *habit alone.* Habit and repetition (leading perhaps to addiction) is the only "resident evil" there is, and in that form it is a *result of immoral behavior not the cause of it* and it dies with the organism. It lives on in others in only the same ways: *through ideas and habits of thought and practice* — imitation. Evil is a virtual reality. It is a purely human phenomenon, a product of the virtual world that is created *by our heads*. It is a function of our heads ... and only our heads can bring it under control.

the true role of religion

Given this clarification, the role of religion, then, should be turned around 180⁰. Religion should **counteract, not reinforce** the belief in the independent existence of evil.   Religion should *restore to us dominion over what we do.* Religion should once and for all refute the bogus claims that there is any other world, resident evil or damnation. There is nothing that forces us to do what we do not want to do. There is nothing happening in the universe except the innocent, intentionless operations of the natural world. There is neither a "God" helping us, hurting us or testing

---

[103] *Of course we are speaking philosophically here, not psychologically. If someone has, by repeated choices and habit, gotten to the point where change is no longer probable, then it is a question for other disciplines, like psychiatry or the courts. Here philosophy simply declares **there is no ontological "resident evil." "Evil" is what and where we think it is.** And there is no divine help beyond what we do with our heads.*

[104] Paul Ricoeur, *The Symbolism of Evil*, Beacon, 1967.

us, nor is there any independent source of "evil" dedicated to our destruction whether in the form of a corruption of our flesh or a Satanic god-person who "goes about like a roaring lion seeking someone to devour."

Jewish theologians insist that the myth of the Garden was created precisely to say that human evil *is human* — it was not created by "God," it does not antedate humankind. The first three chapters of Genesis, they emphasize, are a ringing declaration of the unmixed goodness of God and his Creation. The serpent is a symbol of human rational calculation and the "selfish intent" is nothing but the natural bent of the **conatus.** From this point of view, Augustine's nightmare that the "first sin" produced a metaphysical transformation of our flesh so profound as to *turn evil back into an original organic condition over which we have **no control***, actually reverses the Genesis authors' intention.

Evil, as Augustine would have it, provides justification for the total dependency of the individual on "supernatural assistance." For him that meant the Roman Church. The correlation here should not be ignored or passed over as coincidental. I am convinced that Augustine elaborated the doctrine of original sin in the completely inhuman form he did — gutting the intention of Genesis and insisting *that unbaptized babies merited eternal torment* — with the clear intention of grounding the absolute indispensability of the Church for salvation. I claim that each side of this correlation implies the other. You can't have an independent "resident evil" without precipitating the search for a "supernatural" mechanism of salvation ... and you cannot have a Church that is "absolutely necessary for salvation" without a belief in a supernatural "evil" from which we need to be "saved."

spinoza and the "inclination to sin"

There is an aspect of the human phenomenon that original sin traditionally addressed in a unique and, for many people, persuasive way. And that is what is called the "inclination" to sin. It was exactly Paul's complaint voiced in Romans which he felt he had to say twice in chapter 7:15-20:

> *I do not understand my own actions. For I do not do what I want, but I do the very thing I hate. Now if I do what I do not want, I agree that the law is good. So then, it is no longer I that do it but sin which dwells within me. ... I can will what is right, but I cannot do it. For I do not do the good I want, but the evil I do not want is what I do.*

Now if I do what I do not want, it is no longer I that do it, but sin which dwells within me.

The denial of responsibility — the equivalent of "the devil made me do it" — is familiar to us all. These notions have become embedded in our subconscious. Paul's expression of personal moral impotence resonated so intimately with Augustine's experience of his own sexual addictions that it provided the foundational dynamic of the latter's *entire theology*. Augustine's thinking about sin, free will, grace, redemption by Christ, the application of that redemption through the Church's sacraments, and of course his "doctrine" of original sin, were all elaborations of that key experience and insight. The death of Christ, according to Augustine, saves us from *ourselves as corrupted by original sin.*

Paul's experience was an intense personal anguish that ended with his lament, "wretched man that I am ... ." That lament has echoed down through the ages for it was not only an experience of Paul and Augustine, but of many others. Augustine explained it as the "effects" of original sin, and many have become convinced that there can be no other reason for such a universal phenomenon. We experience powerful forces roiling within us that seem to have a life of their own and do not obey the commands of our minds. Something must have happened to explain this. If not original sin, then what?

the *conatus*

Baruch Spinoza, a Dutch-born Jewish Philosopher who died in 1677, suggested an answer to that question that did not require an "original sin." He said it was the natural effect of *"being-here"* in God's world. It was nothing else but the innate *instinct for self-preservation* that comes along with every *existent* — every bit and particle of anything that exists. It is the energy of existence, derived from the source of existence itself — "God" — *esse in se subsistens,* "self-subsistent being." He called this force the **conatus** and insisted that it was an energy proportional to the organism or substance it energized. The animals experience and manifest their *conatus* in activities dedicated to feeding, defending and reproducing themselves. The "violent" urges that we humans fight against, he explained, were nothing but complex manifestations of this same urge for self-preservation — survival and life — as it works its way through the complex labyrinth of human social reality, well beyond the simple needs of physical survival. There is nothing sinful or other-worldly about it. It is an irrepressible urge implanted in our bodies and minds. It comes with our physical existence; it is intended to help us stay alive and reproduce our kind. It is involuntary and insistent. It is understandably intense for it is focused on survival. It will derail us, he counseled, if we fail to realize what its purpose is, and how to control the objects toward which it will spontaneously direct itself if left without the guidance of reason and decision. He wrote his greatest book, *Ethics,* in order to make clear the simple wisdom behind controlling human behavior. Don't fight nature, he said; nature is good. Work with it and direct it to its proper ends ... *but don't think for a minute that there's anything "evil" about you or the "God" from whom you and your drives emanated.*

Let's look at an example. You perceive that what someone has said insults you. Your culture has interpreted your place in the virtual world of society *as essential to your survival.* Your **conatus**, therefore, springs immediately to defend your bruised "ego" with all the energy meant to guarantee survival. No one is threatening your life, and yet it *feels* that way. In Spinoza's system, the first thing you do is *to recognize* that the intensity is the knee-jerk reaction of the **conatus** and you will be neither shocked nor surprised by it. But you do not let your culture tell your **conatus** what is essential for survival. You bring your *rational mind* to bear on it. **You** make the decision. The *conatus* is not intelligent and the culture may be immoral. Alone or together, they cannot be trusted to determine the correct moral reaction. Our instincts reflect the force of organic life, they are good ... their intensity is even a reflection of the divine existential *necessity to exist* and therefore it has a mystical dimension ... *but they are not inerrant guides to behavior.*

So what's the value of this approach? The first is that you stop thinking you are "evil" for having intense reactions. And then, secondly, you do not assume that *the moral content of your reaction* accurately reflects reality — it comes from a cultural pre-set and must be evaluated. Spinoza claims that most people do not question their spontaneous feelings. They allow the culture to focus the aim of the **conatus** *and it can fool them because it feels like it's coming from themselves.* And so it runs their lives. Having some way of subordinating our spontaneous reactions to our conscious judgment goes a long way to bringing some measure of rationality to what we do ... it makes for "solutions" rather than exacerbations of problems.

You may say, "what's the difference ... whether the offending urgency comes from the **conatus** or original sin, I still have a major battle to get my feelings under control." The emotional struggle might be the same, but the deeper issue is not. It is the question of *relationship*. Original sin nourishes a false self-perception that that we are evil. It undermines the possibility of a *positive relationship* to myself and the source of my existence; in other words, it poisons ~~faith~~ and religion. It places the focus on correct behavior alone and creates a dependency relationship on "moral miracles" provided by an intervening "saving" deity. Spinoza's *Ethics* is really a challenge, if not a contradiction, to all that.

the cultural imprint of "doctrine"

Religious doctrine, over time, imprints itself on the culture. "Eternal verities" that are accepted as absolutely true eventually become part of the horizon, assumed and unchallenged. Give it enough time, and the culture shapes the personalities of those that live in its virtual world. It is simply not possible that people born into a particular culture can extract themselves from its control without a considerable amount of challenging experience and the hard laborious effort both intellectual and moral to change themselves. And even then, their success depends upon inserting themselves into another virtual *gestalt* — another cultural community — that substitutes for the original. We are the products of the virtual worlds that our collective heads have conjured to make sense out of a random universe. The doctrine of original sin has penetrated the inner psychic reality of the people who are formed in western culture and reversing its defining power is not an easy task. The almost negligible impact of Spinoza's rational approach to ethics, despite the admission on all sides of its wisdom and humanity, is proof. People still consider themselves innately corrupt.[105]

---

[105] Even a Christian as modern and "progressive" as Chris Hedges repeatedly ascribes an innate moral corruption to human nature. This is clearly on display in his book directed against the "new atheists,:" *When Atheism Becomes Religion*, Free Press, NY, 2006.

II: REDEMPTION

Paul the apostle is credited with writing 14 letters found in the New Testament. They constituted the foundational theology of the new-born Christian movement. What is most striking is that in all those letters Paul cited Jesus' words only once. This was a strange way to treat the "divine" founder of the religion he was promoting. What explains it?

The answer is not very complicated. It was not Jesus' life and message that interested Paul, but his *death*. It wasn't as Jesus, the rabbi, but as "Christ," the messiah, the chosen of God, that this man became significant for Paul. This pronounced yaw from Jesus' own description of his mission has a source and a reason. For Paul, the Pharisee-theologian, the death and suffering of the messiah, as *"foretold by the scriptures,"* saved us.

Christianity's defining phrase that came out of apostolic times was: *"Christ died for our sins."* Christians say it means "redemption;" and redemption says in one word what *existence* is all about. Redemption was accomplished by the death of Christ. We ourselves are so accustomed to the phrase that we cannot imagine Christianity without it.

But the remarkable thing is that "redemption" stands *in stark contrast to what Jesus thought he was doing.* Jesus' message, discernible in his words as reported in the gospels, was about life and how to live it. He saw his own death as a faithful expression of that — *a lived example of the commitments he invited his listeners to make.* Jewish Christian thinkers like Paul, however, were more focused on the *fact that Jesus died and what that meant to "God,"* than how he lived and *what that means for us.* For Paul, Jesus' life was secondary to the transcendent significance of his death. For Jesus, in contrast, his death was secondary to the kind of life he encouraged his followers to lead.

The original witnesses to Jesus' life were convinced he was the Jewish messiah. In the wake of his death, therefore, they had to find a way to explain what seemed to the world like a complete disaster. They searched the scriptures and came to the stunning conclusion that Jesus' execution by the Roman occupational forces was not a defeat at all; it was actually the triumphant climax of his mission. Everything Jesus ever said was seen by Christians as pale in comparison with the ultimate gift that "saved" us — his death on the cross. Today, some might call it "spin." But for the first generation of Christians, both Jewish and Greek, it explained everything.

Two thousand years of Christian theology may be characterized very succinctly as the attempt to justify the claim that "Christ died for our sins." *and not* that Jesus, a Jewish rabbi, tried to change a world of Imperial plunder by proclaiming the "reign of justice" of Judaism's "loving Father" ... *and failed.* The Church's fatal embrace of the absurd "doctrine of original sin" was made possible by the fact that *Jesus' death and not his life or teaching* came to completely dominate western Christian thinking on who Jesus was and why he was significant. "Original sin," a myth taken as a literal historical event, helped to turn Jesus' death into a myth — a theological projection — that taken literally makes no sense. As literal fact, "redemption" diverted Christianity from Jesus' message. This had far reaching consequences. The inability to focus exclusively on what Jesus was calling for, set up the conditions that led to the expropriation and co-optation of Christianity by the Roman Empire 350 years later. The rest of this chapter will be yet another attempt to understand what actually happened in the transition from Jesus message to Christianity and what that means for us.

the "contract"

For his Jewish followers, the death of Jesus represented a completely reversed understanding of the traditional Covenant — the contract — between Israel and Yahweh. The contract established at Sinai was understood to be a *quid pro quo* between Israel and Yahweh. The mainstream understanding was that Israel promised to promote Yahweh's "glory" through cultic observance and mandated behavior, and in turn Yahweh would grant Israel economic prosperity and victory over its enemies.

Jesus saw things in a different light altogether. For him, the Jewish "contract" with "God" was a *relationship of imitative love* not unlike that between a loving Father and his children. While his view would have been considered somewhat out of the mainstream, it was far from an innovation. It had deep roots in ancient Judaism. Doubts about the standard view of a *quid pro quo* contract can be seen emerging very early, as early as the Book of Job in the 6th century bce. Job was a just man who suffered horrible torments ranging from the loss of his wealth and family to the deterioration of his body. He complained that he was complying with his side of the deal, so why was he suffering? Job's questioning was more than one man's bitterness about an excess of bad luck ... *it called into question the very meaning of the contract itself and the reliability of Yahweh.*

These misgivings deepened through the reflections of the prophets in the same century as they agonized over the breakdown of the Jewish state, the utter destruction of the Northern Kingdom and the decimation of the population of Judah in the aftermath of the humiliating exile of 587 bce. How could such disasters be permitted by a powerful "God" who was supposedly holding up his side of the bargain?

As they wrestled with a disaster of no less proportions, it began to dawn on Jesus' friends that the Jewish relationship to *Yahweh* was not as they had thought. They came to realize *that the Covenant was not about national or personal prosperity in exchange for obedience or moral right-eousness. The covenant was simply about love.* Rather than a business deal it was more like a marriage — *to have and to hold ... for better or worse.* And just as Job decided to love God and accept that "God" loved him despite the overwhelming losses he was made to suffer, Jesus' death represented the ultimate sign that the relationship to "God" was simply loving trust — no matter the context. There was no guarantee of recompense whatsoever, and the clearest way to announce that realization definitively was to say that the symbol of our relationship to "God" was Jesus' death on the cross. With such a vision, "resurrection" was an afterthought.

resurrection

Jesus' close companions scoured the scriptures looking for answers after his humiliating defeat. This process is recapitulated in the episode of the two followers on the road to Emmaus whose "eyes were opened." The stranger who had joined them explained "all that the prophets had spoken ... that the messiah should suffer these things and so enter into his glory."[106] The gospels clearly are suggesting that this was the paradigm of the "discovery" that spawned Christianity, first as a radical sect within Judaism and then later as a religion in its own right. The core of the discovery was that as far as the relationship with "God" was concerned, worldly success was not the issue. This insight was foreshadowed in Job

---

[106] Luke 24:13-35

and the prophets. Suffering was somehow *redemptive.* Here is Isaiah ch.53:

> *Surely he has borne our griefs, and carried our sorrows: yet we es-teemed him stricken, smitten of God, and afflicted.*
>
> *But he was wounded for our transgressions, he was bruised for our iniq-uities: upon him was the chastisement that made us whole; and with his stripes we are healed.*[107]

It is not hard to imagine the powerful impact those words would have on Jesus' followers, who were intense believing Jews, convinced that their leader was the messiah but who had just been executed in the most de-humanizing manner possible.

I believe that the trope of resurrection was generated indirectly and *by implication.* That means it was secondary, derivative — an inference con-structed out of wispy experiences like that on the road to Emmaus where a mysterious stranger temporarily joins a conversation, makes important insightful contributions and suddenly disappears. Post resurrection ac-counts in the gospels are all of that surreal quality, including Paul's vision on the road to Damascus. I believe they *are symbolic extrapolations* of the new understanding that "the death of Christ was the redemption of Israel." They were the articulation of that insight *in symbolic form.* Resur-rection was its primary symbol ... *but it was only a symbol.* The core of the insight was that Jesus loved his "Father" to the end; the "resurrection" was a metaphor for his Father's loving reciprocation.

According to the interpretation I am suggesting here, Jesus' "resurrec-tion," by moving from being a *symbol* of the "victory" of the cross, to being taken as the **literal reward** for his fidelity, fatally diluted Job's profound insight: *that the contract, the relationship to "God," has nothing whatsoev-er to do with prosperity of any kind* — in this world or the next. In the drama written by the Apostles, as I read it, Jesus' resurrection is similar to the rewards showered on Job for being faithful through his ordeal. Both events are *an anti-climax.* Job loved "God" *even though there was no answer.* Job's "story" should have ended there. *That there was no an-swer,* **is the answer.** The rewards meant nothing; for despite them, Job had to die at the end of his life anyway and would have to face the same challenge all over again *and this time without any hope of reward.* Jesus

---

[107] Isaiah 53:4-5 (RSV)

died trusting his "Father;" that in itself was his reward. It was a victory of the human spirit. **Loving trust is its own reward**. There is no other answer. Quiet as it's kept, **that is the answer to life.** And if it is the answer to life, then it is all the "redemption" we should ever expect.

According to traditional Christian belief, Jesus died *knowing* he would rise. To my mind that is not credible. If it were true, then I ask: what was all that anguish and isolation painted so vividly for us by the gospels ... *pure midrash ... or worse, theater?* I'm sorry. It seems obvious to me that those who wrote the gospels believed what they wrote, *whether it happened exactly that way or not*. If the narrative in any way faithfully reflects events, then Jesus died *not knowing* he would rise again. *His trust was all he had*. What drove his fidelity was not the hope of resurrection but *his relationship to his Father*. Anything less would be a betrayal of his message. After eschewing "reward" in his preaching, would he have had recourse to it himself? *Even if he did literally rise, that was not the point*; and we should disregard it, or the clear lines of his vision become blurred. He knew his Father loved him; that was enough. That was all he had; and please notice: *that's all any of us have.*

Literal resurrection introduces a false clarity. The recognition that Jesus' death was "the answer," did not in itself supply any clear outcome. It was hope ... an *amorphous unspecified trust* based on knowing a loving Father. *The only thing secure — the only thing known for sure — was the relationship*. I claim the metaphor of resurrection was an "as if" ... just like all metaphors. It was saying something like, "We should think of Jesus' death *'as if'* it were followed by his resurrection." In this form it serves to evoke a relational response, not identify an actual, literal *quid pro quo* reality. *There are no quid pro quo's in life. The old "contract" was an illusion.* The relational response can only be trust. Jesus leads us to trust our loving "Father" — for us, the source of our existence — even unto death. Our trust takes wings from his trust. That's how he "saves" us. That's all he could do for us. That's all any of us can do for one another.

Did the apostles intentionally "design" this symbol to mystify others about resurrection? No, I am saying the symbol sprang into their heads *spontaneously* because "victory over death" implies it. I believe the fantasy that dominates the minds of all of us that have lost the person we loved most in life — *that they can't really be dead* — took over their collective imagination. This is not a stretch of the imagination, by any means; it is a common phenomenon. Widows have this experience all the time. His close friends saw signs of his living presence everywhere. Combine an intense worshipful love for an extraordinarily good person ... with a religious tradition that had apocalyptic expectations, and resurrection becomes more than a spontaneous fantasy, *it becomes a conviction*. Nobody was "lying." But his followers were caught in the thralls of a collective illusion based on scriptural proofs, mechanisms of grieving and eerie coincidences like that on the road to Emmaus. They also had a deep insight into the integrity of Jesus' vision of the meaning of the Torah — the *sh'ma Ishrael* that Jews nailed to the doorposts of their homes and hung from the tassels of their garments: *"love Yahweh your God with your whole heart and soul and strength ... and your neighbor as yourself."*

To return to the point that initiated this reflection, Jesus' exclusive focus on "life in this world" was irreparably deflected by the emphasis on the resurrection. We follow our leaders wherever they go. Instead of following Jesus into the kind of integrity and resistance to oppression that led to his death at the hands of the Roman overlords, Christians became focused on following Jesus into the other world where it was supposed he was alive and living with his "Father." It dovetailed with the Greek obsession with immortality. This confluence of factors resulted in an historical trajectory for Christianity that led it further and further away from a just life on earth and toward a reward of eternal life in another world. The Romans then, exploited the shift to help them keep their moribund empire running.

"redemption"

The Latin word *redemptio* was used to translate the Hebrew word *kopher* and Greek *lytron*. The word's religious usage did not originate with the Christian application to the death of Christ, but was rather a traditional Jewish term that came from Temple worship. The Jews, like most ancient peoples, had a custom of dedicating the first fruits of the fields and the first born of humans and animals for sacrifice to "God." It was customary to "save" them from literally being sacrificed, by buying them back (redeeming them) for a certain price (in money or produce) paid to the priests.[108]

By Jesus' time the term simply meant "to save" and had come to be applied to actions of "God's" powerful salvation of Israel from its enemies, and so it was the term used to describe the anticipated re-establishment of Israel's prosperity by the messiah. *The term, therefore, simply evoked the work of the messiah.* It was of generic significance. The two on the road to Emmaus lamented the defeat of Jesus, whom they had hoped "would redeem Israel." It was a phrase-label for the messiah. What they learn from their mysterious companion is that Jesus' death is exactly that redemption.

"Jesus died" ... but why *"for our sins"*? What does "sin" have to do with messianic restoration?

"Sin" for the Jews was not primarily a personal moral lapse as much as "infidelity to the contract," the failure to hold up one's side of a business deal. The Jews were already thoroughly convinced that their political degradation could only be due to their infidelity to the contract — *"sin"* — because *Yahweh* was faithful and that left only one possibility. If "sin" was the exclusive reason for Jewish abasement, then the *triumph of the messiah* had to mean the conquest and elimination of "sin" both by forgiveness and by a restoration of a right relationship with "God." This was exactly what his followers concluded about Jesus, but it was not Jesus' claim as recorded in the gospels. It was the semantic result of a reasoning process.

Even though Jesus did not claim to be the messiah, the theme and significance of Isaiah 53 were relevant to his message. It is hard to imagine that he would not have discussed it often with his closest friends and followers. In other words, what was dawning on all of them at that time was a new understanding of the meaning of the "contract," and a definitive movement away from the traditional interpretation that it meant prosperity

---

[108] Gigot, F. (1911). "Redemption in the Old Testament". In *The Catholic Encyclopedia*. New York: Robert Appleton Company. Retrieved May 21, 2011 from New Advent: http://www.newadvent.org/cathen/12681a.htm

in exchange for moral righteousness and ritual compliance. Isaiah 53, following Job, was a critical piece in that reappraisal.

I maintain that the coining of the phrase "Jesus Christ died for our sins" was actually a **verbal** tag drawn from the logic of the evolving Jewish understanding of the contract using the traditional words of the prophetic text. It was an identifier, not an explanatory notion. It is simply saying, "Jesus is the messiah, the man in Isaiah 53." It included a *vague sense* drawn from the tradition of animal sacrifice that the sufferings of the messiah somehow atoned for sin. There was no more intelligible depth to the phrase than that. It was poetry; and like all poetry its significance evaporates if it is analyzed scientifically and applied literally ... *and over time that is exactly what happened.*

So, here is my reading: The statement "Jesus died for our sins" was a **verbal formula** — traditional terminology that conferred a messianic identity on Jesus. It was the conclusion of a chain of reasoning. It was the application to Jesus of an interpretation of sacred texts. He himself never made any such claim.

So can we still use the phrase "Jesus died for our sins" in any literal or metaphysical sense? *No we cannot.* Then how does Jesus death "save" humankind? Answering that question as posed assumes that we have an obligation to preserve the traditional intent of the phrase in some way. We do not. For me, the cross is an extraordinary symbol of the poignant reality of the human condition. I personally feel that Jesus' trust in *Yahweh,* despite his brutal treatment by the Roman authorities and the defeat of his anti-imperial project, stands as a triumphant display of resistance in a world of where exploitation and repressive control had become systemic. No death can be more bitter for human beings than knowing that they are being dehumanized by fellow humans in an attempt to make them despicable in the eyes of others. I believe that to assert the value of human life, even in the teeth of death's most intolerable forms, is a challenge we all have to be prepared to face. For me, the death of Jesus speaks to the human condition as does no other. I believe this is the unique source of the perennial appeal of Christianity and why I consider myself a follower of Jesus. Jesus died with us, like us, and, by proclaiming that our humanity was once and for all beyond the torturers' reach, *for us.*

But there is no literal *supernatural* salvation reversing a "death penalty" imposed by original sin. Also, without original sin there are no grounds for the claim that evil is permanent and resident in human nature, justifying the insistence that the cross is the *only* valid symbol of man's treatment by man. The whole scenario smacks of a self-fulfilling prophesy and an indirect justification for fatalism. More fundamentally, to even suggest that there is something "redemptive" in the fact of physical suffering and death, especially a sadistic political execution like that of Jesus, or that the spilling of blood literally pleases or appeases "God," is repugnant, destructive, meaningless and impossible. These are poetic images drawn from the animal sacrifices of old. They do not function literally in the real world. *They were metaphors even for Jewish Jesus two thousand years ago* and may be used by us only if their figurative character is clearly acknowledged.

conclusion: what to do with "original sin"

"Original sin" is the fulcrum of the western Christian theological system. And while it is, in terms of the inner logic of the western theory of redemption, the most indispensable link, in terms of credibility it is the weakest. If it falls, the whole construct falls with it. It is not only unbelievable as formulated, it seems clearly damaging to our psycho-social and spiritual development. I see no "remedy" short of total repudiation. The doctrine as traditionally understood must be publicly acknowledged as erroneous and destructive, and it must be publicly rejected. Abandonment by neglect is not enough. Any literal interpretation of the fall must be totally abandoned and the story of Adam and Eve must be returned to the way the Jews originally meant it: as an allegory of origins.

On the issues raised in this chapter — evil and redemption — even Catholic theologians less inclined to wholesale rejection of the notion of "original sin" than I am, call for the doctrine to be "rethought" based on experience, science and history.[109]

Is there any chance of that happening? By way of an answer, I would like to cite another paragraph from the *Catholic Catechism* of 1992. It is the "official" teaching of the Roman Catholic magisterium on the question of the salvation of infants who die without baptism. On p.321, paragraph 1261 of the *Catechism* says:

---

[109] Wiley, *op.cit*, p.207

As regards children who have died without Baptism, the Church can only entrust them to the mercy of God, [and] ... hope that there is a way of salvation for children who have died without Baptism.

We will remember that Augustine's theology declared baptism necessary for salvation, and infants who died without it, therefore, *necessarily went to hell.* The unbelievable stupidity of such a position has been traditionally circumvented by a "theory" that "God" would put such infants in a place called "limbo," where they would not suffer, but would also not be granted access to the beatific vision. The paragraph quoted from the Catechism makes no reference to "limbo" but still says the Church is at a loss to explain how children who die without Baptism can be saved. The Church may not draw Augustine's absurd conclusions but it still stubbornly clings to his equally absurd premises.

Paragraph 1261 is an example of the refusal to acknowledge theological untenability. When theories like Augustine's are obviously impossible, that in itself should be sufficient proof that those theories are false. A theory that requires that "God" send innocent infants to hell is *utterly absurd.* It doesn't need a "limbo" corrective, *it needs to be trashed* along with the premises from which it was drawn ... *end of story!* It is a complete contradiction of Jesus' "loving father." The inability of the Roman Catholic Church to acknowledge that, is evidence of an irrationality so dense as to suggest an ulterior motivation. But ... what could be so important to the Church that it would be willing to betray the reputation of "God," rather than abandon? Dr.Wiley identifies a possible motive:

... the doctrine of original sin located salvation exclusively in Christ and the church, **fostering a dismissal of salvific possibilities in other religious traditions**. Religious denigrating of non-Christians, when allied with political power, becomes religious imperialism.[110]

By insisting on its exclusive role in the channeling of salvation the Church prioritizes its own power. The call of Vatican II for religious dialog was *exactly* a recognition of the "salvific possibilities in other religious traditions." Dr.Wiley identifies original sin as directly inimical to such an ecumenical effort and calls for a long overdue "review."

The next chapter explores what seriously pursuing such a dialog might entail.

---

[110] *ibid.*, p. 208, *emphasis mine.* Cf also endnote #7, p.264

Chapter VI

to whom shall we go?
doctrinal truth and spirituality in an age of dialog.[111]

PART I: CHRISTIAN DOCTRINE

We live in an age of religious dialog. Great distances separate us from our brothers and sisters of other traditions, and we want to dialog in a spirit of ecumenism encouraged by the 2nd Vatican Council. But in another sense, maybe a sense we are not comfortable admitting, we want to dialog because we may feel we have something to learn. Our own tradition may have lost something of its sustaining power; perhaps it no longer provides the answers it once did. We dialog because we are searching.

Raimundo Panikkar is a Roman Catholic theologian and a Hindu mystic. In thirty-odd books over his lifetime as an academic, he has pursued what he sees as a key area of religious correspondence: the Hindu-based mysticism of India, and the Western **apophatic tradition** of spirituality and theology.[112] While "apophatic" spirituality is known only by a minority among Catholics, it has always been recognized as authentically Christian and even as the highest to which one can aspire. But, by its very definition, it is "speechless." That is what apophatic means — a speechlessness based on the premise that "God" is unknowable. Hindu mysticism is similarly based on the unknowability of Brahman.

It is a Christian axiom that we cannot know God. And so the very apex of Christianity's spirituality stands in sharp contrast with Catholicism's perennial claims to be in solid possession of the "truth" about "God" and

---

[111] Much of the material in this chapter was written in 1999 and self-published in a booklet of the same title.

[112] Cf Raimundo Panikkar, *The Silence of God*, Orbis, 1990.

the human relationship to "God." The ramifications of this paradox have yet to be fully explored; but on the very face of it, the fact that we cannot know "God" must have a profound effect on the way traditional doctrine is articulated and how we relate to other traditions. Specifically it will require a sharp turn away from the *reification of religious symbols* — taking doctrine literally — and from our claim to have "objective" knowledge of the Godhead. This provides a firm ground for sincere dialog. What we don't know we can only speak of "as throiugh a glass, darkly." It calls for a *thorough critique* of Christian doctrine and with it a new appreciation of *metaphor* as a vehicle for religious expression.

I believe moving in that direction is a natural process, an evolution, ultimately impossible to contain, which in our times has already begun. The role this reflection will play, hopefully, will be to prepare our side of a long-overdue conversation. Perhaps at a later time we can steep ourselves in Hindu mysticism and follow Panikkar to the mountaintop. But first we need to purify ourselves, make ourselves apt partners. To this end I offer a *critique of Christian doctrine* and a *proposal for a new spirituality* based on the re-interpretation of doctrine as metaphor.

the roman church and the roman empire

Mainstream western spirituality has been prevented from evolving in this direction because it has been bound up inextricably with a doctrinal complex driven by a *non-religious agenda*. That agenda is the need to make the Roman Catholic Church indispensable. That indispensability was itself the by-product of the need of the Roman Empire to justify its conquests and universal control on hieratic, religious grounds. Catholicism was the state religion of the Roman Empire.

The Roman Empire was a theocracy. Long before the advent of Christianity, a major source of its credibility derived from the ancient belief that the gods "blessed" those who were destined to rule. Heaven had determined that the world was to be ruled by Rome; its very wealth and power proved that it was chosen for this role. That the "divinely established Church" and the "Holy Roman Empire" were one and the same thing was essential to that projection. It not only justified the plunder of foreign lands, but it was the source of internal stability — it elicited the voluntary compliance of citizen and slave alike.

This conjunction produced a set of Christian beliefs that are major problems for dialog. "Problem doctrines" are what I call those that, in support of Roman authority, attempt to make Christianity the exclusive path to God. Such exclusivity, as Dr.Wiley quoted in the last chapter pointed out, undermines respect for others' religions. It makes sincere dialog impossible. But the critique I propose not only says that these doctrines are "problems" for inter-religious dialog. It goes further. It says they became doctrines in order to accommodate Christianity to the Greco-Roman mindset and its socio-political structures. Later, Christianity became a part of the Imperial state apparatus and served to justify the Empire's theocratic pretensions.

From that point forward the Church had an institutional investment in the advancement of the political interests of Rome. It was an attachment that through the centuries has solidified the Church's pursuit of institutional wealth and political power. The odor of theocracy has dogged the Church's reputation ever since.

The point I want to emphasize is that *these doctrines were not part of the message of Jesus; they evolved as presently articulated from the needs of social survival for the Christian community in ancient Mediterranean culture.* They reflected the religious, moral and authority values of the Roman Empire.

Of the two historical phases of this institutional modification the first permitted the expansion and integration of Christianity into the Hellenic world. It involved the Christian appropriation of Greek religious categories, initially the imagery of the mystery religions. It imagined Jesus like the god-man Dionysus who died and rose again from the dead, and whose *initiates* believed they would gain eternal life by immersing themselves in the *mysteries* of their god.[113] Subsequently the educated upper

---

[113]From the *Encyclopedia Brittanica, 1979, vol 15: 615,* "The Study of Religion:" *"... in the early empire, the mystery cults, ranging from the Eleusinian mysteries of Greece to those of the Anatolian Cybele and the Persian Mithra, together with philosophically based religions such as Neoplatonism and Stoicism, had the greatest vitality."* cf also Edith Hamilton, *Mythology,* 1942, Warner Books, p.55ff. For an extensive overview in the Western tradition of the ancient myths of gods that die and rise again, see Sir James Frazier, *The New Golden Bough,* revised and edited by Theodore Gaster, 1959, Mentor Books, Part IV p 339ff. In this respect cf. also Justin, Martyr. Justin was so clearly aware of the parallelism between Dionysus and Jesus that he ascribed the Dionysan myth and cult to "demons" who, knowing of the messiah's character from OT prophesies, *created the fable and cult of Dionysus to pre-empt belief in Jesus!* Justin, Martyr, *First Apology* ch 54

class hierarchy took control of discipline and ritual and separated itself from the laity. Christian theology in this phase also marched in step with the philosophical preferences of the upper class. Vestiges of an earlier alliance with stoicism were abandoned in favor of a two-world ritualized Platonism. It incorporated Greek philosophical notions like the "One" of Plato with his craftsman *Demiourgos,* called *"Logos"* by Philo."[114] In this phase, the basic profile of Hellenic Christianity emerged in such foundational doctrines as the divinity of Jesus and his cosmic role in creation and redemption. But, however early they may have become part of Christianity's self-definition, it's clear that these foundational doctrines *were not part of Jesus' own message.* We will come back to this.

The second phase was the stabilization of doctrine and authority structures at the time of Christianity's legalization by the emperor Constantine. Freely evolving developments were frozen in place and Christianity's ultimate promotion to official status followed in the next generation. The earlier adaptations to Greco-Roman customs made Christianity a reasonable choice for Rome, and whatever did not already dovetail with the needs of the theocratic state were quickly put in place. This stage produced the *homoousion*[115] of Nicaea in 325, and 75 years later with Augustine, the doctrines of original sin, sacramental efficacy and the universal necessity of the church. This more or less final formulation responded to the new requirements for credibility and control, made inevitable as the Church became identified with the destiny of Rome.

It's not insignificant that as the inner reality of the Church changed so did its name. The Roman Imperial Church was no longer simply "Christian" as it had been for centuries; it became "Catholic," from the Greek, meaning "universal," derived from its status as the Official Religion of the Empire that ruled the entire known world. "Catholic" was an Imperial Title, and "Roman" identified for later ages which empire it was.

---

[114]A Christian "apology" called "Athenagoras' Plea" included in Cyril Richardson, *Early Christian Fathers,* Macmillan, NY 1979, pp.291-340, has some of the clearest examples of Platonic concepts and terminology as applied to Christian beliefs as will be found anywhere among the ancient documents. The date of the piece is given by Richardson as 176-177CE.

[115]A.H.M.Jones, *Constantine and the Conversion of Europe,* Collier NY 1962, p 135ff. A Greek word meaning "of the same substance". It was the term resolved upon at the Council of Nicea 325 CE to establish the definitive separation of "orthodox" christology from Arianism, which was thereby condemned. It is reproduced in the Creed at mass as "of the same substance as the Father".

Throughout its history Christianity has shown itself to be fundamentally intolerant of other religions. This intolerance is, I believe, a corollary of the absolutist intent embedded in the "problem doctrines" to which I've been alluding. We must remember that prior to their elevation by Constantine, Christians suffered persecution for their rebellious refusal to worship the symbols of Roman authority. It was idolatry to call Rome and the emperor "divine." But afterward, as the official religion of the Empire, the "Roman Catholic" Church blithely commandeered the Roman legions to persecute and eliminate its rivals, heretics and schismatics, with the instruments of state power. It's difficult to imagine that the intolerant Imperial Catholic Church that emerged from the Constantinian era was the same persecuted community that in the days after Jesus' death preached a radical universalism:

> And Peter opened his mouth and said: "Truly I perceive that "God" shows no partiality, but in every nation any one who fears "God" and does what is right is acceptable." (Acts 10: 34-35)

The influence of Rome was determinative. The *symbiosis* between Christianity and the Roman Empire molded the church and Christian doctrine in inauthentic ways. It is this inauthenticity that I believe is an obstacle to dialog.

apophatic mysticism

Apophatic" is a Greek term that has been used traditionally to mean that "God" cannot be described in human terms. "God" is ineffable because "God" is unknowable. This mysterious feature has always accompanied religious experience. It is attested to as far back as religious records exist and accounts for the strange metaphors used to describe it. Jacob said it was like wrestling with an angel, Moses heard a voice that came out of a burning bush.

In scholastic philosophical terms, this characteristic has been "explained" by the view that "God" is Being itself. "God's" essence contains all essences and so is totally beyond the grasp of the human intellect which knows only by distinguishing essences. We cannot "know" "God" the way we know other things. We know *that* "God" is, but not *what* "he" is. All we know is *what "God" is not*. Aquinas says:

> The Gift of Understanding ... creates a mind purified of illusions like those that attribute anthropomorphic qualities to "God" ... it also corresponds to an *imperfect vision* of God, in which even though we may not see what "God" is, we *do* see what he is *not*.

> And in this life the accuracy of our knowledge of "God" is directly proportional to how well we understand that he exceeds anything our mind can conceive.[116]

The mystics have always used "apophatic" descriptors — terminology that highlights the unknowability of "God." Moses called "God" *Yahweh*, which means "the Nameless One," who had only an empty tent to indicate his imageless residence among his people. Elijah experienced *Yahweh* as "a gentle breeze;"[117] John of the Cross met his Beloved "on a dark night," and described what he met as *"nada"* — nothing. And two anonymous Christian monks 600 years apart found "God" in a "cloud of unknowing."[118] There are also a host of mystics from other traditions who attest to the experience in similar terms. Some Buddhists speak of *sunyata*, "emptiness" as the essential experience. But this is beyond our scope.

Apophatic mysticism came to have a significant impact on European thought and spirituality in the middle ages, when a treatise was discovered called *Theología Mýstica*, whose author claimed to be Dionysius "the Areopagite" a contemporary of Paul, mentioned in Acts chapter 17. "Pseudo Dionysius" as he came to be known, insisted on the way of *negation* not only for theology but for spiritual development as well. *All we know is what "God" is not.* The ineffability of "God" was intrinsic to divine transcendence and a guide to spirituality.

Mediaeval theology attempted to synthesize mystical experience with traditional philosophy. "God's" Hebrew name, *Yahweh*, had been translated into Latin by Jerome in the 4th century as "I am Who am," and was erroneously interpreted to have the sophisticated philosophical meaning of the scholastic definition given above and to reflect the teachings of Dionysius. But while the exegesis may have been faulty, the essential insight was not. For it is now the accepted interpretation that the name *Yahweh* signifies, *"I am who I am,"* or in other words, *"I'm not telling you my name."*[119] It meant the "one true God" would in no way be subject to the

---

[116]St Thomas Aquinas, *Summa Theologíae*, 2-2, 8, 7 (tr.and emphasis mine)

[117]1 Kings, 19: 11-12

[118]The two I'm referring to are the anonymous Syriac monk of the 6th century known as Pseudo-Dionysius, and the unknown author of the 14th century English correspondence called *The Cloud of Unknowing*.

[119]cf Even Philo, (20 BCE-50 CE) understood "Yahweh" as a refusal to "be named": see "on the Change of Names", (11) *The Works of Philo*, trans. by C.D.Yonge, Hendrickson, 1993, p. 342. In this respect see also Justin Martyr, *First Apology* ch 10 and ch 61.

magical control of the ritual incantations that used the names of the gods in order to gain power over them. It was a way of saying that by being "nameless," "God" is absolutely transcendent. It therefore corresponds in all important respects to the intent of the philosophical formulations of the schoolmen *and* the doctrines of pseudo Dionysius. These teachings are traditional in Christianity, even though rarely offered to the masses by the pastoral programs of the church.

The early Christians, from as far back as documents attest, even to the new testament writings of "John" and "Paul", have been in fundamental agreement on the basic outlines of apophatic mystical doctrine within a Christian world-view. It could be summed up briefly along the following lines:

- *"God is unknowable ("no one has ever seen God, ..." Jn1).*
- *We, and all of humanity, grope in darkness; we did not realize that God is already intimately present to us because in him we live and move and have our being. (Acts 17)*
- *It was Jesus of Nazareth who called us to understand that God is a "loving Father" and to trust "him."*
- *We heard him, and so came to trust God as he did.*

Christianity's fundamental reference was to the *experience* of God, and Paul's vision on the road to Damascus was its symbol — he experienced God in the risen Jesus. It was only later, after the intrusion of Roman Imperial requirements, that Christianity became the Ideological Guardian and Moral Whip of the political state. Only then did the afterlife come to function as a Skinnerian mechanism of behavioral control, the reward or punishment of an autocratic "God" who was the image and likeness of the Emperor of Rome, the symbol and underpinning of political authority. This association with state authority and public morality — what may be called the theocratic imperative — has been a feature Christianity ever since. The Roman Catholic Church is still convinced that one of its primary responsibilities is to set public policy.

monasteries

A significant change occurred subsequent to Nicaea — *monasticism* appeared, perhaps a response of Christians wishing to flee the religious laxity that came in the wake of Imperial favor. This phenomenon was quickly absorbed into what had become a two tiered church — a division between an upper-class elite and the ordinary people. It also provided a way to quarantine those contemplative "dreamers" who posed a threat to the social control which theocratic Rome required of its religious arm. Mystical experience came to be associated almost exclusively with monastic life. It evolved into the post-mediaeval position that mystical experience is extraordinary — something special and apart from normal Christian life, not required for salvation, therefore not for everyone and better avoided unless accompanied by proper hierarchical supervision and guidance. But even while doing everything possible to insulate the ordinary people from these doctrines, *the church never denied them*, nor did it ever refuse to admit that they were the apex of Christian life. For those interested in a bridge to others and to the future, I believe that this is the key to continuity and dialog.

The church marginalized mystical doctrine by confining it to the monasteries — along with other socially disquieting practices like voluntary poverty, shared manual labor and communitarianism. Mystical spirituality refers to and encourages the pursuit of a *self-justifying experience* of "God." As such, it is politically threatening to the authorities for it contains the seeds of religious autonomy.

Mystical spirituality also exhibits common characteristics across creedal boundaries. It is obviously not exclusive to Christianity and so it stands as living witness to a religious universality. That challenges the well-known key doctrinal positions of official ecclesiastical ideology which claim exclusivity for the Christian religion. And it shouldn't come as a complete surprise that those key doctrinal positions are the very ones that we've been calling "problem doctrines." Besides establishing a supposed indispensability to the Empire's version of Christianity, these doctrines contradict the manifest universality of mystical experience and its clear implication of an unconditioned, open access to God.

If we accept what Paul says in Acts 17, that "God"

Made from one every nation of human beings to live on the face of the earth ... that they should seek God in the hope that they might grope after him and find him. Yet he is not far from each one of us for 'In him we live and move and have our being'...

then we believe "God" is in an immediate, immanent, permanent, generative relationship with all human beings. It suggests that *there is no exclusive expression of that relationship.* This is the necessary ground of all sincere religious dialog — the key to whatever unity may be achievable among us — that all religions are equally authentic expressions of our sense of the sacred and our search for an authentic response.

Our plan here will be to allow this assumption to guide us through an historical analysis of the Christian doctrines which necessarily appear *inauthentic* by contrast.

the "problem" doctrines

The "problem doctrines" are those that make Christianity and its ecclesiastical institutions the privileged, that is to say, unique, indispensable, *sine qua non* condition for access to God. The "necessity of Christianity" developed in a political context. While it may not be true that Rome actually selected these "problem" doctrines for Christianity, it seems fairly clear that had they not been in place the Christian church would not have been chosen as the official religion of the Empire. The salient point here is that these doctrines were ultimately chosen, promoted, re-shaped if necessary, and finally *set in stone* by the Roman imperial requirements, not by the apostles, much less by Jesus.

They form the core of Catholic ideology. They explain the significance of the death of Jesus as a unique salvific event in *cosmological* terms. They constitute a consistent, interrelated group; they are totally dependent on one another as articulated. The overall purport of these doctrines is to establish that everyone *is obligated* to connect with the Roman Catholic Church as the exclusive agent, conduit and repository of the redemptive death of Jesus. Thus under Rome, faith in Jesus and in the Roman Church was made indispensable — the only path to salvation.

The doctrinal group includes *original sin* which, parenthetically, defined human mortality as unnatural and necessitated the *sacrificial* redemption of Jesus on the cross. Then the *homoousion* of Nicaea establishing the *co-equal Divinity of Christ* with "God" the Father, crediting Jesus with sufficient ontological status to make divine restitution for Adam's sin possible; it also coincidentally assured the Roman Empire that assuming a new religion would not mean any diminution of the "divine" status it had come to enjoy with the gods of Olympus.[120] Then, the indispensability of the Church as the continuation of Christ's presence and saving work through the ministry of the sacraments comes to mean *extra ecclesiam nulla salus*, "outside the church there is no salvation." The foundation of this is the *ex opere operato* (automatic) function of the sacraments, the *indelible character* of priesthood, and of course, *apostolic authority* whose apex is *papal infallibility*. *Christian mission* is the inevitable implication of all this — to carry the message of *the need for salvation* through Christianity to all.

Let's examine them at more depth.

(1) original sin

This was the subject of the two previous chapters. What follows here are a few additional remarks.

> In Christian doctrine, [original sin is] the condition of sin into which each human being is born. ... [but] the Old Testament says nothing about the transmission of hereditary sin to the entire human race. In the Gospels also there are no more than allusions to the fall of man and universal sin. ...[121]

and from the *New Catholic Catechism* published by the Vatican in 1992:

> #403ff: ... he (Adam) has transmitted to us a sin with which we are all born afflicted, a sin which is the "death of the soul." How did the sin of Adam become the sin of all his descendants? ... the transmission of original sin is a mystery that we cannot fully understand.

While many ancient religions contained some myth to account for the presence of evil in the world, the version that came to be accepted as official in the Christian scheme of things was, consonant with its Greco-Roman origins, characteristically *cosmological and metaphysical*. In the philosophically charged Hellenic atmosphere of the first centuries of our era, the story of Adam's sin of disobedience lost the allegorical quality of the original Hebrew fable. In Greek Christian hands the story was taken scientifically literal and was used to explain death, suffering, hard labor, and all manner of human weakness and defect. In particular, the alleged

---

[120]Rome was a theocracy long before its partnership with Christianity. Cf. *Encyclopedia Brittanica, 1979*, "Roman Religion" vol.15 p.1062

[121]*Encyclopedia Brittanica*, 1979, Micropedia, vol VII "original sin"

connection between *original sin and death* became the linch-pin of the western theory of redemption.[122]

The implication of this connection between death and sin has been a transcendent dynamic in western life, namely, that death is the result of sin and therefore *not a natural condition.* In very broad terms, it served to give sacred sanction to a linear rather than cyclical view of life, an already emerging feature of Greek rationalism. That meant that *our mortal condition, since it was not "natural," was radically reformable.* This belief that *death is conquerable* has had a profound effect on work, medical science and technology, economic systems and other characteristics of western culture that make it very different from other cultures.

In this regard, we also can't ignore the *millenarist and potentially totalitarian* dimension of the Christian vision. Remember that the earliest versions of Christianity were apocalyptic, following a view that many feel was Jesus' own. Paul's letters to the Thessalonians were motivated in part by a need to correct an over-enthusiastic anticipation of what they thought was the imminent return of Christ, *the parousía.*

This literalist identification of the "Kingdom of God" with the Church has been a persistent Christian fantasy through the centuries, and it has indirectly encouraged genocidal attitudes toward those people — the non-baptized — whose very existence was interpreted as postponing the *parousía.* Such a belief has functioned to support pogroms of Jews, crusades against infidels and heretics, religious wars, the forced conversion of dark skinned "heathens," and of course, the "holy" Inquisition.

the psychological dimension

From a psychological perspective, there is another significant human tragedy created by this doctrine. "Original sin" declares that *human beings are born corrupt* and that ordinary manifestations of our natural state like work, sickness, old age, death, even human sexuality and other natural urges, are signs of an unnatural condition. This "corruption" supposed-

---

[122] This classic theory of redemption is a western phenomenon concocted by Augustine. In the Eastern Church, while they still speak of "buying back humanity from Satan," it is clearly metaphorical. The purpose of Jesus' life and death for the Orthodox is rather *theosis,* to allow humanklind "to be divinized." Cf Joroslav Pelikan, *The Christian Tradition, vol 2, The Spirit of Eastern Christendom (600-1700),* U.of Chicago Press, 1974, pp 10 -12 on divinization and pp.181-183 on Augustine's contrasting focus on original sin.

ly caused by original sin has also affected all of nature. I believe it's at the root of our characteristic western alienation.[123] I find it hard to imagine any proposition more damaging to the process of moral and social maturation. It seems almost inevitable that we who were formed in these beliefs would feel we live in a corrupt and hostile natural universe, which includes our own bodies.

The doctrine of original sin was given a curious *sexual* emphasis by Augustine. "Carnal lust," officially known as *concupiscence,* was considered a weakness, a defect of human nature. But Augustine, a Manichaean before his conversion to Christianity, went even further by teaching that *coitus* physically transmitted original sin, generating another human being with the disease. Original sin produced *concupiscence* which inclined human beings to copulate, thus continuing the cycle. The sense of guilt generated by the doctrine continues to function in the general culture, now namelessly, long after many Christians have officially rejected it. Sigmund Freud's focus on repressed sexuality as the source of both a guilty self-hatred and an energy "sublimated" into creativity, adumbrated its ancient ideological roots while incisively uncovering its profound role in the development of western civilization.[124]

(2) the divinity of Jesus

"Divinity" in the polytheist world of Greco-Roman antiquity was applied extensively to every extraordinary manifestation of life. It had none of the awesome exclusivity of the Jewish monotheistic concept of *Yahweh*. To be a "god" in the Hellenic sense was very different from being "God" in the Jewish sense. Even Barnabas and Paul were hailed as gods because they healed (Acts14). The very existence of the doctrine of the divinity of Jesus is a clear indication that Christianity, as we know it, could not possibly have been originally articulated in Jewish terms, and is therefore not anything that Jesus himself would have taught. Jesus, like all Jews, was a strict monotheist. Jesus even avoided being called "messiah" much less "God."

---

[123]cf Max Weber, *The Protestant Ethic and the Spirit of Capitalism,* tr. Talcott Parsons, Scribners, NY 1958, p.105
[124]cf Sigmund Freud, *Civilization and Its Discontents,* tr. James Strachey W.W.Norton, NY 1961 p.83 and passim.

... on no occasion and in no circumstances did Jesus ever claim, directly or indirectly, that he was the Messiah. This is admitted today by every serious scholar of the New Testament, even by those who are inclined to be conservative.[125]

In spite of this, those who wrote the gospel accounts were all convinced that Jesus was the Jewish messiah; Jesus' later Greek "divinity" was a derivative of his messiahship. The doctrine of the *divinity* of Jesus was the "translation" into Hellenic categories of the "messiah-wisdom" imagery of Jewish tradition that the early Christian community used to describe Jesus. The Greek parallels were the Dionysus mysteries celebrating the death of a god-man who came back to life, and Plato's creative *Demiourgos*, what Philo called the *Logos*.

It's very revealing to what a remarkable degree this early Christian imagery, especially the identification of the *Logos* with Jesus as the Jewish messiah, resembled the Hellenic syncretism taught by Philo of Alexandria, a contemporary Jewish philosopher. Philo anticipated Christian formulations by calling the Greek *Logos* "the first-begotten Son of God."[126] Once transplanted into the Mediterranean world, *"messiah"* developed over time from a *Logos-Dionysus divinity* to the full-blown philosophical over-kill, the *homoousion*, at the Council of Nicaea.

hellenists and judaizers

It is instructive to view these early developments of Hellenic Christianity against the background of the Jewish monotheism from which it emerged. There seems little doubt that the controversy recorded in Acts and referred to in Galatians between the two factions of early Christians the "judaizers" and the "hellenizers," was both bitter and determinative. My conjecture, while I have only indirect historical testimony to sustain it, is that the divisions between the two Christian factions went far deeper than "meat sacrificed to idols," discussed and resolved at the Council of Jerusalem as recorded in Acts. I believe what was at stake was the incipient Hellenic articulation of the *divinity of Jesus*. I base my opinion on the following:

The Jews themselves, around the time of Jesus, were divided on the theological issues that affected their traditional belief in Yahweh. Mem-

---

[125]Albert Nolan O.P., *Jesus before Christianity*, 1976, Orbis, p.107
[126]L.H. Feldman, "Philo of Alexandria", *Encyclopedia Brittanica*, 1979, vol 14 p.246

bers of the Alexandrian Greek-speaking Jewish community, like Philo, had for some time been exploring a syncretistic convergence with Platonism on the concept of God. But there were problems for the Alexandrian approach, since the Greek "One" also generated a *"Logos."* Philo considered the *Logos* an intermediate divinity between "God" and man which he syncretized with the OT "Wisdom" and the "Word of God."[127] Not all Jews would accept this. Feldman says that Philo's views "were considered too dangerous" by the Palestinian Jews.[128] At any rate, it's clear that the authorities in Jerusalem attempted to maintain ideological control over the *diaspora,* to the point of arresting and punishing "heretics" like the Christians who held views similar to Philo's. Would such measures have been applied for anything less than "blasphemy"? Apparently this was the very activity Saul the Pharisee (later *Paul*) was engaged in when he had his own "mystical experience" on the road to Damascus.

What's most important for our discussion is that as Christianity began to penetrate Greco-Roman society, it became clear that the Greek-speaking converts not only believed Jesus to be the messiah (whatever that might have meant to them), but also, accustomed to many gods *and many offspring of divine-human liaisons*, tended as a matter of course to ascribe "divinity" to Jesus. Jesus "divinity" was conceptualized in the terms suggested by Philo. Unquestionably, such ideas would have been anathema to many Jews. The Acts of the Apostles records event after event where diaspora Jews used or provoked violence in an attempt to prevent what they saw as *blasphemy* from being propagated in their area. There must have been *Jewish Christians* who shared this same sense of outrage.[129]

There is ample evidence that the controversy over "Hellenism" within the very early church was not put to rest by the "Council of Jerusalem" recorded in Acts. After examining the textual and archeological evidence in his book on the primacy of Peter,[130] it is Oscar Cullmann's opinion that the Neronian persecution, in which it was traditionally believed Peter and Paul were executed, was instigated by "Judaizing" Christians in an attempt to put an end to the "Hellenizing" of the faith. I find it very hard to

---

[127] ibid.
[128] ibld., p.247.
[129] By *Jewish Christians* I mean followers of Jesus who, like him, were Jews.
[130]Oscar Cullmann, *Peter: Disciple, Apostle, Martyr*, Philadelphia, PA: Westminster, 1953

believe that, if Cullmann's theory is correct, such extreme measures were motivated merely by an argument over *kosher food*. What was at stake, in my opinion, was unstated — the "divinity" of Jesus.

This would also corroborate the view that Christianity separated from its Jewish origins and took the Greek road very early. It's my conjecture that the controversy over the "divinity" of Jesus was a key element in that separation, an issue that was not fully resolved until the Council of Nicaea. I would suggest that at the root of this was the confrontation of two apparently contrary religious image-systems: Hebrew monotheism and Greek polytheism which were elegantly merged in the hybrid, undeniably Neo-Platonist, "doctrine" of the Trinity. By resolving the *kind of divinity* that was to be imputed to Jesus, the Council of Nicaea finally brought the controversy to a close in 325, a mere dozen years after Constantine's decriminalization of Christianity. It seems historically indisputable that what came to be known as Arianism, the belief that Jesus was divine but of *secondary status to "God" the Father* (stock platonic and Philonic characterization of the *"Logos"*), had represented an acceptable if not original Christological current[131] until Nicaea, where it was condemned and systematically eliminated by the Empire thereafter along with its literature.

---

[131]Herbert A.Musurillo, tr.and ed., *The Fathers of the Primitive Church*, Mentor-Omega 1966 p.183. In speaking of Hippolytus of Rome (died as a martyr 235 CE) Musurillo says, *"he adopted a **subordinationism** that was very similar to the positions of Origin, Justin [Martyr] and Methodius. He believed that the Logos or Son of "God" is a divine spirit, who is somehow **subject to** the Father, in whose divinity he shares."* In this respect see also Cyril Richardson op.cit, Justin Martyr, "First Apology" ch 63 p 284f. *"Those who identify the Son and the Father are condemned..."* Justin, here calls the Son the *First-Begotton Son of God* which was also Philo's phraseology.

On this same question, Bihlmeyer-Teuchle, *Church History, Vol I,, Christian Antiquity*, p.158 refers to the Trinitarian doctrines of Justin, Hippolytus, Tertullian and Origen and says they were, *"... following the theosophy of Philo, the Alexandrian Jew. ... These views subordinated the Son to the Father because they questioned the eternity of his subsistence as a Person and made his generation not so much an eternal and necessary act as a temporal and free act of God. ... this so-called Subordinationism did no particular harm at the time; ...* and on p.246f.: *"Quite a few ... held that He [the Son] was more or less subordinate to the Father. ... some thought that his generation was somehow related to the creation of the world and thus denied his eternity or at least the eternity of His subsistence as a person; others considered the Son less than the Father because they believed that He had received His divine being from the Father and hence His divinity was derived from the Father (Origen)."* The authors admit that Arianism in fact differed little from this subordinationism except insofar as *"Arius espoused it deliberately and taught it boldly."* p.247

It appears that what Arius did was simply to insist on the logically consistent philosophical implications of the "subordinationism" that had been believed *"ubique, semper, ab omnibus."* A sub-

constantine and nicaea

The Emperor's personal intervention resolved the issue of the divine status of Jesus. Nicaea was a *tour de force* of Constantine himself who played a key role in calling the Council and in settling its deliberations. As attested to explicitly by Eusebius of Caesarea, an early historian of the church and himself a participating bishop at the Council, the choice of the term *homoousion was Constantine's himself*. It was accepted reluctantly by the Fathers even though Constantine was not a baptized Christian.[132] In the final analysis, the decision to eradicate Arianism was his.[133]

This association of dogmatic preference with political power gives rise to the suspicion that there were reasons, perhaps short-range political, perhaps connected with Roman ideological underpinnings, that were factors in the Nicean decision. In any case, it was clearly unacceptable that a "divine" empire and emperor could be associated with a religion founded and mediated by a mere mortal or even a "god" of secondary status. A religion founded by "God" in Person can have no rivals; and an empire that "*in hoc signo vincet*" has little need of further justification for conquest and control. Rome's political interests were indeed well served by the existence of the doctrine of *homoousion*.

But aside from the possible political motivation of the Roman State, the doctrine of the *homoousion* dove-tailed neatly with the cosmological theories of redemption by Christ.

(3) christian soteriology

There was more than one theory of *Redemption* generated in the first three centuries, and they shared the characteristic *cosmological* dimension to which I've referred. The one that predominated in the West for over 1500 years was elaborated by Augustine in the 5th century and re-

---

ordinate "Son", said Arius, was a created being, therefore while possibly "divine", was not "God" in the same sense as the Father.

[132]Jones, op.cit. p.135, says, "... *Constantine dropped his bombshell on the Council. He suggested the relation of the Son to the Father might be expressed by the word "homoousios," of one essence.* **Eusebius is explicit that the Emperor himself proposed this term,** ..." We should remember that Constantine, personally, did not accept Christianity and was not baptized until he was on his deathbed. The word *homoousios* was accepted reluctantly by the assembled bishops even though previously the term had been condemned.

[133]ibid.

fined by Anselm of Canterbury in the 12th. It can be called the *Theory of Restitution.*

An earlier theory focused on the notion of "ransom from slavery" or from "captivity by Satan." It's the Christian origin of the use of the words "redeem," "redemption," and "redeemer." Redeem means "to buy back." The imagery was that of a humanity *enslaved* to sin (and death), captive to and *owned by Satan* who required payment to liberate the human race. Satan's *"price"* was the death of Jesus. The demand was met and humanity was freed. The "slavery" motif is obviously an expressive image, all too familiar in the ancient Mediterranean world.

But the importance accorded to Satan in this story is evidence of Persian influence, which saw the world divided between a "God" of light and a "God" of darkness. It was characteristic of a post-exilic Judaism historically impacted by Mesopotamian culture. So we can say with some justification that the earliest cosmological theories of redemption were probably of Jewish theological inspiration. But notice there is an inescapable odor of "fable" about this version — as if "God" could ever be "forced" to negotiate with the devil. The *motif* is also found in the book of Job. This property would not be expected to sit well with the rationalist "scientists" of the Greek tradition. It's not surprising that later it came to be considered a mere catechetical device, an allegory, and discarded in favor of other theories, like the *Theory of Restitution*, which were understood as literally and scientifically true.

What needed interpretation was *Jesus' death.* According to early Church interpretations as recorded in the gospels, it was foretold by him, and also by the prophets like the Songs of the Servant of Yahweh in the book of Isaiah (ch.53) applied to the future messiah. Isaiah said the messiah would suffer and thus "save" us. There was no further explanation. It was left for later generations to figure out "why"? What could possibly account for this bizarre "plan" of God that turned expectations for a political messiah upside down, and seemed to make death a victory? If Jesus was, in Isaiah's words, like a "lamb led to the slaughter," wouldn't it imply that his death, like the lamb slain at Passover, was a "sacrifice"?

sacrifice

"Sacrifice" was a concept common to all the religions of the ancient world — a ritual performed for the purposes of securing the favor of the gods and turning away their wrath. Though it was also established practice among the Jews, routine animal sacrifice figured prominently on a much greater scale in Mediterranean religious life. As the Hellenic culture came to characterize the Christian community, this familiar feature became central in the Christian theology of redemption. The death of Jesus *understood as a sacrifice* offered to God, was a theory that became "fact" in Roman times when the Catholic Church was expected to play the role in public life that once belonged to the traditional cults of the Olympic gods. Sacrifice offered to secure favorable outcomes to state endeavors, for celebrations and other public functions was a well established routine.

This reinforced the interpretation that Jesus' death was a *payment to "God"* for the supposed insult that came from the disobedience of Adam. That "God" could be angry and needed to be placated with gifts to deter him from punishing people was an anthropomorphism of such antiquity and universal acceptance that it was never challenged. In the hands of the sophisticated theologians of the Roman world, like Augustine, the concept of *laesa majestas* functioned in the background to explain it.

laesa majestas

Laesa majestas (Eng. *lese majesty*) was a legal category that outlawed any slight to the dignity of the ruler. Adam's disobedience, to no less a personage than the Divinity itself, was considered a crime of the greatest magnitude, deserving the death penalty, not because of what he did, but because of whom he offended by doing it. *Laesa majestas* meant that what would have otherwise been a *minor offense*, (eating a forbidden fruit, for example) became a *major crime* because of the importance ("majesty") of the individual offended.

"Majesty" derived directly from "God's" own inner reality; even "God" could not waive the requirements of *laesa majestas*. In terms that would be familiar to the Roman legal mind-set, the sin of Adam, a sin of *lese majesty,* was a *tort* that needed to be set right by an adequate restitution. This legally inescapable condition-of-guilt was then resolved by the death of Jesus which was considered the restitution required. And Jesus' death had the necessary juridical weight to accomplish this cosmic repair because he was *homoousios*, co-equal to the Father.

This juridical fiction inevitably welded the Christian doctrine of "God" to the autocracy of the times. The fine points of Roman legal thinking came to be lost on future generations. The doctrine eventually resulted in what became a *monster-God*,[134] feared by the trembling masses of Western Europe. For what kind of "God" but a *monster* would require the death of his own Son to assuage his injured dignity? It was exactly the same kind of "God" that could condemn without remorse unbaptized new-born babies to hell, as Augustine believed. So besides directly contradicting Ezekiel's command that *"it shall no longer be said among you that children shall be punished for the sins of their parents" (Ez 18)*, this view of things also disregards what Jesus taught: that Yahweh is like a "loving Father" who knows how to give good things to his children ... that Yahweh cherishes every sparrow that falls from the sky and clothes even the wildflowers with the splendor of kings.

(4) *extra ecclesiam nulla salus*

If *lese majesty* is the background for the western Christian theory of salvation developed by Augustine and Anselm, the doctrines of original sin, sacramental efficacy and the powers conferred by holy orders comprise the foreground pieces that rationalize the death of Jesus, on the one hand, and the indispensability of the church on the other. All these elements conspire to transfer the death of Jesus from the moral to the cosmic plane, and in the process similarly reinterpret his message, life, and therefore ours. Henceforth, evil — now identified as an *ontological, not moral, condition*, a disease we catch at birth — could be cured *only* by the ontological medication of the sacraments, which were the "death-of-Christ" in dosable form. The rituals of the Church incrementally reestablished the benevolent relationship between "God" and humankind throughout the moments and phases of people's lives. It was *not* a moral process of personal transformation; it had become an automatic, almost physical function, the application of medicaments that worked whether the minister was worthy or not and even in the absence of full motivation on the part of the recipient. This is what is meant by the term *ex opere operato*: the sacraments accomplish their work by the very fact that they are performed.

The automatic "hydraulic" efficacy of the sacramental ritual was in every way the counterpart of the cosmological "salvation" accomplished by

---

[134]cf Gerald Bullett, from *The English Mystics,* cited and reproduced in *A Quaker Reader,* Pendle Hill Publications, Wallingford, PA 1962, pp. 32-38

the death of Christ "atoning for the sin of Adam." Because of Jesus' *ontological status* as co-equal "God," his sacrifice was infallible, it could not be rejected, salvation was automatically accomplished once and for all. The sacraments, as the ritual re-enactment of that salvific event, functioned with a similar infallibility. The Church as the minister and repository of the sacraments was therefore absolutely indispensable for all, everywhere and at all times. "Outside the church there is no salvation," *extra ecclesiam nulla salus,* is simply an inescapable corollary of the infallible function of redemption applied by sacramental ritual.

It was a development of the 5th century with Augustine and very different from the early "mystery" perspective that created the sacraments. That fact might serve someday as a basis for its serious review and renewal. Taken as *symbolic* rituals that use mimetic effect to motivate spirituality, the sacraments can provide sense of solidarity with Jesus and the community of his followers without evoking a "hydraulic" definition of holiness as "grace infused automatically."

The doctrines regarding the *powers reserved to holy orders* correlate directly with the *ex opere operato* function of the sacraments — one implies the other. *Apostolic Authority,* and of course, *papal infallibility* are adjuncts necessary to preserve intact an institution whose absolute and immutable necessity has been established by the definitive redemption by Christ. Nothing can possibly change in this arrangement without causing an implosive contradiction. All of these "necessities" are inescapably linked to the theory of Redemption. And the Augustinian theory of Redemption is squarely based on the doctrine of original sin.

(5) apostolic succession and rome

Alongside the development of the cosmological theory of redemption, the doctrine of the *indispensability of the church* has been maintained by claims that divine authority was directly conferred on it by Jesus himself in a doctrine known as *Apostolic Succession.* The divine origin of the church is found in the gospels in the context of the investiture of Peter with leadership by Jesus (Mt 16). Statements that Peter had supreme ecclesiastical authority given to him directly by Jesus are found *only* in the gospel of Matthew, one of the latest of the canonical gospels.

Peter was the most important member of the early community to embrace the change from a Judaic to a Hellenic emphasis. Paul was its ideologue and spokesman, but Peter's commitment gave it legitimacy and authority because he held leadership among the original twelve. Given the fact that Acts seems to assume the primacy of James in Jerusalem earlier (Acts 15), we can conclude that the transition of Christian focus to the Hellenic world, symbolized by Matthew's declaration of the "primacy" of Peter, was well under way or perhaps already accomplished by the time that late gospel was written (90 CE). It appears that the passage indicating Jesus himself chose Peter as the foundation stone of his community of followers was written by the leaders of the "Hellenists" for the specific purpose of establishing that the ascendancy of Hellenistic Christianity was the "will of God."

I'm suggesting that the Hellenism that came to dominate Christian doctrine was the result of a conscious plan on the part of the progressive organizers of the early church. Following a path adumbrated by Jesus himself who related equally to gentile or Jew, they saw the future of Christianity in the universalism of the Roman world, not with the Jews. The Jews had not embraced Jesus as messiah and Christians thought they had been clearly rejected by "God" as a result. That was considered proven by the destruction of Jerusalem in 70 ce, a full generation after the birth of the Christian movement.

In their enthusiasm for this universal vision, Christians were willing to radically reinterpret their own ancient Jewish traditions. In the process, Jewish categories had to be translated. Christianity as we have received it from the original organizers, was the result of these creative missionary efforts. Christian doctrine is a Hellenistic metaphor, so to speak, for the message and significance of Jesus as Jewish messiah.

Such efforts pose obstacles for us as we try to get behind the cultural translations and rediscover the original message and personality of Jesus. But these missionary techniques are also an invitation to repeat, in our times, what is fundamental to the process of religious renewal, *metaphorization*.

metaphorization

The early Christians were Jews who not only furnished Hellenistic translations for Jesus' message, but also reinterpreted their own ancient Jewish covenant with Yahweh *as* an allegory — effectively, a *narrative metaphor*. This is very significant. They reinterpreted the entire Jewish tradition and turned it into a *predictive symbol*, "prophesy." This methodology had already been explored extensively by Philo of Alexandria, who used allegory to syncretize the Jewish scriptures with Platonic and Stoic philosophy. Philo was a beacon to the early Christian community. Using these new exegetical criteria, Christians came to understand the election of Israel to be a simple foreshadowing of the "more definitive" Christian arrangement which included the entire human race. *The Jewish people became a metaphor for all humanity understood as included in the Church.* The *literalness* of the Jews being "God's" chosen people was discarded, but *the tradition* of a contractual relationship between "God" and people was preserved. The "old contract" became *a symbol* of a larger perspective. I wonder if we can appreciate how earth-shattering this must have been for orthodox Jews of the 1st Century. It fundamentally wiped out any claim of Jewish exceptionalism. It is no wonder few Jews accepted Christianity.

The point of this study is to propose that, if we want to dialog *sincerely* with other traditions, we should try to do the same thing with these "problem doctrines" to make dialog impossible ... *we should take them as metaphor.* The next section will attempt to reinterpret Christian doctrine as *metaphor* for a new understanding of "the sacred."

PART II: A CHRISTIAN SPIRITUALITY FOR OUR TIMES

Without an analysis of these issues, we can't responsibly perform the difficult work of separating "the baby from the bathwater." The purpose of this separation is to liberate and energize ourselves for the search for "God" which perhaps we have abandoned. Our intention is the rebuilding of what seems broken: a religiosity for our times but perhaps in ways different from our Christian traditions, once considered absolutes. Those ancient formulations have lost their significance for us; for they were once wedded to conditions and accepted wisdoms that no longer exist. We don't believe, for example, like the ancients did, that death is unnatural and therefore a *prima facie* evidence for "original sin."

This essay is really an attempt to achieve closure on these beliefs and with it, silence. And silence means the internal stillness to listen, maybe for the first time in a long time, for the quiet voice of the source of our existence. This source — this "God" who penetrates our bones and sustains our being — we may imagine is asking us to listen, even as Moses listened with his shoes off in Sinai.

But listening begins with a *critique* which was unfortunately necessary to establish definitive separation from the world-view they represent. Simply claiming "no one believes these things anymore," or that they will disappear by simple neglect, disregards a few important realities.

The first is represented by the existence and character of the very recent 1992 *Catechism of the Catholic Church*, which we've cited frequently. Traditional Catholic doctrine is still being taught as it has been historically formulated. There is no indication that it is disappearing or being significantly modified. This is a phenomenon for which we all have to take responsibility. Do we want these doctrines, like the doctrine of original sin, as traditionally formulated and interpreted since the days of Augustine, to control the formation of future generations of Catholics?

Second, there is always the possibility of theological suppression as evidenced by the Papal Bulls *Ex Corde Ecclesiae* in 1989 and *Ad Tuendam Fidem* in 1998, and the admonition *Dominus Jesus* of September 2000, written and promulgated by a Vatican commission headed by Joseph Ratzinger, the man who became the present Pope. All are reminiscent of the inquisitorial mind-control that has been so characteristic of the Catholic church throughout most of its history. The last-mentioned document unambiguously and unapologetically arrogates the determination of all religious truth to the judgment of the Roman Catholic Church. Indeed, such arrogance is quite traditional for Christians who began their history by expropriating and re-interpreting the Jewish scriptures in accord with their own beliefs.

But even more dangerous, I would add, is the residual cultural reverberation of these "obsolete" doctrines in our daily lives. Thus, something like the belief in an insulted and punishing "God" assumed by "original sin" can function as a subconscious archetype for generations even after formal belief in the doctrine has disappeared, poisoning our trust, undermining our love for life and our enthusiasm for others. This is true of other by-products as well ... belief that the matter of our bodies is "corrupt" creating a sense of undeserved guilt ... belief in the "particular judgment" that exonerates us from all concern for anyone's "salvation" but our own ... belief in our destiny in the "other world" encouraging disregard for this world and its injustice ... the magical (male) priesthood ... salvation as the earned accumulation of merit ... the monarchical episcopate ... all the doctrines relating to the absolute superiority of Christianity over other religions. I believe we have a responsibility to deal with these residues. They can cripple us even without our acquiescence.

poetry and religious truth

Truth" in the west has been identified with "science" from well before the advent of modern times. The ancient Greeks sought a rational understanding of the world we live in; they called their quest philosophy, the love of wisdom, but they thought of it the way we think of *science.*

Theology was born in this context. At the dawn of western science there did not exist any clear separation between theology and physics as we have it today. For millennia, theology was not only considered a science, it was *the* science, the instrument that reached to the inner nature and operations of reality.

But science had to compete with poetry. That was a problem for the scientists. Socrates, you'll remember, had great difficulty with the poets because they *could not use other words* to explain what they wrote.[135] He considered them alien to the rational-scientific quest he was pursuing.

---

[135]Plato, *The Apology* in *The Works of Plato,* tr.Jowett, Tudor, NY, vol.III, p.107.

I believe Socrates was blinded to the value of poetry because of the solid possibilities that logic seemed to offer: clarity, precision, verifiability, therefore "truth." Poetry seems to have none of that. Multi-layered, peppered with mixed imagery and allusions, full of intense personal feelings, poetry seemed entirely subjective. Socrates wanted to know "what the poets meant." They answered by telling him to go back and re-read their poetry; apparently they felt their words had been very precisely chosen. There was no other way they could say it. Socrates could not understand that. His demand to "explain your poetry using other words," was, as far as the poets were concerned, an attack on the jugular. What better way to tell a poet s/he's failed? Perhaps there was an odist or two among those who voted for the hemlock.

One modern poet calls his own poetry a "raid on the inarticulate."[136] He speaks of "shabby equipment," words — the poor, worn implements of daily life — that were never meant to carry the weight of the realities that the poet imposes on them. So, because words are not quite adequate, the "methodology" of the poets is special. And it's used to communicate a special truth, a truth that is in a class apart from the measureable realities of the so-called exact sciences. The methodology is *metaphor,* and the special truth is "relational truth." What do these terms mean?

relational truth

"Relationship" is a very specific feature of our lives as human beings. It is a complex and interior experience of inter-personal connectedness of which our own participation is an integral part. Our relationships are difficult enough to perceive accurately but even more difficult to communicate to others. How do I express the unique relationship that I have with someone I love. I am aware that scientific descriptors, even from a science specifically dedicated to human perceptions and emotions like psychology, are totally inadequate for this purpose. Enter the poet. Her task is to try to find that combination of metaphors — symbols and images that lie outside the range of ordinary speech — which may convey with greater *human accuracy* the multi-faceted dimensions of the relationship. "Human accuracy" here is "truth" and refers to the ability to evoke in another person, an experience as close as possible to the poet's experience in its

---

[136]T.S.Eliot, *Four Quartets,* "East Coker" V

individuality, complexity, scope and depth of feeling. Solomon's poet, for example, might say:

> *"You are beautiful as Tirzah, my love, comely as Jerusalem,*
> *terrible as an army set in battle array."*[137]

How is the poet's "love" as "terrible as an army set in battle array"? You may "get it" or you may not. But if you connect with it, you will *understand* what experience the poet is trying to convey, and in that act of *understanding* you will provide a "third party verification" both for the experience and the accuracy of its articulation. Poetry is not (only) entertainment, an elective pastime for the *literati*. It's the only instrument we have for communicating "truth" at this level, *relational truth.*

So, I believe Socrates was wrong. The poets labor with as much commitment to *accuracy and clarity* as any sincere scientist or philosopher. Their art is the attempt to find those *precise* phrases, that *precise* sequence of words, that evoke human relational experience. And religion is our human relationship with the source of our existence ... *whatever it may be.*

My point is that "relational events" or "inter-personal events" differ as object from other objects and therefore are communicated by a different kind of discourse. These "relational realities," which include the existential relationship — i.e., *my relationship to the source of my existence* — are experienced by the knower as objects that *include his/her self. The resonating subject is the predominant component of the object known*, making the object inaccessible to another subject except through a recognized similar experience. So communication in this area involves "constructing" (*poiein* in Greek) something that evokes the same experience in the hearer. The "constructor," the *poeta*, tries to create external conditions (words, dramatic dialogue, paintings, music, dance, ritual, etc.), a symbolic "construct," a *poema* that accomplishes that task. And metaphor is its instrument of choice because it uses words not as concepts that try to comprehend and define the object, but as *symbols* that *refer to* and evoke the object in the experience of others. Evocation invites the hearer *to find the object within* his/her own file-cabinet of experience and thus interpret, compare *and verify* its truth. There is no other way these complex, interi-

---

[137]Song of Solomon 6:4

orly experienced realities can be communicated and verified except by speech that of its very nature can only evoke and not denote, describe and not define, invite and not impose.

Traditional western theology has historically been considered an exact science in the rationalist sense. Realities that we know in and through our own experience, and whose inner workings apart from us we can only adumbrate, we in the west have historically claimed to know with quasi-mathematical precision. All our religious discourse, doctrine, creed, dogma, even ritual formulae, have been infected with this rationalist contagion. Religion has been subsumed under the heading of "truth," and "truth" in the west is prejudicially the result of rational inquiry.

But what gets lost in our scientistic scenario is that "true" religious speech is indeed critical to our lives but in a way that antecedes and bypasses logic. Religious discourse, — ritual, creed, doctrine — is not science; it is *poetry* and as such it provides evocative descriptions of our *relationship* to realities whose inner mechanical workings *are irrelevant to the relationship* whether I do or even *could* come to know them or not.

For example, the perception in which I relate to my wife *does not include knowledge of the vegetative functions of her organism or the neurological operations of her brain.* And yet I claim to have an accurate grasp of "who she is." I may call her a butterfly today and a soaring eagle tomorrow, but even though literally she is neither, I know exactly what I'm talking about, *and so does the reader.* The ruling element that gives those words meaning is *relational experience.*

Now, in the case of "God," the relationship stands on its own: *I understand myself* to exist and that *I am not self-originating.* I immediately understand — from my side — the relationship I bear to the existential source of *existence ... even if I don't know what it is.* It's at this point that religion enters the picture. Religion is the reflective description of *my* experience in the form of "doctrine," which is symbol, metaphor, *poetry.* I say "'God' is my Creator." Literally, scientifically, I know neither "God" nor what it means to create. All I know for a fact is that I am not self-originating; but that is sufficient to establish the relationship. Both "God" and "creation" are metaphors for *what I do not know* but to which I bear a constant and inescapable relationship. In Dickens' *Great Expectations,* Pip had no knowledge of his anonymous benefactor, and his conjectures were upended in mid-stream, but his awareness of what he had received and his sense of loyal gratitude was the same regardless.

Doctrine's interpretative tool, *theology,* comes next. It is simply a kind of literary criticism *that evaluates religious poetry in the light of the "facts" and how well the words chosen convey the indicated experience.* At no point in the process does the presumption of claiming *to know the object* — "God" — apart from the relational experience of it, intrude. *All I know for a fact is that I am not self-originating.*

metaphor

> ... an implicit comparison between two unlike entities ... The metaphor makes a quali-tative leap from a reasonable, perhaps prosaic comparison, to an identification or fu-sion of two objects, to make a new entity partaking of the characteristics of both. Many critics regard the making of metaphors as a system of thought anteceding or bypassing logic.[138]

Metaphor is a symbol. As a symbol it does not conceptualize its ob-ject, it "refers to" it ... or, as Wittgenstein might say, it "points to it." Meta-phor is a linguistic device that applies words to realities they were not meant to define. Metaphor is a word adequate for one reality which is used "improperly" *to stand for* another which has no adequate word, or whose usual word has been judged inadequate. *"My love is like an army set in battle array."* Metaphor does not define, it rather evokes and sug-gests; it "points to." But the metaphor's very "impropriety" accounts for its evocative quality, for it throws the listener back onto his own experience for *understanding.* It contributes a new, fresh and vital element that other-wise would be absent. *"The winter wind with its long fingernails tore the canvas to shreds."* The wind does not have hands and fingernails, but the imagery evokes the destructive action of the wind. "Long fingernails" are symbols. They do not define any "scientific" reality; they rather describe how the wind's action *makes us feel* — and therefore how *we relate to it.*

Poetic metaphor is a most appropriate instrument for speaking about our relationship to "God." For, besides more accurately communicating the experience, its symbolic character guarantees and protects *apophasis:* "God" *remains ineffable, undefinable, unknowable.* Metaphor is concep-tually empty. Metaphor makes no pretense at grasping and comprehend-

---

[138]*Encyclopedia Britanica*, 1979, Mic VI, p.831

ing its object. The believer using a metaphor is consummately aware that its employment is improper, therefore temporary, provisional, and compelling only in the personal sense. *No one is compelled to assent unless their own experience verifies it.*

If we say that the concept "God" is itself derived *only* from human experience, it means that the "objective" element in our knowledge of "God" *includes the experiencing subject.* I am not using the word "objective" to mean "the thing in itself apart from its being the object of a knowing subject;" there is no such thing. In the case under consideration here — knowledge of "God" — there is nothing known outside of the inseparably subjective feature of experiencing "God" in the *intimate realization of our own "non self-origination."*

Does this mean that "God" is not real? ... only on the gratuitous assumption that what can't be *verified independently* of experiencing subjects is non-existent. But no one would say that. The most that even a scientist would claim is that you cannot *compel assent to* the existence or character of things that are not independently verifiable. That in itself does not *prove* that they do not exist, nor does it establish their character, i.e., *what they are like.* Unfortunately, the word "truth" has been arrogated by the over-enthusiastic scientism of our times to refer exclusively to "knowledge" that has been subjected to the kind of probity demanded by science. Relationship — the intentional valence between conscious organisms — may be accessible to scientific measurement as far as its emotional resonance or other observable by-products are concerned, but no one would say that *those things were themselves constitutive of the relationship.* The emotions of elation that accompany a realization, for example, might be measurable, *but they do not constitute the realization.* Religion is not about *what* things are, but how *we relate* to them. I relate to *the source of my existence* as to "God," and the nature of that relationship is determined by *the nature of my existence* and how I experience it, not by what I have been led to think "God" is. I articulate the *nature of my existence, i.e., that it is not self-originating,* and celebrate it in poetry.

I call metaphor a tool of poetry and that poetry reaches "truth" — but not a scientific truth that is verifiable *independent of the experience of the subject,* demanding acknowledgement without concurrent experience. This "poetic truth" that I speak of, however, is also *truth*, it is objective *and it is verifiable*. It's the communication and sharing of experience; as such *it cannot be communicated without being verified.* You verify it with your own experience, however, not some independent measuring device or a logical syllogism.

Religion tries to turn the experience of "God" into words. Poetry is our almost exclusive tool for communicating truth in these interpersonal regions. But I want to emphasize, it's aim is *truth: what is real and really there — the relationship.*   We are not talking about fabrications of the imagination.[139] I am objectively related to the source of my existence — in which I live and move and have my being, *whether I scientifically "know" what it is or not* — and I express that relationship in religious poetry. Poetry uses metaphor, symbol, fables and allegory, to express *relational truth* that cannot be expressed in any other way. The very nature of the realities we've been talking about, realities whose existence is *knowable only as interpersonal relational events*, must *necessarily* use metaphor for their expression.

This is true of all relationships. Who would ever deny that the relationships between spouses, or friends, or siblings, or parents and children were *real*, even though there is no physical or chemical or laboratory test that could verify their existence?

> *A propos of these epistemological questions, I'd like to summarize a relevant but potentially distracting technical discussion of the Thomist position on analogy vs. metaphor.[140]*
>
> *Analogy is a category of conceptual attribution. It claims to speak scientifically about "God" using words and concepts drawn from known realities which themselves supposedly really share characteristics attributed to "God." Metaphor on the other hand proposes to speak poetically about*

---

[139] H. and H.A. Frankfort, "Myth and Reality," in *The Intellectual Adventure of Ancient Man,* U of Chicago Press, 1946 & 1977 p.7; and also "The Logic of Mythopoetic Thought," pp. 10-11: *"[Myths] are the products of imagination, but they are not mere fantasy. It is essential that true myth be distinguished from legend, saga, fable and fairy tale. ... True myth presents its images and its imaginary actors, not with the playfulness of fantasy, but with a compelling authority. It perpetuates the revelation of a "Thou". ... "Myth, then, is to be taken seriously, because it reveals a significant, if unverifiable, truth ... It is concrete, though it claims to be inassailable in its validity. It claims recognition by the faithful; it does not pretend justification before the critical."* H. and H.A. Frankfort, "Myth and Reality," in *The Intellectual Adventure of Ancient Man,* U of Chicago Press, 1946 & 1977 p.7; and also "The Logic of Mythopoetic Thought," pp. 10-11

[140] Thomas Aquinas, *Summa Contra Gentiles,* Bk I ch 34 & passim; *Summa Theologiae,* I, 13, 5 & passim.

God. It functions in the realm of meaning and human significance, not "things."

For the scholastics analogy is scientific knowledge and metaphor is not. Analogy supposedly stretches the comprehension of the literal term by "elongating" it from finite to infinite without changing its meaning. Metaphor, on the other hand, uses a word whose meaning is improper — it cannot be taken literally either because of signification or proportion or both — but has evocative power.

The West has never considered metaphor sufficient to ground theological "truth." But I am saying that the very category of "analogy" was a massive circularity — a begging of the question. There is no "analogy of being" which permits us to say "something scientifically true" about "God;" there is only metaphor which can only use "silly" words, so-to-speak, that may come to mind to express our experience. I am denying the validity of any conceptual determination of "God;" I say we cannot know "God" as we know other things and in that sense no speech about "God" is scientifically valid, even by extension. Ricoeur agrees:

> [The] express purpose [of the Thomistic doctrine of Analogy] is to establish theological discourse at the level of science and thereby to free it completely from the poetical forms of religious discourse, even at the price of severing the science of "God" from biblical hermeneutics.[141]

If "being" is taken as <u>existence</u> it has only one meaning. For, insofar as they exist, all things are doing exactly the same thing. "To be" is the same for a person as for a paramecium. That would make the concept of being univocal not analogical.

*Thomas on the other hand, following Plato, elaborated the idea of participatory existence, and connected it with Aristotle's notion of analogical knowledge. Thomas thought that since things are different from one another in **what** they are, their existence itself as existence (**that** they are) must also be proportional. This means that for Thomas there are modulations in the intellectualized concept of "being" that are not derived from the concrete experience of existence, which is invariable, but rather from their essences, our conceptual definitions of them. We have to be clear about the import of this thinking for the Christian theologians who developed it. "Participation-in-being" seemed to be the only philosophical bar-*

---

[141] Paul Ricoeur, *The Rule of Metaphor*, University of Toronto Press, 1977 p.273, emphasis mine. CF also Study 8, "Metaphor and philosophical discourse", 257-313; especially see fn# 36 of the same study, p.359.

> rier against pantheism, for all finite essences are conceivable ... and thus <u>distinct</u> from the divine essence which is not conceivable.
>
> Some have claimed, however, that the entire western metaphysical edifice is nothing but smoke and mirrors, built on a simple but cata-strophic error. Plato confused abstract concepts with reality — and the concept "reality," of all concepts, can be the most easily confused.[142] The properties of a reality seen through the lens of "essence" are not neces-sarily the properties of reality-as-existence, as phenomenon. So the unicity of "being" in the concept was considered a transcendental attribute that in no way supported the "univocal" character of existence as experi-enced. The doctrine of analogy then, was developed to support an intel-lectually elaborated "concept of being." The project was circular and gra-tuitous.

The root of religious speech is human experience which is *historically and culturally conditioned*. Speech about "God" that was forged at a par-ticular time and place bears the stamp of that particularity and will need constant translation and renewal if it is to correspond to what is experi-enced by other people at other times and under other circumstances. The words of one age do not necessarily communicate in another. "Original sin," for example, may have corresponded to a Greco-Roman's intuition that something was radically wrong with life under the oppression of the Empire, but a modern South Asian may find such an idea unthinkable and an insult to the goodness of God. "In our countries," says Sri-Lankan Catholic theologian Tissa Balusuría, "the idea of humans being born al-ienated from the Creator would seem an abominable concept."[143] Meta-phor preserves the relativity of local expressions.

Moreover, the *uniqueness* of metaphorical projection introduces a fra-grance and intensity to religious communication that more adequately corresponds to the nature of the human experience in question here, mys-tical experience. The mystics speak of "the cloud of unknowing," for ex-ample, a haunting image to describe the ineffability of God. If this evoca-tive quality should be lost, religious truth, as we are defining it, *would not be adequately transmitted*; metaphor is critically important in this respect.

---

[142] cf a discussion of this in Bertrand Russel, *A History of Western Philosophy*, Simon & Schuster, NY, 1945, pp 48-52

[143] Sri Lankan Catholic theologian, Rev.Tissa Balasuriya on original sin, quoted by Celestine Bohlen, *NYT* article 1/15/97

Again, in this same connection, while metaphor communicates, and communicates well, it also retains the quality of *indefinability*, which we discussed at length earlier — a fundamental characteristic of all interpersonal encounter. It evokes, it does not define. The "doctrinal terms" are temporary because of their evocative function. Once they cease to evoke, they no longer communicate. The experience to which they refer, however, remains always what it was. New conditions may require new metaphors.[144] This is most relevant to our reflection. For it means that metaphor preserves inviolate the *apophatic* principle of Christian tradition, that is, *the radical unknowability of God*. For *metaphor is essentially empty*.

Theologians must analyze, weigh and judge all these terms used to define elements of religious experience. It hardly needs saying that much of what is most sordid and shameful in the history of humankind is directly traceable to the unwarranted ascription of *literal scientific objectivity* to locally conditioned religious experience and the metaphors used to evoke them. The conviction that one has the absolute truth about "God" and how one should live has provoked and excused wars, pogroms, conquests, slavery, persecutions and xenophobic hatred of all kinds. What's at stake, as we've unfortunately come to realize in these times, is nothing less than genocide carried out in the name of "God."

doctrine — the christian metaphors

The Christian west has elaborated a rich tradition of metaphorical speech about God, developed during two millennia of religious history and disseminated throughout the vast extent of Christendom. I'm referring to what we call "Christian doctrine." Under the influence of Greco-Roman thought, these "teachings" emerged early in the history of Christianity. They evolved into a philosophically sophisticated, internally consistent system within the first four centuries and have endured virtually unchanged to our day. These are the "core truths" that define Christianity: creation, original sin, incarnation, redemption, the trinity, the role of the Church. We dealt with them in Part I of this chapter. Many are what I call the "problem doctrines."

---

[144]Eliot, op.cit."East Coker V",

The negative side of these doctrines notwithstanding, my point in this section is to say that they also represent an immense collection of luxuriant and treasured spirituality that has flourished on the imagery that underlay them. This spirituality has existed alongside and in spite of the dubious origins and questionable purposes of the doctrines. It speaks to the irrepressible thirst for "God," *the unknowable source of our existence,*— a thirst that will find the "God" who is everywhere, *anywhere*, even in shoddy and erroneous doctrinal expression.

This is key. We can point to the insanity of individuals, the exploitation of classes and the rapacity of empires for the development of erroneous and pathogenic doctrine ... and we can accuse faulty doctrine of causing untold damage to individuals and nations ... we can stand appalled and in horror at the historical fall out in plunder and genocide in the name of "God" which rolls on generation after generation for centuries and even millennia ... but we cannot deny that alongside the stench and rubble there has always emerged an indomitable simple humanity that "saved" Christianity from destroying us altogether. There were always people with the simple compassion, sense of community, cooperation, forgiveness, zest for life, love of people and gratitude to *existence* that makes life bearable. This, I say, is what saves us: *our organic, bodily, natural humanity*, driven to love and survive. Alongside a morbid and morose Christianity there have always been sane and healthy Christians who — as even as many of us may remember — searched for and found "God" in Christian doctrine.

Others can find "God" there too. Not because, as the religious authorities have claimed, "God" cannot be found elsewhere, but rather because the people of our tradition have watered these doctrines with their tears searching for the beloved source of their *existence*; they have made them fertile for us. They are the *poetry of our people* that sings about the source of the life and existence. Our ancestors were in love, and they did not fight it. We are overawed by that volcano of joy at being human that exploded from these forebears of ours who expressed their blazing insight into *their own worth and goodness*, by declaring that "God" *in Person walked among us* and validated our humanity by dying as we die banishing forever any doubts we may have had about the ultimate value of our life. Whatever egregious falsities may have existed in these doctrines, sometimes at a depth and to a degree of intensity that should have poisoned everything for all time, these "little people" — our people — found a way to turn it to the advantage of their exuberant and compassionate humanity. *Christianity has not saved humanity, the humanity of its people has saved Christianity.* And they did it by disregarding the literal claims of their doctrines and taking them as metaphors of what they knew they needed.

For, once the meaning of these metaphors — "incarnation, redemption" — are heard and understood, we see that, really, there is nothing new here. For in what way do they alter the message expressed earlier *and forever* by the gift of our humanity — the message of existence itself — a message that perhaps we never sat still long enough to hear? These doctrines fundamentally do no more than call us back to our connection with our source, but as Eliot said, "now under conditions that seem unpropitious."[145] The original creative contact, embedded in "God's" gift of ourselves to us, which is really "God's" self-gift to us, had lost its ability to communicate. Why? The ancestors had a metaphor for that, too. "Original sin." They said it had corrupted our hearts and darkened our vision. We don't find that metaphor helpful any more.

The awe of existence had to be restated again and "*in other words,*" more understandable to them, with the images and drama that they could relate to. "Incarnation", "redemption", "sacrifice", expressed this loving relationship with our source and matrix in other words, *in their words.* It used as poetic symbol the story of the political assassination of the man, Jesus, and his indomitable resistance to Rome's dehumanizing pretensions.

This transcendent need and capacity of people to find ever new ways to proclaim their embrace of the *source-of-all-things*, is itself an evidence of the generative power of the relationship by which we are sustained in existence. "In 'God' we live and move and have our being." The wellspring of our *humanity-being-generated* is our source, *whatever it is.* I love it, *because I love being-here and being me.* This proclamation is the song of those grandparents of ours who forged our language, our art, our stories, our laws, and our religion. *"Come sing these songs of ours,"* they tell us, "*live with gratitude and generosity as we lived, stand before the lions as we stood, dance and sing as we danced and sang. These are not the only songs. But they're ours. It's all we have to pass on to you, our*

---

[145]*ibid.*

children. Use these songs to learn to sing. Perhaps someday you will sing your own songs."

Yes, it's time we sang our own songs.

the song of "creation"

We begin with *existence* which as a Christian "doctrine" is called "creation." "Creation" is a metaphor. In traditional terms it literally means that a personal "God" planned and fashioned all the forms and features of the universe. We no longer use that imagery; it does not conform to reality as we know it. The primordial presence of *existential energy* set in motion the evolution that has fashioned us. It is the sheer fact of *existence itself, as much here and now as at the beginning of time,* that must be recognized as the source of it all.

Existence in the form of *matter's energy* is both the place and the time where our "God" *is,* even now, as I write and you read. We are actively *existing;* here and now is where we are in contact with our "creator." The existence we project is not ours to generate, sustain, guarantee or control. *We are not self-originating,* neither in the past nor in the present. We exist like tiny sponges in a great sea of suffusive *existence — material energy* — that bears us along. So we ourselves and all these things around us are the expression of this sustaining *existence.* As for Moses, "Yahweh" is right here. *Yahweh,* is a metaphor for the *existence* in which we swim. *"Take off your shoes, the ground you are standing on is holy."*

By "us" of course, I mean all things, of which we humans are an integral part — of hydrogen and helium, potassium and iron, protein and cell, sinews, bone, flesh and brain. We are the fabric woven with these threads — *we are what they have made of our common "matter."*

"Creation" remains a metaphor. The energy of matter is the energy to exist. It makes all things come to be. *Matter's energy* is like "God" to us. We really don't know how our own reality can be a "participation" in this "God's" very own existence without us being "God" ... *but, perhaps we are in some sense.* "God" is itself a metaphor, a symbol, for this energy to exist and power to make things be.

the metaphor of "God"

We have never seen "God," yet we *understand* our fashioner and sustainer as the source of *what* and *that* we are. We describe and communicate it as best we can. We use images and symbols.

We have many traditional images of "our creator" and the "act of creation," some are hopelessly anthropomorphic. Others, like the philosophical concept of participation-in-being, are an intellectual exercise rather than a description of experience. All of them represent an attempt to express what we *understand* by other means. *They are metaphors.*

What *are* those other means by which we *understand* "creation"? We are not *self-originating existence*, and I believe that is the foundational realization that flowers in *"apophatic mystical experience,"* a term we've been using throughout this essay. The abstruse words are unfortunate for I believe that we *understand* ourselves and "God" in this fairly simple, commonplace experience. *We are not self-originating.* I *know* I cannot account for my *self* — *a self that, despite being entirely and exclusively mine, remains ever a mystery to me.*

I am not self-originating. It is a personal realization that my very self is a "project," elaborated, evolved, set in motion — from *a source not myself.* This awareness does not involve knowledge of the purposes or mechanisms by which this may be happening; nor does it clarify the nature of the "source-not-myself" any more than it clarifies the very *self* — my *self* — that I do not fully understand. I float, unanchored, over the abyss. The experience has no necessary concrete dimension, no content outside of the random circumstances that happen to accompany the moment. I may feel at a loss to describe this experience, so I have recourse to a concept, like "creation," which has been elaborated by my people over millennia to describe exactly this awareness *in other words.* There's nothing necessary about that word either. However, in their attempt to express this profound and simple insight, they generated images, metaphors that are at our disposal. These images include the determination that the "source-not-myself" will be called "God"; they include creation stories, and later philosophical musings on the meaning of participatory existence. The imagery is designed to clothe the experience in "usable" terms. But there's nothing *literal* in any of these symbols or expressions. In the final analysis the concept "creation" is nothing but *a metaphor* for a mystery. It is poetry. It's a traditional symbol for this experience — which I call "mystical." The very meaning of "mystical" is *an experience had and expressed in symbol.*

Am I offering this as a new "proof" for the existence of "God"? Not at all. Nor am I insisting that the word and concept of "God" is the best way of expressing the experience for every individual. I am not describing the phenomenon in order to transfer it to the plane of "objective" or scientific knowledge or even less to use it to justify Christian doctrinal formulations. I would like to communicate it as it is, a personal event, an interior experience, an intuition, a realization — *I am not self-originating*. Nevertheless, this realization is self-sustaining, self-evident, and self-justifying. It is communicable only by evocation, by symbol, by metaphor many of which are traditional. Either you know what I'm talking about or you don't. I am *not* operating in the sphere of the knowledge of "objects," but I am "pointing to" what is absolutely true.

That *"I am not self-originating"* is a proposition in the realm of tautology, *and it creates a relationship which you and I experience.* In this regard I am entirely dependent on you — your own experience — verifying what I'm talking about if we are to travel together beyond this point.

existence is the only religious "fact"

A religion based on the mystery of existence — that we are not self-originating — is very different from a religion based on ecclesiastical dogma and ritual. A problem arises when some "Church" tries to take the place of creation and manipulate our sense of being conditioned. Instead of inviting us to find "God's" presence in the *existential energy* that is driving the evolution of matter, it attempts to supplant that experience, calling creation "profane," and directing our attention to itself as the only authentic manifestation of "God" — the only thing sacred in a profane world.

"God's" *self-expression* is the material universe itself, as it is, as it is evolving, in all the myriad forms of being and species of living things — for "purposes" that we *do not know*. But maybe there is no purpose, besides just existing. We are at a loss to understand what is at the root of all this life — *and* the death and dissolution that seems intrinsic to it, the common lot of us all. It has always been a temptation of ours to turn away from the whole, to deny our connection with our sibling species from whom we evolved, with whom we share this perishing material existence. We abandon our spontaneous sense of a sacred world. We build ourselves a world apart from the incomprehensible frenzy of life that envelopes us. We would like to deny our place in this maelstrom; for we are exhausted at what we see: the apparent recklessness of it all. We separate ourselves from the universe out of whose very entrails we have emerged. We build a shelter for ourselves; we withdraw from the world into a castle-fortress, a basilica. We close the windows and bolt the doors, and in everyway possible try to substitute a world of our own making for the incomprehensible world that "God" is making.

the metaphor of death

We vanish but there is constant regeneration. We know that after our turn in life our own "stuff" gets re-cycled and other forms of things, living and not living, re-use "us." Who can stand it? I am not happy being a temporary coalescence in a mass of stuff in flux. I don't want to die. And this thirst to go on living comes from the same unfathomable depths that well up my existence — the **conatus** — what makes me, *me.* I know what I want, I want to *be-here.*

Thus is set in place what seems to be our eternal dilemma. We are not resigned to our impermanent place in this mysterious world. Where does this desire come from, a desire we share with all living things? For all things defend their life and continuance ... and die reluctantly. The process of living day to day is the work of staying alive. And yet at the end of it all is death? Who can stand it?

There really is no positive evidence to support claims that our "personalities," traditionally called "souls," live on after death. If this claim is *true* then the dissolution of the body we call death is really a simple transition to life in another plane and is therefore not really death at all. Death in this case is only a metaphor because it would only *symbolize* dissolution.

If this claim of "spiritual" immortality is *false*, however, meaning that we have no separable, immortal souls, then we are only the material of which we are constructed. My *self* would then be the temporary coherence of a substrate ... and the substrate may be here forever. So, in this case also, since *I am* that substrate, then, metaphysically speaking, death is a relatively insignificant modulation, a mere fluctuation from one configuration to another. There is no dissolution, no disappearance here either, because all my "stuff" continues on forever. In all cases death is *a metaphor for the mystery of matter — the void.*

the "resurrection" of jesus

The man Jesus, claimed that "God" was a loving Father. In my terms, he had an experience of the benevolence of *existence* with such depth and duration that it led him, trusting, even through his execution by the Roman thugs who had taken over his country.

His absolute trust in "God" sustained a serenity of purpose that, even as he died before their eyes, convinced his followers that in his case, death was overcome. Death had "no dominion over him," which in the vocabulary of his time could only mean he would rise again. And, perhaps he did, or perhaps he will. That part, I claim, is irrelevant. Follow me here. Whether he *rose*, or *will rise*, is the same thing. And whether he will rise *as we imagine that resurrection to be* or in another manner is also irrelevant; for to rise this way or that is the same thing. Perhaps, as Teilhard de Chardin imagines, following what was suggested by Paul, *it is the whole cosmos that will reach an Omega Point and we with it.* But It really doesn't matter. In all these cases our "stuff" perdures, *existence* goes on, our trusting relationship to "God," our source and sustainer, continues.

Jesus did not literally escape death, because he died. What he conquered, however, was *the fear of death,* death as symbol of dissolution. It is that conquest that is *symbolized* by the resurrection. What Jesus knew and communicated to us was that "God," our source, *can be trusted.* "Resurrection" performs a virtual role in a virtual world. It is *a metaphor* for the conquest of *death-as-metaphor.* The real human event here is Jesus' experience of the real Father-of-life as Love. The factual reality here is *existence* — "God" relating to us, giving us the gift of ourselves. And Jesus' message was to establish *definitively* that *that* relationship is absolutely reliable. The significance of death is not determined by the "facts," because we really know nothing at all about death. *It is had indirectly through our relationship with "God"* which is, after all, our very selves. Jesus encourages us to follow our instinct *and trust existence.* The **conatus** is not a deception. Jesus trusted it implicitly.

Are we denying the literal reality of the resurrection? Are we being fooled here by some semantic sleight-of-hand? Is the impermanence, the obliteration we so dread really eliminated? Let's follow this question out to the end.

we say "god is love" . . .

What Jesus accomplished by living its consequences in his own flesh, was to "prove" that "God" *can be trusted even through death.* But it was not a rationalist "proof." It was a "street level" proof that we all understand. "You think I'm kidding"? we ask when the argument gets hot, and we answer "watch, I'll *prove it* to you." We mean we are willing live the consequences of our claims. All Jesus *did* was to die, nothing more. That was his "proof." The claim that he rose as the "first fruits" of an imminent universal resurrection collapsed within a few generations of the birth of Christianity for there was no evidence that anyone else ever rose, even his eye witness followers who fostered belief in it. This entailed a shift from belief in an imminent bodily resurrection to a shadowy afterlife for immortal souls threatened with eternal punishment. It amounted to a stunning sea-change in the Christian vision. It was an impoverishment from which Christianity never recovered. The resurrection lost its central meaning for Christians and served thereafter only to support the divinization of Jesus along with the Empire that used him to legitimize its depredations. All that remained human of Jesus and available to suffering humans was his death. It was his only testimony to the "truth," his proof. It was his poetry, his song ... *and we heard it.*

What about the rest of us? Will we rise, as the Church claims, at the "end of time"? Some like Teilhard de Chardin suggest that perhaps the totality of this turbulent universe of matter, including us, will evolve itself into something so god-like and eternal that it eludes our capacity to imagine. Perhaps this is the resurrection "God" has "planned" for us, a collective "salvation" as Paul believed. But frankly, it's all conjecture, guesswork. No amount of theological ratiocination can convince us that we know anything at all about what death means or what may await us or our universe in the future. *We have only one choice; to trust or not to trust the source of our existence.* But ... do we really have a choice? Our natural inclination, springing from *our existence itself* is to trust. Can we really choose *not* to trust, when the very apparatus we must use to despair is this magnificent and improbable humanity?

But what if the reality is entirely different? Is it possible ... *(can we accept this?)*... that at death we are dissolved back into the elements from which we were formed, to be reused over and over until the whole meets its ultimate destiny ... which may *not* be a Teilhardian *Parousía*, a Second Coming to our taste and preference, but perhaps another cycle — an implosion to singularity and another big bang, a new universe. What if our little heads and our little hearts are not equal to the unfathomable magnanimity of a "Father" who, more like a "Mother," wishes to share, and share, and share Herself (and us as part of Herself) *endlessly*, we might even add, *purposelessly* ... for the sheer joy of *the relationship* ... to share *being-here* with ever new things and new "people" out of a generosity and self-donation beyond our capacity to imagine ... or *endure*? What if "She" never rests? What if "She" never stops reusing us to give Her gifts to others? What if "God," and we as part of "God," are **pure kenosis**, *bottomless eternal self-emptying*? Are we still willing to "be like 'God'"? Do we want to go to *that heaven*? Are we really as convinced that "God is Love" if it would mean *that much love*? Are we willing to share *what we are* endlessly with others, as "God" does, and find ecstatic joy in it, as "God" does? Could we forgive our "God" a generosity we ourselves cannot bear? Do we love our existential source and the universe it has made, as it really is — or only as we want it to be?[146]

In such an event, there is no dissolution. If our personalities are a particular convergence of matter (our body), when de-convergence occurs the particles continue to exist available for re-convergence into other entities. Our personalities no longer function — the virtual *self* disappears but our "stuff" persists. The relationship to "God," therefore, goes on ... forever. What if we are *thus* so integrally part of the whole?   Could we live with it?

agnosticism or ignor-ance ... the incarnation

Please note. We are *ignoring* the literal reality of the resurrection-as-imagined, and we are also *ignoring* the "divinity" of Jesus in the form we've inherited from Nicaea. As "facts" they are irrelevant. The only bearing they have on religious experience in any case is their metaphorical value —i.e., *what they evoke in us*. For even if the incarnation were a *fact*, it's value for us is what it says *as a metaphor*: *"God became human out of love for us."* What could possibly require "God" to repeat the "message" of existence *in which "God's" very existence became ours*, ... except to recall it *in other words*.

If we really want to imitate Jewish Jesus, therefore, we will trust in "God" as Jesus trusted. The only "objective" reason for an "objective" incarnation would be the "objective" repair of an "objective" cosmic disaster such as is claimed by the doctrine of original sin — which is why the Hellenic scientists had recourse to that whole imaginary fantasy. *The entire Christian theological edifice we've inherited from these ancient Greeks*

---

[146]"The beginnings of Islamic mysticism is ascribed to Rabi'ah al-'Adawiyah (d.801), a woman from Basra who first formulated the Sufi ideal of a love of "God" that was disinterested, without hope of paradise and without fear of hell." *Encyclopedia Brittanica, 1979,* "Islamic Mysticism," p.943

hangs perilously on the single thread of an incredible Cosmic original sin. Without it there's no reason for "incarnation" and "redemption."

But, is Jesus God? Did he rise again? In my opinion, there is nothing in the spiritual posture of authentic Christianity, in its traditional "mystical life," that would change if either of those two statements were not literal fact. In all cases Christian spirituality remains the same. Our songs of thanksgiving to "God" remain the central focus of our lives, uniquely evoked and sustained by the message and the martyrdom of the man Jesus, who conquered death, for himself and for us.

So is Jesus God? *My* answer to the question is: *it is irrelevant.* It simply does not matter. It is Jesus' *humanity* that's the key to our hearing and following him. The metaphor of his "divinity" — that he was "God" — may have been important to an earlier epoch that was convinced that the cosmos had been taken over by satanic powers and required divine "redemption." Who are we to deny to our ancestors the metaphors they needed to express the horrors the ancient slave-based empires, from Sumeria and Egypt to Rome, had perpetrated on the populations they conquered and bled dry? It seems those people had come to think their very humanity must be intrinsically flawed. Who can refuse to be moved by the expressions of self-loathing exhibited by Roman writers of the first century at the corruptions and injustice of empire.

What we, in our times, require in a "redeemer" is a *human being* who can encourage us to be in such secure possession of our own awesome humanity as to live generously and serenely amid the involuted ego-frenzy generated by the insecurity of the mass market-place we call society. We are not helped one bit by being told *that it takes a divine being to do the most basic human things*, feed the hungry, thirst for justice, live with humility and compassion. What energizes us is that the man Jesus, a human being like us in every way, found among the resources of his own natural humanity, the clarity and courage to be fully human in the face of the dehumanizing greed of the Roman thugs: "Give Caesar his money, it's got Caesar's face on it; and to God, everything that has "God's" face on it." (Mark 12)

Did Jesus speak "as one with authority," because he was "God"? Or was it because his unconfused *humanity* saw clearly that "the sabbath was made for man, not man for the sabbath,"[147] and in an instant dismissed religious legalism by the authority of his (our) humanity alone. Was Jesus "lord of the sabbath" because he was the Son of "God," or because, as he himself insisted over and over again, he was the "son of man," the quintessential human being,[148] acting on the authority embedded in his human nature by his Father, and ours.

It's also not surprising that a human being like Jesus, who vested such ultimate authority in ordinary people, would be murdered by a conspiracy of the corrupt ruling classes, who were well aware of the danger he represented. This point of view is powerfully expressed by the "Legend of the Grand Inquisitor" in *The Brothers Karamazov*.[149] Dostoevsky's fable suggested that Jesus was a threat because he respected the worth of the ordinary human being. Autonomy is based on the individual's moral intuition, which comes with the gift of human nature. Exploitative, parasitic authority, like that exercised by the Roman Empire, is threatened by individual autonomy; and under the guise of love for the masses, it tries to save us from the burden of our freedom. And toward that end, it utilizes every contrivance at its command — from death, to dogma.

The key is humanity. Why else would it be most characteristic of Jesus to teach in parables? Jesus' parables — metaphorical by nature — assume that his audience can figure out what he's talking about. The parable format *implies that the listener already knows the answer.* What a parable teaches is not knowledge, but *understanding* — significance, relative importance, priority, *wisdom.*

Jesus didn't teach anything new. Scour the synoptic gospels. He never spoke of any of the things that later became core Christian doctrine ... not original sin, not the trinity, not grace, not the sacraments, not the necessity of the Church ... and certainly not his own divinity. All these doctrines "developed" in the course of history and the most problematical of them only after the Roman expropriation of Christianity. What Jesus the Jew taught was that, in the search for "God," the priority over every other consideration, was *humanity.*

---

[147]Mark 2
[148]cf Nolan, op.cit., p.70ff
[149]Fyodor Dostoyevsky, *The Brothers Karamazov*, "The Legend of the Grand Inquisitor".

In a world that believed that the Roman Empire and the Emperor, regardless of the brutality and greed they displayed were unquestionably divine, the "divinity of Jesus," defined and set in dogmatic stone at the instigation of the Roman Emperor himself, served to co-opt a potentially dangerous *human energy* that at one time — the era of the persecutions — heroically opposed the Roman program. To prevent rebellion, it seems the "Great Whore of Babylon"[150] had to kill Jesus twice. First it took his life, ... *then, by insisting he was co-equal to "God," **it took his humanity*** in an attempt to prevent spawning other human beings like himself.

original sin

In many ways our reflections in this essay are centered on the incredibility and injuriousness of the doctrine of original sin, the fulcrum and logical center-piece of the entire western Christian speculative construct of Redemption. For to say "Jesus died for our sins" can have many interpretations. But to give it the one meaning we've received from western Christian tradition depends entirely on the concept of a cosmos-changing original sin. I believe the Christian doctrine, a Jewish allegory mis-taken as literal fact by Christians, is patently erroneous and represents much of what is distorted in Christianity and from there, in Western Civilization.

My interest in this phase of the reflection, however, is to reinterpret the doctrine *as metaphor*, which is, simply to do nothing more than return it to its original meaning as the Jewish authors intended it, and therefore rehabilitate it as a potentially positive feature of a new spirituality. This is not a giant step at all, because for the human beings among us who enjoy "a profound and available sanity,"[151] original sin never functioned as anything but fable anyway.

The original purpose of the Hebrew authors of the Genesis parable was to make it clear that evil is *not* part of "God's" original creation, but was the foolish choice of human beings. The lesson intended was that each time sin is committed it robs us of the happiness natural to life in "God's" universe, *this paradise we live in*. The purpose of the story is to blame human unhappiness on faulty human choice and not on the work of

---

[150]Apocalypse, 17
[151] Daniel Berrigan

a good God. *There is nothing physical or metaphysical about "evil." "Evil" is in the mind and choice of man.* The fable of the Garden is an allegory of the first sin, and therefore establishes a paradigm for every sin. But it was never meant to claim a cosmic deformation. It was a catechetical device of an ancient pre-philosophical people designed to encourage gratitude to God, love of life, serenity of mind and heart, generosity and compassion toward others.

Ironically, by taking the Genesis myth literally instead of poetically, the Greco-Roman rationalists effectively turned this Jewish message on its head. The "Christian" version now says that "God" was *implacably offended* by the sin of Adam, implying it was an unforgiving "God" who made this world. The doctrine says that the entire universe, including us, became *intrinsically corrupt.* Therefore *corruption* is the natural state into which we are all born and inexorably live out our existence. The unhappiness that we experience is not due to reformable moral error but is part of the very fabric of the universe and therefore inescapable. And as if life weren't hell enough in this scenario, for the unforgivable insult to "His Majesty" by our paleolithic ancestor, Augustine's Monster-God would send us all to eternal damnation ... *including innocent new-born infants, unless we were baptized into the Roman Empire's "Catholic" Church.*

This is totally incredible. The Church must not only stop teaching this rubbish, but it must be *denounced and repudiated* and the Genesis story returned to the metaphor that the Jewish authors originally created.

Taking myth literally, as in the case of original sin, inevitably entails profound distortions. But by looking at our traditional doctrines as metaphor, we may get some insight into the processes that we ourselves have developed for interpreting the vast and unfathomable depths of the sacred in which we are immersed like sponges in the Sea. We generate symbols to express our sense of this sacred compenetration, this relationship to "God," which is also our relationship to our very selves. Every age creates its symbols. It's time we shouldered that responsibility.

God as person.

Is "God" really a "person" as we know it, or is "person" the only term we can use that will *evoke in us* the depth required by a *real and accurate* relationship to the unknown source of ourselves. *Person is a metaphor.* It's purpose is not to speak about the ontological characteristics of "God" but rather the way *we relate* to God; it is not a scientific concept, it's a *poetic* concept.

The insistence on defining "God" *literally* as a "person," on the other hand, explains our perennial difficulty with the "problem of evil." The philosophical nuances of our traditional approach are, in fact, lost on the ordinary person who continues to expect "God" to act like we do — i.e., *like a person.* So it has remained a recurring obstacle to our grateful relationship with "God" to think that "God," is somehow a "person" like we are but does not respond to our pleas for help and permits utterly incomprehensible atrocities to happen to us.

This expectation of a personal response from "God" prevents us from appropriating some of the powerful insights of Buddhism, which offers a different perspective on the problem of evil. For Buddhists suffering is an inescapable fact that has nothing to do with "God." It cannot be avoided but the intensification of suffering that we cause ourselves through greed and false expectations can.

As the scientific world view continues to explain ever more of the realities around us, we come to realize that events we used to call "evil" are simply part of the natural order. *The lion is not supposed to lay down with the lamb.* That was poetry. The *real "God"* sustains a universe of violent interaction among species and natural forces, where death is natural to all living things, not the result of original sin. This is the "God" the Buddhists are familiar with, and it's the "God" ecologists, biologists, physicists encounter daily in their work.

Calling "God" a "person" is a metaphor. It symbolizes my sense of ecstatic gratitude at *being-here* and *being me.* But it cannot be taken literally. "God" is not a "person." We have to come up with other ways of saying what we mean.

the trinity

Is "God" a *Trinity* of Persons, the Second an intellectual emanation of the First and the Two spirating ("sighing") the Third as if a Personal Embrace? Or is this description of "God's" Internal Act-of-Love really a Mega-Metaphor, a unique image elegantly crafted by a Greco-Roman world-view that, unlike Jewish monotheism, lived easily with a plurality of interrelated gods? The trinity is a poetic Neo-Platonic fantasy built on a sexual and family model. The philosophers *projected* that these were the characteristics of the Source of the *pervasively sexual* reality we see all around us.   We are deeply indebted to those visionary-poets who provided the Fathers at Nicaea with the *"Ultimate Metaphor For Everything."* What could be more apt than this poet's vision of our pulsating universe(s) as the residual aftershocks of a primordial Act of Love?

In an almost predictable elaboration of the *sexual* implications of the metaphor of the Trinity, Julian(a) of Norwich a 14th century English mystic, calls the First Person of the Trinity "Father", the Second Person, again and again, *"Mother"* and the Third Person "Love."   She identifies the Second Person of the Trinity as the *Mother of creation and the Mother of "desire"* which she portrays as holy:

> *"I saw that the Second Person, who is our Mother with regard to our essential nature, that same dear Person has become our Mother in the matter of our sensual nature. ... So Jesus Christ ... is our real Mother. We owe our being to him - and this is the essence of motherhood! ... he said that sweet word, 'It is I ... I who am the Wisdom of Motherhood ... I who am the sovereign goodness of every single thing; I who enable you to love; I who enable you to long. It is I, the eternal satisfaction of every genuine desire.'" (Revelations of Divine Love, 58,59)*

This is the function of metaphor; it reveals the insight of a mystic poet. She sees the *Logos,* the eternal Wisdom in which our two-gendered universe of living things has come into being, as the paradigm for all that is, both feminine and masculine. The "trinity" is human poetry, projecting what we love in life — sex, love and the families it creates — onto the source of *existence.* But it must be emphasized, *it is poetry.* It does not tell us *what "God" is.*

But the religious "scientists" — the theologians — have dared to invade the Parental Bedroom and claim to have literally dissected the divinity, articulating in great detail the Act-of-Love in which we were conceived. Is nothing sacred?   At mass we say *consubstantial* of the Son, and that the Spirit *proceeds* from the Father and the Son ... as if we knew! These are not meant as poetry; they are obsolete scientific terms inherited from an antiquated metaphysical system that thought it knew the very inner workings of "God." As science they are a stumbling block to faith and dialog. But as metaphor, as poetry, as prayer, they take us, in a cloud of unknowing, to the mountaintop. For we don't know what "God" is like. But we know the kind of world "God" has evolved. Can we be forgiven for projecting its features back onto its source? ... *only if we admit it is a projection.*

the whole nine yards

Cement trucks carry nine cubic yards of wet concrete mix. What's salient about the image is the secondary image it evokes, namely, if you don't use the whole nine yards, what do you do with what's left? It suggests that things should be used as a totality.

In our case the entire world-view that the early Christians developed, taken as metaphor, as symbol, and *as a whole*, speaks with a clarity and power that we don't want to lose. For these people had an unusually intense and all-embracing convergence of insights that once and for all put an end to the hieratic justification of four thousand years of systemic dehumanization in the "almighty" slave-empires of the ancient world culminating in Rome. Christianity, prior to its Roman Captivity, was an anti-imperialist phenomenon. People were sick of empire and were searching for a way out. Christianity was only one of a number of religions that provided escape hatches from its dungeons. Searching for a symbol, a standard to rally behind, they focused on the events of the life and death of the *man* Jesus, who "spoke as one with authority," who loved "God" as if he were his child, and treated people like sisters and brothers. He was murdered, like so many of us have been murdered, by the same mob of thugs that have murdered us since time immemorial in the name of "God," order, "peace", and of course, profit and their own glorious destiny.

But Jesus trusted "God" and by his "obedience unto death" threw that murder back in their faces robbing them of the power to abase his humanity. His simple trust took away death's sting. This was the symbol people were looking for. They saw the world starting over again, fresh, clean, just and pure, full of joy, a world worth facing the lions for. It was almost like a new creation. How could they express this sea-change except in cosmic terms.

The ancient Christians refused to offer incense to the Imperial System. Those uncontaminated flames have continued to ignite a deep respect for the autonomy of human beings even to our day, to the chagrin of modern Torquemadas and SOA graduates who organize and direct the death squads, and the torture chambers. The ancients rediscovered their own human integrity in the midst of that "desolation-called-peace" created by the Roman Empire, *the Great Whore of Babylon, the Beast.* Our ancestors were "saved" from the death of their humanity by the death of the man

Jesus, executed like so many of us, for being human ... just *too* human. *It was Jesus' humanity that threatened the empire — that's why they made him "God."*

a global metaphor

Early Christians' entire vision was a complex global metaphor, a poetic panorama, that used the word-hoard of Greek metaphysics, the most transcendent terms they could come up with, to communicate what had become transcendent in their lives. Christian doctrine was simply another attempt at expressing the inexpressible mystery of existence and of humanity, another attempt to speak of the ineffable, another "raid on the inarticulate."

"The letter kills; the spirit gives life." If we insist on taking the Christian dogmatic complex literally, the nine yards of concrete hardens in distorted form. It loses its vitality as a message and becomes a set of obsolete objective propositions — ersatz *facts* — scientifically indefensible on the one hand, and spiritually valueless on the other. If we say, **literally,** the human race was punished because "God" was insulted by Adam, we make a monstrous and childish fool out of "God" and a thing of loathing out of ourselves just for being born. But if we take it as allegory and poetic symbol, as the Hebrew authors originally intended, we encourage that trust in *existence* and compassion that brought Jesus, in total serenity, to conquer death itself. Jesus' *humanness that attracted us all* was formed by the Jewish interpretation of Genesis, not Augustine's. Jesus, we must continually remind ourselves, was not a Christian, *he was a Jew.*

dialog

This reflection began focused on the question of dialog. We know that the Catholic claims to objective truth make dialog impossible because they preclude taking any other religious tradition seriously. We have suggested that, as a matter of fact, Christian doctrine is *metaphor*, nothing more and also, nothing less. As metaphor it expresses most powerfully the quality of our western search for "God" and our cultural presets for guessing what "God" is like. Our doctrines teach us about ourselves, not about God.

"God," the object of our search, in spite of a seemingly endless self-display in creation, remains hidden from direct sight, adumbrated by our metaphors. The best metaphors of our tradition are *apophatic*; they confirm and preserve that God is unknown. The very first dialog is with ourselves; and the first thing we need to do is reconcile these profound metaphors for an Unknown "God" — *the Nameless One, The Cloud of Unknowing, The Dark Night* — bequeathed to us by our mystics, with the pretensions of our dogmas. Perhaps then we will be ready to dialog with others.

Tony Equale,
November, 2000 ... revised 2012

Epilogue

theology and the "new atheism"

This book has been about religion, not about atheism. Even though the prologue used the criticisms of the "new atheists" to help set the focus, and even though I share some of their outrage at traditional religion, their ideas did not figure prominently in my efforts in this book either for support or rejoinder. In this epilogue I am going to use them, obliquely again I'm afraid, to help identify what I feel are potentially false steps for religion as it faces the future. We need religion, and I oppose short-sighted defensive strategies that will only insure traditional religion's continued alienating effect on human life and its inevitable irrelevance. My efforts here are intended to show how traditional theology, by failing to engage these "new atheists" who in many ways are the representatives of common sense, reveals the flaws that render it obsolete. This epilogue is meant as a summary of the book, but it will do that by way of a reflection on theology.

Some defenders of religion have attempted to respond directly and in detail to the "new atheists," among them Georgetown University Professor John F. Haught in his *God and the New Atheism*.[152] I want to use Dr. Haught's work to examine the elements of an argument with the new atheists that might have become a dialog but did not.

The reasons for this impasse exist on both sides. The new atheists came at the issue with a fury born of a visceral revulsion at the self-proclaimed act of Islamic religious *jihad* carried out on September 11, 2001. I believe the atheists quickly realized that the hieratic structures that made *jihad* possible remain the unrepudiated bases of all the religions of the West. Hence, from Islam their target immediately widened to encom-

---

[152] WJK Press, Louisville 2008; cf: Karen Armstrong, *The Case for God*, Alfred Knopf, NY, 2009; Chris Hedges, *When Atheism becomes Religion*, Free Press, NY, 2006

pass "religion" ... and from religion it was expanded, naturally, to the Abrahamic "God" of the book — the *"one ring that rules them all."*

Clearly, the new atheists were not interested in dialog. But even if they were, the possibility was obviated by the defenders of religion who realized that their own tradition could not avoid coming under the same condemnation as Islam. They reacted so defensively to the attack that they tended not to hear new atheist complaints ... or at least not give them serious attention. All concessions by the religionists were mentioned in brief asides and the focus was quickly redirected to the counter-attack. The believers' rejection was so total that some even questioned the motivations of the atheists, casting umbrage on their rationality or intellectual integrity. This is heavy stuff. For what's left? ... an unexpressed insinuation that the reason for their hostility is either pathological or malevolent ... *not an entirely untraditional way for religion to deal with critics and dissenters.*

John F. Haught

I want to concentrate on the theology of John Haught, because he is a senior Catholic academic who is both respected for his orthodoxy and supportive of science. It is that combination of loyalties that explain his response to the new atheists' attack, and, I believe, the shortcomings of his "theology" and it is his theology that interests me in this epilogue.

Haught is known for the work of a lifetime in the controversial field of science and religion. He has taught systematic theology at Jesuit-run Georgetown University for 30 years. He is a proponent of evolution and rejects any suggestion that "Intelligent Design" (ID) is *science.* His expert testimony as an esteemed Catholic academic, was persuasive for the celebrated 2008 decision in So.Dover PA not to allow the teaching of ID in the classroom. He has written 18 books on the compatibility of science and religion. So it would seem of all people he would be the best prepared to counter an attack on religion coming from the side of science.

But I believe his work illustrates the difficulty that those who would defend traditional supernatural religion have in maintaining rational coherence. Haught's solutions, while they appear to let religion "contact and confirm" science (and *vice versa*), fail to achieve the thoughtful integration that would heal the schizoid mindset — the disconnect between science and religion — that dominates modern life. In short, Haught is inconsistent; and the anatomy of his inconsistencies mirrors the structure of his loyalties. I offer this in support of my hypothesis, *viz.,* a theologian of traditional supernatural theism cannot be consistently rational because *the position is not tenable.* I do not question Haught's honesty and personal integrity but rather a vision seriously compromised by ecclesiastical absolutes.

Haught seems to have mounted a two pronged reply to the new atheists. He says that what the new atheists attack is *not really religion,* and that the basis of their attack is *not really science.* In support of the first, he avoids openly justifying the current versions of Christianity and concentrates on another that he identifies only as "theology." We are given glimpses of what he means by that throughout the book. For the second he claims the new atheists work from an irrational set of unproven beliefs that he calls scientism or scientistic naturalism — not science. His efforts using the second tack are principally directed at trying to reduce atheist arguments (and motivations) to absurdity. My criticisms have to do not with these polemics, but with his theology.

science and "god"

The new atheists are incensed at "the undeserved place of privilege" granted to religion by society. Religion, they say, has no right to such deference. Religion is an ancient science, they insist, that has been proven erroneous and obsolete by modern discoveries. It has outlived its relevance to human life because it no longer describes or explains the world as it is. There is no "God" who made the world and oversees its running. Religion should be treated like any other eccentric club that panders to the fantasies of its members — like Sasquatch watchers or UFO enthusiasts.

Haught retorts that the atheists project a false definition of "God." Hence, he says, they are attacking a straw man — a "God" that the religions do not really believe in. For my part, I agree that they attack a "God" that does not exist; but I disagree that it is not the "God" of religion. In fact, I believe it is the very same "God" that Haught limns in his own supposedly updated "theology."

The attacks of the new atheists, admittedly are a broadly focused, unnuanced over-kill of the stereotypical fundamentalism that sophisticated theology claims to eschew. But their criticisms are, I believe, aimed exactly at the heart of the problem. For no matter what way you twist and shout, traditional religion rests on the base of "theism" which necessarily includes a chronic spirit-matter dualism, an anthropomorphic "God," and, in institutions like the Catholic Church, a doctrinal authoritarianism so entangled with privilege and power that it is incapable of reform. I believe "theism," and that includes Haught's sophisticated version, is unable to avoid the identification with the pre-scientific myths on which it is built and therefore with the archaic theism attacked by the atheists.

It must be acknowledged that fundamentalism is on the march in America. Haught virtually ignores the question. But it is my opinion that in the context of the globalization resulting from the economic domination of Western culture, borne forward at this point by the US, it seems hardly prophetic to say that in a few centuries time, unless current trends change, this culture will displace native cultures everywhere. That doesn't augur well for religion. Because of the unusual strength of Christian fundamentalism in the US, we could be on the edge of a transformation of all religions into some imitation of this phenomenon; for when cultures change, *their religions change with them.* We have already seen the Catholic Church reverse course from the progressive leadership role assumed at Vatican II and regress into a dogmatic and moral fundamentalist reaction that most would not have believed possible in 1967. These things can and do happen. To excoriate the new atheists, as he does, for leveling their attack at the very versions of religion which actually threaten to return us to the dark ages, seems short-sighted.

Since Haught insists that he disagrees with fundamentalism as much as the new atheists, instead of resenting them for *not* excluding his esoteric version of Christianity from their screed, it would seem more appropriate to join them in denouncing what they *together* find so unacceptable, and then go on to clarify the "theology" that he promotes. Strangely, he doesn't do that; and my suspicion is that it's because he feels a loyalty to the common theism he shares with those religions, and has little zest for an alliance with atheists however appropriate and partial.

theism

Haught accuses the atheists of using a theologically obsolete conception of "God" and thus of not knowing what religion really is. He dismisses the imagery of an all-powerful "Intelligent Designer" micro-provident miracle-worker and angry punishing warlord as false and atavistic. Religion, he says, has evolved beyond all that and the "new atheists" refuse to acknowledge it.

But I believe while the atheists may have missed a few gnats here and there, they correctly identify the camel Haught's "theology" has swallowed. For the essential nature of the "God" of "theism" that Haught endorses, is no different from the "God" of the "Book" and he admits as much. Haught says

> ... my reflections arise out of my belonging to a theistic religious tradition that is, one that professes belief in a personal God, a God of infinite power and love, who creates and sustains the world, ... [It is an] essentially biblical understanding of God ..."[153]

All theism, including Haught's, projects a divine *entity* separate from and opposed to the material universe, responsible for its creation, even though it may not be the intelligent designer who crafted it. This "God" is a *"person" who inexplicably refuses to act like a person* because he does not respond to human pleas for help. Haught imagines "God" humble and with all sorts of liberal virtues, but his "God" is simply a more nature-loving, companionable version of the fire breathing monster of Calvin and the evangelicals. This modern "God's" morality, like his science, is up-scale and up-to-date; he uses evolution to create the universe and psycho-therapy instead of exorcism; he is *in every way the mirror image of the system of human values held by those progressive Christians who project his existence and humanoid character.* Haught's "God" makes better choices, but *earthquakes still kill 250,000 Haitians* as "he" looks on, and genocide is still carried out in his name with no protest from him. Haught cannot explain these things except by having recourse to the permission of "God" who *consciously chooses* not to intervene. Haught's "God," even though enlightened, is still an inscrutable despot; and his religion is still based on a world parallel to the one we live in even though ruled by a divine onlooker who doesn't interfere ... *but he could, goddammit, he could!*

Here's where I part company with Haught. There is no such "God." And "explanations" that simply shift the kinds of choices this *"choosing"* personal, all-seeing, all-powerful "God" makes, are a theological revisionism — a superficial tinkering that leaves the system intact. In my opinion, it is theology in name only because it does not conceptually integrate the notion of "God" with the *scientifically proven knowledge we have about ourselves and the world we live in.* Haught simply "glues" the miracle-

---

[153] Haught, *God and the New Atheism*, WJK Press, Louisville, 2007, p.xii

working "God" of the Book to a new set of miracles, modern and politically correct: evolution, psycho-therapy, modern medicine, etc. For Haught, "God" and modern science are extrinsically juxtaposed — like "pinning the tail on the donkey" — it is not a physically and metaphysically integrated and coherent view of the world. In his model, science and religion occupy two separate spheres of reality, roughly corresponding to spirit and matter, and the one does not encroach upon the other. This is the heart of the problem. Such a view does not concur with reality. Theists think there are two worlds; but *there is only one*. And while there may be different layers of understanding, they must refer to the same reality. Hence their explanations ultimately must be demonstrably compatible. We must be able to see and say clearly how these interpretations work together. Haught's solutions offer no such integration.

The scientific anomalies I am referring to are generated by the central tenets of theism. The theist "God" is *rational* and chooses to do things *for reasons*. The "creation" of the universe — accomplished by evolution — was *planned and willed* by the theist "God."

The theist "God" also has a personal interest in the ongoing developments of human affairs. "He" has the ability to intervene in history, even though, because of our freedom, "he" chooses not to. The doctrine that covers this is called "divine providence" and its central tenet is that all events — including natural and human disasters — are "permitted" to happen by "God" *for a reason* even though we may never know what it is.

Another corollary is that this "God" enters into a personal, intimate *episodic* interchange — a *"relationship"* — with human persons (and groups) in which the communication and initiative is not only from the human but also from the divine side. Traditional theism believes that "God" is deeply invested in the behavior and proper attitudes of human individuals, judges each individual person after death and assigns a reward or punishment depending on conduct during life. This "God" is "spirit" and not matter, just as the human individual is essentially "spirit" (a "soul"), separable from the matter of her/his body and will survive it after death. Therefore this relationship as imagined requires a dualist metaphysics for a context.

Since for Haught, "God" is a rational "person," every part of the theist projection rests on **"God's will,"** *even when contrary evidence is overwhelming*. Some examples of this: theism holds that, according to tenet #2 above, "God" providentially rules over the natural order and can intervene at any point. That's why we pray. But if in fact, it appears that "God" *never does* intervene, even when events result in the death and suffering of untold numbers of innocent victims, according to theism there can only be one reason for that: the omnipotent *"God"* **chooses** *not to intervene.* It is explained as "God's" respect for human freedom. But this is strange. For if human beings **chose** not to intervene under those circumstances whatever their reason, it would be considered immoral. Again, "respecting human freedom" may seem to make theoretical sense for catastrophes like the holocaust, perpetrated by humans, but it doesn't make sense even theoretically for natural disasters in which "God" similarly "refuses" to intervene, even when the human devastation is massive and the victims are mainly children. I would dare say the Haitians did not see "God's" *respect* for the geotectonic forces that killed a quarter of a million of their people in 2010 as *an act of love.* Perhaps Haught's "God" might have considered consulting them on how they would like to have been loved under the circumstances.

"God's" failure to act is regularly exonerated by theists on the grounds that he "sees and wills" an unforeseen future benefit. The fact that no such benefit is ever clearly identified is a clue that it was nothing but a rationalization from the start. The possibility that "God" is not a rational entity, and that "intellect and will" are humanoid projections that have no meaning when applied to "God," is never permitted to enter the discussion, much less are the implications *for theology* ever entertained or explored.

Similarly, theism claims "God" is the omnipotent Creator. Now, the theist "God" could have created the world by *fiat* literally in seven days as the Genesis myth said, but if the evidence shows that the universe was actually self-elaborated in an evolutionary process requiring over ten billion years for the emergence of life, and another four billion for intelligence, then theism must assert that "God" **chose** to create that way. This is the extent of Haught's "theology of evolution." Haught imagines "God" making these choices ... and then he argues that no one can **prove** that it didn't happen that way ... *and he calls that theology!*

These are all gratuitous "just so" explanations. In fact they are not explanations at all, for each of them involves anomalies and contradictions down the line for which theism has no explanation. For example, if creation was "God's" goal and purpose, why did he **choose** the circuitous time-consuming and potentially dead-end route of evolution? Haught will

epilogue

say *"to display his humility and self-emptying love and to "give" matter an independent existence and autonomy."* But it is not immediately clear how a tortuous process that has meant the extinction of 99.9 percent of all genotypes is a display of "love." Nor does he explain why, if it was a "display" it was so well-hidden and for so long: no one before modern times even heard about evolution. Moreover, the fact that more than half of all believers even today, 150 years after Darwin's publication, are scandalized by evolution and reject it as contrary to their understanding of the divine initiative in creation,[154] *means it continues to fail as a communication.* If the Genesis account and evolution were **both chosen** by "God" as his principal means of *revealing himself*, he seems to have selected conflicting forms of expression because most believers do not recognize them as compatible.[155]

As an "explanation" it is incoherent. But you can never prove that it's not true. Haught's "theology" is not designed to understand reality and the real "God" and move knowledge and understanding forward, but rather to allow for the continued existence of the traditional religious imagery and anthropomorphic understanding taken literally and held intransigently by the institution that employs him. It is a defensive theology dominated by ecclesiastical priorities.

Haught claims that "faith" speaks of things that science cannot. But what he defends as "faith" is really a set of beliefs that originally were offered *as science* by their ancient authors. To now suggest that these same doctrines, like the Genesis account of creation, were *never* taken as science is simply not true. Besides, to say that the *method employed* in Genesis — direct divine action — was a metaphor, but that *the decision to create* was not, is gratuitous; and it means the words "creation" and "providence" retain their traditional signification which is quite literal. While Haught insinuates these doctrines are mere metaphors, he himself is careful *never to say exactly what he means* and follow out its implications. So in this case, unless theology clearly admits that it is only *symbolic* to say that "God" "created" the universe or "providentially acquiesces" in the events of current time, the words are misleading, and in fact most believers are misled.

---

http://en.wikipedia.org/wiki/Level_of_support_for_evolution
[155] http://news.nationalgeographic.com/news/2006/08/060810-evolution.html

Theists' insistence that "creation" and "providence" are metaphors is only a feint, a diversion used to distract the opposition; for in fact theists could never admit the doctrine of creation or providence was metaphor, for then, *since everything would be done by other agents,* there would be no role for "God" at all. That is unacceptable. *The theist "God" has to "do" things or "he" stops being "God,"* because "God" for them is an *all-powerful thinking, planning and choosing entity.*

evolution and the "descent of god"

How does Haught say "God" should be thought of as the creator and provident guardian of an evolutionary universe? In his 2007 volume *Christianity and Science: Toward a Theology of Nature,* he introduces a notion which he calls "the descent of God."[156] As he presents it, the term *kenosis* (self-emptying), used in the NT to describe Jesus' life and work,[157] is extrapolated to refer to "God," but he doesn't mean it metaphorically. Jesus reveals "God," says Haught; therefore it is reasonable to suggest that "God", like Jesus, is *kenotic.* "God's" very nature is to empty himself. This self-emptying *kenosis* is "God's descent." Haught continues:

> An evolutionary theology ... would picture God's descent as entering into the deepest layers of the evolutionary process, embracing and suffering along with the *entire* cosmic story, not just the recent human chapters. Through the liberating power of the Spirit, God's compassion extends over the totality of time and space, enfolding and finally healing not only human suffering but also all the epochs of evolutionary travail that preceded, and were indispensable to, our own emergence.[158]

Haught goes on to suggest that we

> ... envisage the divine descent as the ground of creation itself. That is, even as a condition of there being any world distinct from God at all, the omnipotent and omnipresent Creator must be humble and self-effacing enough to allow for both the *existence* of something other than God, and an ongoing *relationship* to that other. If the creation is to become truly other than God, and not just an accessory attached to God's own being, then the divine omnipotence and omnipresence would become "small" enough to allow room for what is truly distinct from God — although, it must be added, that this self-constraint is paradoxically a function of God's greatness. It is out of the infinite *largesse* of the divine humility, therefore, that the otherness of the world is "longed" into being by God. Creation is God's "letting be" of the world, a re-

---

[156] *Christianity and Science,* Orbis Books, Maryknoll, NY; 2007; pp. 42, 93, 129 *passim*; Joseph Hallman, *The Descent of God,* Fortress Pr., Minneapolis, 1991
[157] Philippians
[158] *Ibid.,* p.92

lease that makes possible a dialogical relationship (and hence an intimate communion) of God with the finite created "other."

    Once God's "other" ... emerges as a historical reality, it can sustain its otherness
only by becoming more, not less, differentiated from its Creator.[159]

Well, here we have an example of what I am tempted to call "theology
by *fiat."* Haught's imagination seems to know no bounds. He is determined to "cut and paste" the standard mainstream "God" of the book, newly converted from thundering warlord to humble loving companion, to the
findings of evolution, no matter how baseless and incoherent it might be.
Haught's imaginary "God" in the above paragraphs is said to **"heal"** the
wounds that *his own chosen process of evolution* has created. Am I the
only one who finds this incomprehensible? Why would "God" choose a
process of "creation" that was so "sickening" that we would need him to
"heal" us from its effects? And another question: why would we suspect
that after having *generated* the universe in the selfsame act in which he
generated the Logos (according to Aquinas[160]), that "God" would then
devise evolution (a new *Demiourgos?*) as a way to let the universe be
"other than himself" just so he could then turn around and draw it into
"intimate communion" with himself? Such a torturous "explanation" seems
redundant and senseless. Haught himself calls it "conjecture."[161] How
does a **mere conjecture** qualify as "systematic theology;" or, for that matter, how does it even merit consideration as a replacement for traditional
creationism which, however unscientific and unacceptable, was at least
internally coherent?

    Haught clearly holds that "God" is still Creator, for he says "God"
"call[s] the world into being"[162] through evolution, as if evolution were a
creation-tool fashioned and selected for that purpose by a rational mind.
But evolution is completely the opposite of rational. There is no purpose
or "mind" in "selection" until you get to human beings who really do "select" because they know what they want. The "natural selection" Darwin
was referring to is a misnomer really, coined by him in an analogy with the
breeding of animals. "Natural selection" is actually not selection at all; it is
rather the survival of those traits and species that *happen* to achieve "re-

---

[159] *ibid.*, p.93
[160] *ST,* I, 45, 6c
[161] *Ibid.*, p.129
[162] *Ibid.*, p.105

productive success" because of their appropriateness to a given environment. So if evolution is the adventitious result of the irrational drive to survive, why would a "rational" God, whose motive is to "reveal himself" (presumably as rational), intentionally devise and exclusively employ a creation-tool like evolution characterized by randomness and irrationality? What would be the point? Why would "God" intentionally make creation seem random and haphazard when he himself is rational and purposeful? Is "God" trying to confuse us about who he is, or disguise his true nature? And, with regard to a "divine providence" that permits the holocaust and other forms of genocide in order to "preserve human freedom," why would the absolute ground of morality **choose** to even appear to be complicit in immorality?

Or is there another answer altogether? (This is what theists will not even consider.) Does a groping random process of universal development give us an unmistakable clue to what "God," the true source of our existence, is really like? Exploring *that* possibility, however, will take us very far from theism. We will look at this shortly.

When Haught speaks of "God" it is always in *humanoid* terms. "God" "descends," "chooses to be humble," "restrains himself," "calls the universe into being," "relates" to it, "enters" into intimate communion with it. This is all projection. We have no right to extrapolate from our human experience and claim that "God," like us, chooses, longs, descends, restrains himself. Even less do we have the right to circle back from those unwarranted extrapolations and use them as premises to then say that "God" set evolution in motion in order to create other beings like himself (or in Haught's fantasyland, *unlike* himself). These are not rational explanations; besides being gross circularities, they are pure guesswork, and incoherent.

Haught's theism, *as systematic theology*, is also inconsistent with the very tradition he claims to defend. According to the norms used by classic theology, "God" does not choose in time, and *"God" is not rational*. A rational mind has *reasons* for what it does. *Reasons* are the purposes, the ends, the goals that are sought, *planned for,* and so they explain why actions are taken. We humans exist in time, we cannot achieve our survival without planning for future goals — making something materialize in the future that is not here now ... getting something we don't have. Hence we act for *reasons*. Haught speaks as if that is exactly the way "God" acts. But it is entirely unorthodox. The traditional "God" *wants nothing* because he has everything, and he doesn't plan because he doesn't need to; everything has been preplanned from all eternity. He lives in an "eternal now," there is no difference for him between present and future so he would never need a reason for anything, *ever.* Reasons, "final causes," are exclusively human. If Haught is going to propose a different way of thinking about "God," like the rest of us, he has to justify it and refute those who think otherwise.

a philosophical interface

Theists like Haught seem to have given up on philosophy, and because they have nothing to take its place, they revert to what he calls an "essentially biblical understanding of God." What can that possibly mean except the anthropomorphic deity of the "book" that the atheists denounce and perennial theology itself rejected. That "God" is metaphor. Haught has no choice. If he is going to speak about "God," he has to use metaphor as if it were literal reality.

OK, you might say, the idea of "God's rationality" is a human projection. So what ... Haught projects. We all do it. Even scientists do it. They spontaneously imagine other species as if they were human. The teleological "explanations" given to account for the random events of biological evolution are prime examples. From the camouflage of butterflies wings to the advantages of gene mixing in sexual reproduction, biologists explain behavior and selection in terms of *purpose.*

Granted. But however understandable, *none of it is literally true;* and both "religionists" and "scientists," when they are trying to be "systematic" and precise, need to clearly define their statements. They have a right to their metaphors, *but they do not have the right to use them as if they were literal propositions.* They have a right to their poetry, but they must acknowledge that it is poetry.

Haught's imagery, as poetry, is valid ... and at times, perhaps even moving. Poetic, metaphoric statements lie in a different realm of discourse from literal scientific propositions. This means that while the *literary genre* might be different, the "thing" (in this case "God") is the same for both. Exactly what "thing" science and religious poetry may concur in describing needs a third discipline — an interface — to identify and articulate it. That interface is philosophy ... but not any philosophy. It must be a philosophy that shoulders the responsibility of mediating between scientific facts and religious metaphors — a discipline that provides a rational interpretation of scientific facts and can distinguish what is literal from what is metaphoric.[163] Haught has no way of making those distinctions.

I believe that Haught tries to confront his naturalist opponents directly with his religious and quasi religious metaphors *which he treats as if they spoke literally of the way things are.* Haught literally believes that "God" created the universe through the instrumentality of evolution. He thinks his metaphors, like the "descent of 'God'" are literally true, and he is also asking people like Daniel Dennett to respect the internal human experience to which they correspond. In either case, no communication is possible. In the first, no scientist and very few theologians are going to accept his "descent of God" imagery as fact; and in the second he is asking an atheist to validate the poetry that inspires his prayer-life. Haught's indignation that atheists dismiss his religious experience as illusory fails to recognize that symbols of experience — which is what religious symbols are — communicate only between those who share the same experience. I am sure, and quite edified, that Haught feels "grasped by 'God,'" as he says many times throughout his books; but it baffles me that he would think such a personal description would mean anything to atheists.

I am convinced that there are indeed common data and forms of expression that both religionists and naturalists could accept if they would agree to limit their statements of "fact." And it is philosophy that can provide a common terminology and conceptual framework for the dialog. In such a dialog, both religion and science would agree to the *non-factuality* of all their metaphors, religious or scientific, and that everything else about the phenomenon under consideration would be confined to the empirical. By empirical I mean it can be expressed in literal terms and can be observed and verified by any objective observer, and even possibly measured.

Here's an example how it might work. The heuristic role of the **conatus** is the primary datum and central concept of the philosophy that will mediate this discussion. The **conatus** is the internal drive of everything that exists to remain in existence. In living things it is on display as the instinct for self-preservation. It is observable and verifiable. Among hu-

---

[163] Cf *The Mystery of Matter,* passim.for the limits and methodology of cosmo-ontology: see esp.the end of chapter 2 and the beginning of 3,

man beings, it is the source of our love of our own existence and everything that supports it. From there it is a simple corollary that all other things are "appreciated" by us, singly or collectively, in proportion as they are perceived to assist and enhance our own existence. It is this "appreciation" radiating out from my own **conatus,** that I am calling the "sense of the sacred." This "sense of the sacred" extends to *material energy* itself, which is recognized as the ultimate source, the "stuff" and dynamism of my life and identity.

The universal presence of the drive to survive characterizes *material energy*. Material energy is responsible for every form and feature in the universe, and so it may be said to be *the source of all things*. It energizes the evolution of new species, therefore it is *transcendently creative*. It is, moreover, the matrix *in which all things live and move and have their being*. It is neither created nor destroyed; and it allows everything in the universe to be made of its own substance, in a self-emptying availability, metaphorically a "generosity," without conditions. *But it is not a rational person.*

I am personally related to *material energy* in a most intimate way, for *I am made of it*. My appreciation of it and its living dynamism springs from its apparently limitless abundance and transcendent creativity. It is the basis for the existence and character of my body and my mind, my personal identity and all my human relationships, my family, my friends, my work — everything that I cherish and celebrate in life — *what I live for and even ready to die for*. The spontaneous upwelling of a sense of awe and gratitude in the face of such personally significant *generosity* can hardly be called unwarranted or inappropriate much less an illusory projection. It is an intelligible objective empirical fact *that we all necessarily share*.

All of this is a straightforward datum, like any other in our material world — it is an empirical phenomenon, observable, universally verifiable, undeniable. It is the proper object of philosophy. In my conception of religion it serves as *common ground* between "science" and "religious metaphor," a fact that all can agree on. *No one can deny the fact ... or the experience ... or its unique existential significance for us.* And, in my view, this is the *only fact* on which religion is based. There is no other. The only possible place where religionists and atheists might differ, is the *interpretation* of that experience and the metaphors they use to express it.

Religionists choose to *interpret* the sense of the sacred as an accurate and welcome reaction to a vast, unspecific, non-human, benevolent **subjectivity,** overflowing with limitless and unconditional vitality. They recognize historical religions as past reactions to a similar perception. Because of pre-scientific peoples' ignorance of the sources of that experience, they imagined it in terms of "supernatural" humanoid entities, like rational "personal" gods, that did not exist. Those ancient projections remain valid **as symbols**, however, precisely because they refer to *the same experience.* "God" is a metaphor, coined *from the human side* for the source of *existence* and the universal sense of the sacred that spontaneously arises in us. Religionists, in any case, should limit their "factual" claims to what the observable evidence allows. The rest, they must concede, is metaphor and poetry which is often expressed in ritual and religious practice.

Non-religionists (atheists) on the other hand, while they should acknowledge the existence and validity of the *same experience of the sacred and sense of awe*, choose to interpret it as an erroneous reaction projecting subjectivity and benevolence onto a mindless inert substance and process. They too feel a spontaneous sense of gratitude, because, like all of us, they are ecstatically happy to be alive. To deny it would be to argue in bad faith. But while they understand and respect the poetry generated, they choose to focus on *matter* as it is studied by physics and chemistry. Their acute awareness of the non-rational, random nature of matter-energy's availability prevents them from entertaining any thought that might suggest *a subjectivity capable of generosity.* Hence, for them, religion refers to an illusion.

Nevertheless, in each case, the protagonists can recognize the validity of the experience, reactions and choices. They differ only on how they *choose to interpret* its significance. *The facts for each are the same.* Philosophy validates both interpretations as legitimate. It provides an *understanding* of the facts that is thoroughly consonant with scientific descriptions as well as human virtualities. Religion, then, brings its own poetry to celebrate what *existence **means*** to us; it provides expression for an interpretation of the common fact that awes and astonishes us all.

spirit and matter

The issue of metaphysical dualism — that reality is made of two distinct types of being spirit and matter — lies at the very heart of the "theist" position. The conception of "God" in traditional anthropomorphic theist terms is absolutely tied to belief in the reality of a separate kind of thing — Descartes' "second substance" — called "spirit." Just as human personality has been traditionally grounded in the notion of a "spiritual soul," "God's" divine personality is similarly grounded in his supposed reality as "spirit."

In a 2006 book called *Is Nature Enough*,[164] John Haught claims to have transcended dualism. That would imply a change in the traditional spirit-theism he espouses. If you reject dualism, what are you left with? a monism ... of either spirit or matter. But not Haught. At every turn he slides back into statements that imply the existence of two kinds of being, *spirit and matter.*

Haught cites Hans Jonas' criticism of the reductionist (inert, lifeless) view of matter that we have inherited since the 17th century. Haught describes reductionism as:

> ... a "pan-mechanistic" worldview in which lifelessness is the ground state of all being. The earlier pan-vitalist concern about how to explain death if everything is alive, has now been replaced by the puzzle of how to explain life if being is essentially dead.
>
>   According to Jonas, it was the emergence of dualistic myths and philosophies that made this metaphysical inversion possible. ... especially in modern times, dualism came to divide up the world ever more strictly between life, mind and soul on one side, and mindless and lifeless "matter"" on the other. This worldview received its full-blown expression in René Descartes'' famous separation of thinking substance (mind) from extended substance (matter). Dualism has been attractive to countless religious people because, by separating soul from body, and by linking bodylines to the "evil" realm of materiality, it provides tidy answers to the questions of why we die, suffer and have evil thoughts.[165]

After this admirable denunciation of the reductionist worldview, Haught then introduces the notion of biological information. Information, he says, is intrinsic to the very concept of life. Reproduction and ontogenesis minimally require the instructional modeling of DNA that will replicate organisms and bring them from birth to full maturity. He speaks of the "logical partition between mindless physical reality on the one hand and coded information on the other ..." He asks, "does information introduce into

---

[164] *Is Nature Enough* Cambridge U Press, pp. 11-12
[165] Ibid. p.62

nature a *non-physical* realm ..." or "Is it possible ... that taking stock of information leads only to a **less materialistic** form of naturalism?[166]

What "less materialistic" could possibly mean, like the proverbial "less pregnant," challenges the imagination. For me that is the first clue that Haught has not transcended dualism despite his claims; for either matter itself is the bearer and perceiver of information, or an inert dead matter must necessarily be complemented by "spirit" if there is to be the information necessary for life in the world. We begin to see here examples of Hsught's lack of consistency in the use of terms. If it is not an outright return to a dualism, it at least creates an ambivalence that, in my opinion, is unacceptable coming from a systematic theologian.

He says: "informational causation, therefore, may be no less natural and no more divine than [Aristotle's 'causes']" *but* then, with absolutely *relentless* ambiguity, adds immediately:

> The entrance of information into cosmic process points to a domain of unrealized possibilities that reside **somewhere other than the purely material.** Something quite **natural**, but nonetheless **non-material**, is going on in the emergence of information.[167]

What can "other than the material" and "non-material" mean but "spiritual"? He does the same thing in the next chapter. There, human intelligence is spoken of in one breath as fully emergent *within nature*, and in the next as "going beyond" the capacities of nature (insinuating but never directly claiming that it is due to "spirit"). He makes no effort to clarify or distance himself from the dualist implications of words like "beyond matter." But also he continues to insist on using the word "materialism" to refer only to "reductionism" — an inert mechanical materialism that does not allow "matter" to be recognized for what it does as a living dynamism.

Why doesn't he clarify? Is it cynical for me to suspect that *he is perfectly comfortable being misunderstood in the direction of dualism?* Haught can live with dualism because I believe he is committed to the idea that "God" is "spirit." He makes no effort to follow out the implications of his loudly proclaimed rejection of dualism; and he tolerates expressions that are ambiguous .

---

[166] Ibid, p.66
[167] Ibid, p.68 (emphasis mine)

Teilhard's dualism

He does this elsewhere as well. In chapter 5 of his 2007 *Christianity and Science*, Haught offers a way of thinking of "matter and spirit" that he presents as explicitly *not dualist*.[168] He claims it comes from Teilhard de Chardin. The attempt fails, as with his earlier efforts using Jonas, and he quickly slides back into the spirit-matter divide. The subtlety of his recidivism, however, is not immediately apparent. Ambiguity reigns again in this section, and as usual it is sustained by the inconsistent use of terminology.

In the section cited, he *explicitly* states that, *"matter and spirit ... are labels for two polar tendencies in nature's evolution, not two separate types of substance"* ... and even more boldly, *"theology should no longer think of the world as divided into separate domains, matter and spirit"* ... and, most decisively announces, *"there is no such thing as matter."* But even such clear-cut proclamations do not deter him from making the next head-spinning statement, *"it is spirit, not matter, that gives solidity and consistency to the cosmos."* This is stunning. Honestly, once you have declared dualism dead, how can you possibly say *"spirit, not matter"* in any context except the purely semantic? You could not do that unless you understood two distinct realities of some kind (or one that was only spirit). Once you have said that both spirit and matter are "tendencies" of the stuff of the universe, then *not only is there no such thing as "matter," ***there is also no such thing as "spirit."*** Neither word any longer refers to anything real, and you cannot use them *except as clearly labeled metaphors*. How can you say, as he does in the very same place, that creation is *"matter becoming spirit"*? For if "matter" and "spirit" are simply two different words for one and the same reality, one is not *becoming* the other ... the one substance is simply evolving new versions of itself. This is not just a harmless oversight. The net effect is that he continues to depict a universe in which "matter" and "spirit" each account for separate phenomena of reality. The words "matter," and "materialism" continue to characterize dead, lifeless, mechanical stuff and "spirit" is clearly used to explain "life," "mind," "spirit" and "God."

Moreover, to say *"matter is becoming spirit"* sets up a value gradient in which "spirit" is the ultimate goal for all things and therefore, ultimately, the

---

[168] John Haught, *Christianity and Science*, Orbis, 2007, pp.75-76.

only real reality. Matter is merely the *terminus a quo*, the starting point which must be transcended and left behind. This shows that Haught's vision implies the same denigration of matter as the worst form of dualism. In fact, it smacks of a monist idealism ... a Hegelian vision of all things evolving as the Mind of God. It reveals that Haught is either totally confused, or he is willing to compromise clarity of expression in order to steer clear of anything that would run counter to the traditional religious imagery of "God" as spirit.

From the way Haught speaks one gets the impression the fault really lies with de Chardin whom he uses as an authority here. He quotes him as saying: "[the cosmos] in its complete history is ultimately nothing but an *immense psychic exercise.*"[169] (emphasis mine). If that dramatic phrase doesn't evoke an unmitigated idealism, I don't know what does. In either case, idealist or dualist, we are talking about the insistence on the ruling reality of "spirit" in the universe as a thing or force that is "different from matter" and determines its destiny.

The reality of "spirit" is essential to theism. Theism has to have a "God" that is **not matter**. There is no other way for "God" to be someone no one has ever seen or will see. For if "God" were matter he would no longer be "invisible." *We would be able to "see" or at least experience "God" in some way with our senses or our instruments,* and science could observe, verify and perhaps even measure what we experience. Theists could never accept that, for it would take the "God" experience out of the exclusive purview of traditional religion and its hierarchs.

The "God" of theism needs to be "spirit." But the very claim that "spirit" exists demeans matter, for it implies that spirit accounts for vitality and consciousness and matter is dead and inert. That means that theists like Haught, despite their disclaimers, *actually think of matter only in reductionist terms.* So by "transcending dualism" what Haught really means is a "matter" that is enlivened with another "kind of thing" called "spirit." Funny how much that sounds like dualism. But Haught calls it "panvitalism," a label which he explicitly claims for himself a hundred pages later.[170]

Panvitalism, as Haught has described it following de Chardin, is simply dualism by another name. It is indistinguishable from the dualism of Aris-

---

[169] Ibid; Pierre Teilhard de Chardin *Human Energy*, pp.119-120
[170] Haught *op.cit* 2007, pp.172-3

totle who held that matter and spirit were two distinct "principles of being" each responsible for different observable behavior, even though not two distinct "substances" as in Plato or Descartes.

If "God" were matter, however, as proposed by a transcendent materialism, "religion" would have to be something completely different from what we have inherited. And that is exactly what I am suggesting — a new kind of religion, built on the benevolent living dynamism of *matter's existential energy — an undeniable* **fact** and experience which all religious metaphors throughout the ages have attempted to articulate.

Haught's "matter"

Notice what Haught's blanket condemnation of "materialism" implies: first it assumes that there actually is "something other than matter." By anyone's standards he has no right to that assumption. Then, as "proof" of the existence of spirit he assumes he knows exactly what the properties of "matter" are, and therefore he can identify those activities that "go beyond the possibilities of mere matter." But that begs the question because he gratuitously imputes to matter exactly those limitations which would require the additional presence of spirit.

No one has the right to define matter in a way that excludes *a priori* what matter is actually observed doing. If, for example, you see the brain, which we know is organic matter, performing intelligent activity, *you have no right to deny that intelligent activity is the product of the organic matter of the brain* and insist that *there must be "something else" there* — something that goes "beyond matter" — to account for it. The only thing you are logically entitled to is a revised definition of "matter," nothing else. But that revision is *huge.* It means the reductionists' (*and dualists'*) penchant for defining matter only in the terms used by physics and chemistry (or computer robotics) is not sufficient. We know what matter is by what it does ... *at all levels!* It is one thing to point to something that undeniably "goes beyond" what the sciences of physics and chemistry have up to now observed it doing in the forms they study, *and it is quite another to* make the unwarranted leap of claiming that there must be "something else" there to account for it when that activity is found in living organisms or in human intelligence which are not within the competence of the sciences of inert substances. There is no way of saying whether the limitations are those of matter or those of the sciences that study them in isolated contexts.

That also holds true for every major level of evolutionary emergence whose significant differences have traditionally required assignment to different disciplines. Hence we have physics, chemistry, biology, anthropology and sociology. Each of these disciplines relates to a product of evolutionary emergence that displays characteristics not completely explained by what preceded it. In each case, the expansion of subject matter has been accompanied by an acknowledgement that the earlier levels *had not fully exhausted all the potentialities of physical matter.* Matter itself is capable of life, and matter itself is capable of intelligent activity. That is what we see right before our eyes. If there is any *analogy* to be seen in the emergence of human intelligence, it is not as a *metaphor* for divine activity from another world as Haught intimates, but rather a direct indication that the potentialities (= power-to-be) resident in the matter of this world cannot be limited *a priori* at any given point in time. The incredible qualitative developments in the forms and features that have emerged from *matter* as it has evolved in the 13.7 billion years since the big bang, suggest that the potentialities of matter may very well be limitless. *Matter's energy* has always transcended its current forms. Hence I am fully justified in suggesting that *it may always do so.* If that hypothesis is true, then **material energy is transcendent,** and "transcendent materialism" is a valid and compelling world-view. After this, I can no longer use the word "materialism" without qualifying exactly what type I mean. Inert, mechanical, robotic reductionism is not the only type of materialism there is, and Haught is remiss in not acknowledging that, *especially if he insists that he himself is a "panvitalist."*

What's his problem? Why is it so difficult for Haught to be clear and say: organic matter, as organized and structured in the human brain, is capable of performing intelligent activity? It is an observable fact. The rest, like the existence of "spirit," is pure conjecture. Haught's inability to speak clearly could be an indication of a profound intellectual confusion on his part ... *or a subtle ploy to avoid challenging belief in a different kind of being called "spirit."*

I was originally impressed with the new directions Haught seemed interested in taking. He clearly intends to have religion and science mutually "contact and confirm" one another. But I quickly learned that he does not follow through on the implications of his premises and proposals. For example, in his 2010 book, *Making Sense of Evolution,* Haught criticizes the use that some theologians make of the traditional doctrine of the "direct infusion of the soul" by "God" in an attempt to confine evolution to the body alone. He describes the tactic as "evasive, artificial and theologically shallow" and asks, "is that the best we can do"? But then, without appearing to skip a beat, declares "I am not going to propose that Christian theology drop the idea of the soul."[171] He never takes the time to explain what he means by the "soul," or whether he still thinks that "God" infuses it, or if the traditional doctrine of divine infusion has been gutted by evolution, or if not, why not.

He veers from his initial course — sometimes, as in the above example, even within the same paragraph. I asked myself why? The only thing that I could think of that might cause this otherwise careful and intelligent academic to fall into such lapses of coherence would be *to avoid challenging traditional religion*. The construction of a *new religion* or a new religiosity built on the clear implications of a sincere dialog that "contacts and confirms" science is never really considered. My conjecture: he is not defending *religion,* he is defending *his religion,* the Catholic religion, the religion of his employer.

After a great deal of frustration I have come to the conclusion that Haught's inconsistency in terminology and use of metaphors as if they were literalisms are all due to the schizoid dynamic that rules his "theology." In my opinion he is a perceptive, well-read scholar and a prayerful man informed in science, who is driven into *non-sequiturs* because of the absolutist institution that dominates his thinking.

Have I read him correctly? One never knows. We Catholics are long accustomed to reading our theologians "between the lines" because we are all too aware that a statement or an omission may not reflect what the authors think but only what they need to say to preserve the appearance of orthodoxy. I am simply using his theology to illustrate why a fruitful dialog with the new atheism has not, and probably will not occur. Hopefully, analyzing why his efforts are inadequate will help us uncover the principles that should guide this discussion.   For the atheists are not only wrong, they are *also right.* Let's see what that could possibly mean.

---

[171] Westminster John Knox Press, Louisville, KY, p.46

is "God" spirit or matter?

The ultimate question that this discussion of dualism is leading to, is whether "God" is spirit or matter. And if "God" is matter, what does that do to our imagery about "God"? Can we still think of "God" in theist, *humanoid* terms?

I want to begin this phase of the discussion by tapping an ancient Christian source. In his treatise *On the Making of Man*, ch.23, fourth century Greek theologian and mystic Gregory of Nyssa acknowledged the anomaly of a "spiritual" God who created a material universe:

> 3. ... If God is in His nature simple and immaterial, without quantity, or size, or combination ... while all matter is apprehended in extension measured by intervals, and does not escape the apprehension of our senses, but becomes known to us in color, and figure, and bulk, and size, and resistance ... none of which it is possible to conceive in the Divine nature, — what method is there for the production of matter from the immaterial, or of the nature that has dimensions from that which is unextended? For if these things are believed to have their existence from that source, they clearly come into existence after being in Him in some mysterious way; but if material existence was in Him, how can He be immaterial while including matter in Himself? And similarly with all the other marks by which the material nature is differentiated; if quantity exists in God, how is God without quantity? If the compound nature exists in Him, how is He simple, without parts and without combination? ... so that the argument forces us to think *either that He is material, because matter has its existence from Him as a source*; or, if one avoids this, it is necessary to suppose that matter was imported by Him *ab extra* for the making of the universe.

> 4. If, then, it [matter] was external to God, something else surely existed besides God, conceived, in respect of eternity, together with Him Who exists ungenerately; so that the argument supposes two eternal and unbegotten existences, having their being concurrently with each other — that of Him Who operates as an artificer, and that of the thing which admits this skilled operation; ... Yet we do believe that all things are of God, as **we hear the Scripture say so; and as to the question how they were in God, a question beyond our reason, we do not seek to pry into it**, believing that all things are within the capacity of God's power — both to give existence to what is not, and to implant qualities at His pleasure in what is.[172]

Ancient philosopher-theologians like Gregory were clearly aware of the dilemma involved in claiming that a "God" who was supposedly "pure spirit" created a universe of matter. Notice that Gregory never doubted for a moment that "God" was *only spirit*. How did he resolve the dilemma? The

---

[172] (emphasis mine) Christian Classics Ethereal Library, NPNF2-05 online. URL=http://www.ccel.org/ccel/schaff/npnf205.x.ii.ii.xxiv.html

religious solution was the same then as it is now: *he simply accepted it on "faith."*

If "God" really is "pure spirit" as theists claim, and completely **other than** matter, then how could "God" have been matter's Creator? How was it even possible for "God" to conceptualize matter — to even *think* matter. There would not have existed anything, inside or outside of himself, that could possibly have served as blueprint. And even granting that he *could*, *why* would he ever want to do so? What would be the point?

And again, if he could think matter, doesn't classic theology say that "God" is utterly simple? He thinks only one thing: *himself.* Matter could only have come from the divine mind, *for if not, then where did it come from? At the very beginning, there could not have been anything else but the divine mind.* In classic theology "God" and the product of his thought are one and the same thing. If "God" thinks matter, he *is* matter. Spinoza, who owed his conception of "God" to the *philosophía perennis*, had no problem stating explicitly, "God' is an extended thing."[173] Theism could never accept that. Spinoza was a pan-entheist. And even Thomas noticed the conceptual similarity between "God" and prime matter.[174] Theists insist that when the Book says that "God" is spirit, it is meant literally.

Haught, assuming "God" to be spirit, explains "matter" by saying that "God" longs the world to be *other* than himself, because only by being "other" can he form a love relationship with it.[175] Pardon my astonishment, but where does he get that from? "Opposites attract"? But is that a *theological principle* from which to infer the "nature" of the material universe?

We have no idea what God is like, and if "God" is **esse,** "Being Itself," as Aquinas claims, then union with the divine "being" is the pre-condition of the world's existence. That means communion with "God" is complete *ab initio.* Why would "God" ever need to "achieve" a unity with what was extruded from and composed of his very own being? Haught is offering us a bit of poetry as if it were some kind of literal fact. For if unity with "God" is *the very condition of our existence itself,* then our "relationship to 'God'" precedes any "seeking" on our part. The true "search" would then

---

[173] Baruch Spinoza, *Ethics,* 1677, Part II, prop. 2

[174] ST I,11 ad 3 and 12c; SCG I,43,6

[175] See fn #4, above.

be the process of sloughing off the illusions and distortions that prevent us from experiencing our pre-existent and inalienable identity with "God." The experience of "God," as the Buddha repeatedly preached, is a self-appropriation, *a realization, a self-awakening* and not a search for some-thing or someone "other" and "out there" somewhere else.

Another problem: Haught doesn't explain how a theist person-"God" who lives in complete self-fulfillment could ever "want" anything more ... like this supposed *relationship* with us. And if he's going to insist "that's just the way 'God' is," then he has to at least admit, loud and clear, that he is rejecting two thousand years of Christian tradition, summed up in the theology of Thomas Aquinas. Thomas says there is nothing "God" wants that he doesn't have. Haught says his "longing 'God'" would be open to growth and development ... *just like us.* While all this is beautiful poetry it is, for our traditional "God," theologically absurd.

other possibilities

These are all problems created by imagining "God" as proposed by supernatural theism. The utter failure of theism suggests there must be a different kind of "God"? What if "God" were *not* "theist"? Are there any other possibilities?

If "God" were the *existential energy* of matter, as I claim, then we are the same "stuff" as "God." *Material energy* grows and develops along with us; our yearnings are one and the same — thirst for more existence. No further unity has to be achieved. This imagines a "God" in which we "live and move and have our being." There would be nothing to prevent us from a direct **experienced contact**, for this "God" is not different from us. We are, as Thomas would say, *simul,* "the same kind of thing," and as Nicolas of Cusa said, *non aliud,* "God" is "not other" than us.

Haught explicitly defines himself as a "theist." Theism is categorically different from another way of conceiving "God", quite ancient and tradi-tional among Christians, which is now called **pan-entheism**. It means "all things exist *in* "God." Thomists called it "participation-in-being," and it is pan-entheism that is reflected in Paul's citation in Acts 17 from the pre-Christian 6th century Greek poet Epimenides: "in him we live and move and have our being."[176] The conception is fundamentally Stoic, not Platonist.

Theism thinks of "God" as an entity separate from the world, and so a union between them has to be achieved. *Pan-entheism,* on the other hand, insists "God" is *not* separate from the world at any point in space or in time; existential union with "God" is the very condition of the world's existence. For theism, "God" is imagined as an independent, stand alone entity — a "person" like us, who thinks, wills and acts in ways commensurate with "his" power as an individual. Pan-entheism is very different. It is the ground for the traditional religious notion of *immanence.* "Immanence" refers to the mutual indwelling of "God" and the material universe. "God," it says, is not only present to the world, "God" is its matrix, "in which we live and move and have our being" ... and the world is not only open to and reaching for "God" but actually and *always dwells in* "God" like a sponge in the sea. Haught's concept of a "descending" "God" who establishes a relationship with Creation "as with another," is theism; it stands at the opposite end of the spectrum. Theism imagines a "God" who is "other;" pan-entheism imagines a "God" who is "not-other." The "God who is Other" is *supernatural,* beyond nature and beyond reach. It can be contacted only through "God's" initiative: revelation and grace. The pan-entheist "God" who is "not-other," however, *is completely natural;* no effort is required except acquiescence — he can be directly experienced ... *in fact, the pan-entheist "God" cannot NOT be experienced* for "God's" existential energy is palpable in our own **conatus.**

The very word "pan-entheism" is unfamiliar to most of us. The following long citation, taken from scripture scholar and theologian Marcus Borg's 2006 volume, *Jesus, Uncovering the Life, Teaching, and Relevance of a Religious Revolutionary*, may help explain how *pan-entheism* is different from *theism.*

> The notion that God can be experienced is foreign to many in the modern world. Atheists, of course, deny that such experiences are possible, and agnostics are skeptical. But even many Christians in our time find the claim strange. To a considerable extent, this is because the most common modern Western concept of God, shared by Christians as well as by many atheists and agnostics, is that the word "God" refers to a personlike being separate from the universe. Because this "su-

---

[176]*The Jerome Biblical Commentary* ed Brown et al, Prentice Hall, 1968; ch 45, ¶86, (Vol II, pp. 199-200)

perbeing" is not here, but somewhere else, "out there," beyond the universe, God is not a reality that can be experienced.

The term commonly used for this way of thinking of God — as a being separate from the universe — is *supernatural theism*. This form of theism seems orthodox to many Christians because of its familiarity. Language that speaks of God as a personlike being is common in the Bible. Perhaps the most familiar example is the opening line of the Lord's Prayer: "Our Father in heaven." But when taken as a concept of God, as the meaning or referent of the word "God," it is misleading and inadequate, for it is only half of the biblical concept of God. It speaks only of God's *transcendence*, God's beyondness.

The Bible also speaks of God's presence everywhere and in everything. This is most concisely expressed in words attributed to the apostle Paul: God is the one "in whom we live and move and have our being" (Acts 17.28). Note what the language affirms: we live within God, we move within God, we have our existence within God. God is not somewhere else, but right here, all around us, the encompassing Spirit in whom everything that is, is. Though this notion sounds foreign to some Christians, it really shouldn't. Most of us heard it while we were growing up: God is everywhere, God is omnipresent. The semi technical term for this is God's *immanence*, which means "indwelling." God dwells in everything, and everything dwells within God. For the Bible, and for orthodox Christian theology through the centuries, God is both transcendent and immanent, both *more* than the universe and *present in* the universe.

A term increasingly used to name this way of thinking about God is *panentheism*. Its Greek roots indicate its meaning: *pan* is the Greek word for "all" or "everything"; *theism* comes from the Greek word for "God," *theos;* and the middle syllable *en* is the Greek word for "in." Panentheism affirms that everything is *in* God, even as it also affirms that God is *more* than everything. Though the term is only about two hundred years old, the notion is as ancient as the language of supernatural theism.

        . . .

Whether people use the term "panentheism" does not matter. But whether people think of God as only transcendent (supernatural theism) or as both transcendent and immanent (panentheism) does matter. For many people in our time, supernatural theism is the only concept of God they know, and it often leads to skepticism about God. When somebody says to me, "I don't believe in God," my first response is, "Tell me about the God you don't believe in." Almost always, it's the God of supernatural theism. Thinking that the Word "God" refers to a being separate from the universe, "out there" and "not here," is a major cause of modern atheism, agnosticism, and skepticism. The difference between these two forms of theism matters for an additional reason. For *supernatural theism*, God is not here and thus cannot be experienced, except perhaps in moments of supernatural intervention. This God can only be believed in, not known. We will know God only after death; in this life we can only believe. For panentheism, however, God is here, all around us, even as God is also more than everything. It thus provides a framework for understanding what it means to speak about experiencing God.[177]

mediaeval christian pan-entheism

Thirteenth century theologian Thomas Aquinas was a pan-entheist, though in those days the term was not yet in use. He explained our relationship to "God" as "participation-in-being." Let me try to clarify how that worked in his thinking.

Theists tend to think of *existence* as if it were a "thing" like money. "God" **has** an infinite amount of it, and when he creates me, "he" gives me some. While I have it, it is "mine" and I spend it until it's gone. I have my own *existence* and God has his; my *existence* is limited both in time and quality, God's is not. God and I are two separate individuals, each with our own **existence**. God is present to but is **other** than us.

Thomas would say this imagery is false and misleading. Existence is not a "thing" that we **have,** nor is it a "thing" *that God* **has.** *Existence is "act." It is what "God"* **does,** *and that means what "God"* **is**. Our *existence* is not something that God donated to us at one time in the past or from somewhere else, but rather it is God's presence here and now "in all things and intimately"[178] sustaining us *in his own act of existence* from moment to moment. Our ongoing existence requires that "God" be **present.** Why? Thomas says "God" is present "**in** all things the way an agent is present in what he is doing."[179] That means, for example, the way actors are present in the roles they play, or a singer is present in the song she is singing, or an artist is present in the picture he is painting. Since "God" is **existence**, *existence* is what "God" "does" and "God" shares *existence* by **"doing" us**. Hence we exist "in" God's *existing.* That does not mean we are "God," but it does mean that we do not have our own "stand-alone" *existence* in any form, not even for a moment. According to Thomas, *God must be present for us to exist.* (And conversely, if we exist — if *anything* exists — God must be there sustaining us.)

Thomas says "God" and creatures are "distinct." But he did not mean they are separate and actuated by separate "**existences**" — one created,

---

[177] Marcus Borg, *Jesus, Uncovering the Life, Teaching, and Relevance of a Religious Revolutionary*, HarperOne, an imprint of Harper Collins Publishing, New York, pp. 110 -112
[178] *Summa Theologíae* I, q.8, a.1
[179] Ibid.

and the other uncreated. They are not. There is only one *existence* — **esse** — *and it is "God."* "God" is Being — **esse.** Creator and creature are distinct **only because of the dependency relationship**: one is the source and the other the user. Creatures do not self-actuate their own limited *existence* even for a second. They are not self-originating. Distinctness is not separateness.

How can we imagine this? The analogy of "money in the pocket" mentioned above, is misleading.   There is other imagery that is much better. One is that *existence* is like **light.**

To imagine existence as light, let's picture each created thing illuminated and made visible by light from the sun. "God," would be the sun itself, the source of all light, whose intensity is the equivalent of "infinite," for it totally exceeds our capacities; we cannot even look at it or it will blind us. This light which makes objects visible is the **sun's light,** it is not theirs. And in the same way, our existence is "God's" *act of existing,* it is not ours.

We have to be careful, however, because we tend to think of *light* as if it were shared between independently existing entities. Visible things on earth exist independently of the sun. *But their visibility does not,* and that is the point of the analogy. If there were no sun, nothing would be visible. Similarly, if there were no "God" nothing would exist. *Existence is "God" existing,* it is not a subsequent "quality" bestowed on an already existing thing, the way light is. To be actuated with *existence* is not to be self-energized but to be actively energized by the divine energy itself. *We and "God"* are *distinct but not separate.* That is what Thomas meant.

Theism falsely *imagines* that creation *exists separate from "God."* "God" would not need to be present in order to make us exist. In this mistaken view, "God's" presence to us is considered a voluntary choice, not, as for Thomas, an existential necessity. For Thomas God existing is our very being. God is not only present to us … God's presence **is us.** As the light reflected from visible objects participates in the sun's *shin-ing,* so the *existence* of things "participates" in God's *exist-ing. We ride on God's existence as on eagle's wings.*

The distinctness is there, but so is the *immanence.* This is extremely important. For how we *imagine existence* will determine how we relate to "God." Unfortunately, the usual theist imagery has had the effect of eliminating all meaning to *immanence.* Theism imagines "God's" presence to us as voluntaristic and extrinsic, i.e., "God" personally *chooses* to be next to us, like a guest who is visiting an already existing person.   Hindu-Christian theologian Raimundo Panikkar comments:

> God-immanent has no need of renting a place in my soul or waiting patiently until I allow him a little spot 'within' where he may come and dwell. The idea of indwelling is merely a very pale and distant reflection of true immanence. Man is not the host of an immanent God. ... the name 'Creator' attributed to God (to the [merely] transcendent [theist] God) cannot be predicated of the immanent Divinity, for how could it possibly create itself?[180]

The imagery of theistic "indwelling" doesn't work because it is does not recognize that it is God's *abiding presence* that makes the person exist in the first place. We are not dealing with two separate "things." Theism says "God" is present *to us*; pan-entheism says that we exist *in God*. The kind of relationship each imagines is vastly different from the other. *And religion is relationship*.

Aquinas' analysis of the Creator-creature relationship is pan-entheist. This is a part of our heritage that has been lost. Modern theologians like Borg mourn this loss and are working for the reinstatement of the ancient traditions. Theist theology is, in fact, a relatively recent innovation that does not correspond to the ancient tradition represented by Paul's description of "God" which used pan-entheist imagery. For it was Paul who said "in 'God' we live and move and have our being."

pan-entheism and *matter's existential energy*

Once we come down from the rarified altitudes of Thomas' abstractions, we find that the notional configuration he developed between "Creator" and "creature" is equally valid in a strictly material universe. In other words, the Thomist "equations" for the relationship between existential donor and existential recipient hold true whether *existence* is matter, or spirit, or a combination of the two. The reason is, of course, that **what kind of "stuff"** existence is, is a question for science, not philosophy much less theology. Philosophy and theology *interpret* the significance of the "facts" for human beings — their subject-matter is *the relationship* — but the concrete facts, as always, are the purview of science.

---

[180] Raimundo Panikkar *The Trinity and the Religious Experience of Man*, Orbis, 1973, p.32:

Thomists have always called *pan-entheism* "participation-in-being." It teaches that *the universe exists in "God."* For *what* "God" is, is *what* we are. Thomas said, in the article cited above, "*movens et motum oportet esse simul,*" "mover and moved must share the same motion." Applying that analogy to *existence,* it would translate to "Source-of-**being** and re-ceiver-of-**being** must share the same **being.**" "God" is being. We dwell in "God" as a sponge in the sea.

It doesn't matter to Thomas' analysis of "participation" whether "God" is spirit or matter. Thomas himself was a dualist who did not have the bene-fit of modern science. There is no conflict with what we have learned from science. If we have learned that the universe is matter — always and everywhere, inside and out, wall to wall — matter, our relationship as ma-terial organisms to a *material "God"* is the same as described by Thomas' "participation-in-being."

Participation-in-being is *pan-entheism,* not theism. It says that "God" is "not other." It means that in our "groping" after him, as Paul said, "we don't have to look very far at all; 'God' is near to each of us, for in him we live and move and have our being."

the future of an allusion

Religion is the poetry of our people. It is focused on the most basic and yet most elusive of all virtual realities — **who we think we are.** "God," of course, has always been thought of as our source and designer. So when we spoke of "God" we were really alluding to where we thought we came from and what we believed we were designed for. It was a fairly straightforward project. We were trying to figure out how to live; once our minds came awake, our instincts fell silent on the issue, and we were facing a void.

No one has ever seen "God." In the past, all religions claimed to have some privileged source that provided accurate information — guaranteed — about "God" and what he wanted. And on that basis they told us who we were and how we should live. Many religions still do.

In our day, we are no closer to seeing "God" than our forebears. But there is one great difference; we now no longer believe that it is "God" who determines how we should live. "God" is not in the business of issu-ing commandments. Fundamentally this changes religion from a search for what "God wants," to a search for *what we really are, and what we want for ourselves and our world.*

Since there has always been a close correlation between "God" and "how we should live," this search-shift corresponds to our realization that *"God" is not something other than us.* So it's not surprising in these new circumstances that we are looking for a new definition of "God." We are not only who we think **we** are, but we also know that "God" is (and always has been) only what we think **"he"** is. "God" is the *symbol* — the allusion — we generate that "explains" who we think we are and how we think we should live.

But make no mistake. Even though "God" is a symbol created by us, we did not design, fashion, extrude and sustain our own organisms into existence. *We are not self-originating.* Whatever it is that did that, is our "God." Our poetic allusions may molt and modulate through time, but it's only because our growing knowledge of ourselves — greatly enhanced by science — is constantly suggesting new symbols for "God." But our quest is always for "what," not "whether," *for none of us is self-originating.* Right now I am suggesting that the symbol for our "God" is *matter's existential energy.*

Those who have looked to this book to provide a blueprint for institutional religious reform by "tweaking" traditional dogmas, surely have realized by this time that they came to the wrong place. What I am proposing is nothing less than the acceptance of full responsibility for religion. Religion is a human project. It is not "God's," nor the Church's. It belongs to us. *We need religion* to sustain and deepen our sense of the sacredness — the *mysterion* — that is this universe of matter. Religion is the poetry we create to help us do that. It's a tool of the human spirit. It is in everyone's interest to further that project, and it is everyone's responsibility to make sure it does not become dysfunctional and destructive. That may mean that we no longer leave it to those who have arrogated control of it to themselves and perhaps have used it to conserve the ring of dehumanizing power forged in the furnaces of ancient empires. Religion belongs to us all. Without an *objectively grounded sense of the sacred*, life is fatally impoverished — we cannot embrace the void, we never plumb the depths or the significance of the matter we are made of, we never become fully human. *Who we think we are* remains small, desperate and grasping.

The sense of the sacred emerges irrepressibly from the **conatus** — the drive to survive. It is the soil in which our humanity grows and flourishes. We *understand* the sacredness of *existence* because our very bodies cry out with joy for it. We take our material *existence* for granted ... we don't think twice about it until what seems to be its disappearance looms before us. Then we are shocked ... not just perplexed or dismayed, but *truly shocked*. How could I possibly die ... disappear ... me? ... no longer exist? It is literally unimaginable. These diaphanous minds we are so proud of, are biologically incapable of imagining physical non-experience which we equate with *non-existence*. We are programmed for living in our material universe. We don't know how to do anything else. Fortunately, when death comes it is something that happens to us, it is not something we are called on to do ... for if it were up to us it would never occur. We certainly know how to kill ourselves, and we may even learn how to "let go," *but we don't know how to die.*

That means we have yet to fully embrace the human condition and *the void which brought it into existence.*

-

BIBLIOGRAPHY

A Quaker Reader, Pendle Hill Publications, Wallingford, PA 1962

Albright, William, *From the Stone Age to Christianity,* Anchor, 1960

Anonymous, *The Cloud of Unknowing,* Penguin, London, 1961 (1384)

Aquinas, Thomas,
 Summa Theologíae, Editorial Católica, Madrid, 1958 (1272)
 Summa Contra Gentiles, Image, Garden City NY, 1955 (1264)

Armstrong, Karen,
 The Great Transformation, Knopf, NY 2006
 The Case for God, Alfred Knopf, NY, 2009

Augustine of Hippo, *Contra Julianum,*

Baltzly, Dirk, "Stoicism", *The Stanford Encyclopedia of Philosophy (Winter 2010 Edition)*, Edward N. Zalta (ed.), http://plato.stanford.edu /archives/win2010/entries/stoicism/.

Becker, Ernest,
 The Denial of Death, Free Press, NY,1974,
 Escape from Evil, Free Press, NY 1975

Bhikkhu, Thanissaro, "The Authenticity of the Pali Suttas", *Access to Insight,* 30 January 2011, http://www.accesstoinsight.org /lib/authors/ thanissaro/authenticity.html)

Bihlmeyer-Teuchle, *Church History, Vol I,, Christian Antiquity*, Newman Pr. Westminster MD, 1960

Borg, Marcus, *Jesus, Uncovering the Life, Teaching, and Relevance of a Religious Revolutionary,* HarperOne, New York, 2009

Bromiley, Geoffrey W, *The International Standard Bible Encyclopedia*, Eerdmans, Grand Rapids, 1959

Brown et al eds, *The Jerome Biblical Commentary,* Prentice Hall, Englewood Cliffs NJ, 1968

Campbell, Joseph, *Thou Art That,* New World Library, Novato, CA 2001

Carroll, James *Constantine's Sword,* Mariner Books, Boston, 2001

Catechism of the Catholic Church, Libreria Editrice Vaticana, 1992

Crossan, John Dominic, *The Historical Jesus*, Harper Collins, NY,1991

Cullmannn, Oscar, *Peter: Disciple, Apostle, Martyr*, Westminster, Phila.,1953

Dawkins, Richard, *The God Delusion,* Haughten Mifflin, Boston, 2006

Dennett, Daniel, *Breaking the Spell*: *Religion as a Natural Phenomenon,* Penguin, NY, 2007

Dostoyevsky, Fyodor, *The Brothers Karamazov,*

Eliot, T.S., *Four Quartets,* Harcourt Brace, NY, 1943, 1971

Eriúgena, John Scotus,
Treatise on Divine Predestination, tr Brennan, U.Notre Dame Pr, 1998
Periphyseon, tr Fortuny, Folio, Barcelona, 1984

Flannery, Edward, *The Anguish of the Jews,* NY, Paulist Press,1985,

Frankfort, H. and H.A., *The Intellectual Adventure of Ancient Man,* U of Chicago Press, 1977

Frazier, Sir James, *The New Golden Bough,* ed.Gaster, Mentor, 1959.

Freire, Paolo, *The Pedagogy of the Oppressed,* Penguin, 1993.

Freud, Sigmund,
Beyond the Pleasure Principle, tr Strachey, Bantam, NY, 1959.
Civilization and Its Discontents, tr Strachey W.W.Norton, NY 1961.

Hamer, Dean, *The God Gene, How Faith is Hardwired into our Genes,* Doubleday, NY 2004.

Hamilton, Edith, *Mythology,* Warner Books, NY, 1942.

Haught, John F.,
God and the New Atheism, WJK Press, Louisville, 2008
Christianity and Science, Orbis Books, Maryknoll, NY; 2007
Is Nature Enough, Cambridge U Press, 2006

Hedges, Chris, *When Atheism Becomes Religion,* Free Press, NY, 2006

Heschel, Abraham, *The Prophets,* Harper Torchbooks, NY,1969

Hobbes, Thomas, *Leviathan,* Collier Books, NY, 1962 (1651).

Holtz, Barry, ed., *Back to the Sources,* Simon & Shuster, 1984

Hopkins, Jasper, *Nicholas of Cusa on "God" as not-other,* Minneapolis, U. of MN press, 1979

Jacobs, Alan, *Original Sin, a Cultural History,* Harper One, NY, 2008

Jerusalem Bible, The Garden City, Doubleday, 1966

John of the Cross, *Ascent of Mount Carmel,* tr. Peers, NY Image, 1958

John Paul II, Pope, *Fides et Ratio,* 1998

Jones, A.H.M., *Constantine and the Conversion of Europe,* Collier, NY 1962

Jowett, B., ed and tr. *The Works of Plato,* Tudor Publishing, NY.

Maccoby, Hyam tr., *Judaism on Trial,* Fairleigh Dickenson U. Press, Teaneck, NJ, 1982

Marcuse, Herbert,
Eros and Civilization, Vintage, NY 1962
Negations, Beacon Pr Boston, 1969

Murphy, Nancey, *The Moral Nature of the universe,* Fortress Pr., Minneapolis, 1996

Musurillo, Herbert, tr & ed., *The Fathers of the Primitive Church,* Mentor-Omega, 1966

Newman, Barbara, *From Virile Woman to Woman Christ,* U of PA Pr, Phila., 1995

Nolan O.P., Albert, *Jesus before Christianity,* Orbis, 1976

Panikkar, Raimundo,
The Silence of God, Orbis, 1990.
The Trinity and the Religious Experience of Man, Orbis, 1973.

Pelikan, Jaroslav, *The Christian Tradition, vol 2, The Spirit of Eastern Christendom (600-1700),* Chicago, U.of Chicago Pr, 1974

Porete, Marguerite, *The Mirror of Simple Souls,* tr Babinsky, NY Paulist Press 1993

Pseudo-Dionysius, *The Complete Works,* Paulist Press, Mahwah, NJ, 1987

Richardson, Cyril, tr. & ed., *Early Christian Fathers,* Macmillan, NY, 1970

Ricoeur, Paul,
The Symbolism of Evil, Beacon, NY, 1967
The Rule of Metaphor, University of Toronto Press 1977

Russel, Bertrand, *A History of Western Philosophy,* Simon & Schuster, NY, 1945

Schermer, Michael, *The Believing Brain,* Times Books, NY 2011.

Schwager, Raymund, *Banished from Eden,* Gracewing Publishing, 2006

Spinoza, Baruch, *Ethics,* 1677.

Teresa of Avila, *Interior Castle,* Forgotten Books, 1577, 2007

Vergote, Antoine *In Search of a Philosophical Anthropology,* tr Muldoon, Louvain, Louvain U. Press 1996

Von Rad, Gerhard, *Genesis,* Westminster Press, Phila., 1961

Walshe, Maurice O'C., *Eckhart, German Sermons,* London, Watkins, 1979

Weber, Max, *The Protestant Ethic and the Spirit of Capitalism,* tr.Talcott Parsons, Scribners, NY 1958

Wiley, Tatha, *Original Sin,* Paulist Press, Mahwah, NJ, 2002

Wittgenstein, Ludwig,
    On Certitude, Anscombe et al eds & tr. Blacklwell, Oxford,1969
    Philosophical Investigations, Anscombe, et al, Blackwell, Oxford, 1951
    Tractatus Logico-Philosophicus, Routledge, NY 1922, 1961

Yonge, tr., C.D., *The Works of Philo,* Hendrickson, 1993,

Yoshinori, Takeuchi, ed., *Buddhist Spirituality,* Crossroads, NY, 1997

Zimmer, Karl, *Scientific American,* 9/27/2004 review of *The God Gene*

INDEX

Because of the repetition of ideas and words, I have tried to limit this index to those locations where the indexed term is used in a particularly substantive or defining way. Multiple entries indicate nuanced usage or multiple applications.

.